PHONETICS AND PHONOLOGY

VOLUME 2

PHONETICS and PHONOLOGY

Editors

STEPHEN R. ANDERSON

Cognitive Science Center
The John Hopkins University
Baltimore, Maryland 21218

PATRICIA A. KEATING

Department of Linguistics
University of California, Los Angeles
Los Angeles, California 90024

A list of titles in this series appears at the end of this book.

PHONETICS and PHONOLOGY

VOLUME 2
The Special Status of Coronals: Internal and External Evidence

Edited by

Carole Paradis

Département de langues et linguistique
Université Laval
Québec, Québec

Jean-François Prunet

Département de linguistique
Université du Québec à Montréal
Montréal, Québec

With a foreword by Michael Kenstowicz

ACADEMIC PRESS, INC.
Harcourt Brace Jovanovich, Publishers
San Diego   New York   Boston
London   Sydney   Tokyo   Toronto

Academic Press, Inc.
San Diego, California 92101

United Kingdom Edition published by
Academic Press Limited
24–28 Oval Road, London NW1 7DX

Library of Congress Cataloging-in-Publication Data

The Special status of coronals : internal and external evidence /
    [compiled by] Carole Paradis, Jean-François Prunet.
        p.   cm. -- (Phonetics and phonology ; v. 2)
    Includes index.
        ISBN   0-12-544966-6   (alk. paper). -- ISBN   0-12-544967-4   (pbk. :
    alk. paper)
        1. Coronals (Phonetics) 2. Grammar, Comparative and general-
    -Phonology.   I. Paradis, Carole, date. II. Prunet, Jean
    -François. III. Series.
    P235.S6   1991
    414--dc20
                                                        90-1033
                                                        CIP

Printed in the United States of America
91   92   93   94   9   8   7   6   5   4   3   2   1

To Christine and Daniel

CONTENTS

Contributors   xi
Foreword   xiii
Preface   xv

Introduction: Asymmetry and Visibility in Consonant Articulations   1
CAROLE PARADIS AND JEAN-FRANÇOIS PRUNET

1. Background   1
2. Central Concepts   4
3. On the Special Status of Coronals   12
4. Some Theoretical Implications   21
5. Conclusion   24
   References   26

Coronal Places of Articulation   29
PATRICIA A. KEATING

1. Introduction   29
2. Terminology   30
3. Descriptions of Coronals   33

4. Features Proposed for Coronals   40
5. Discussion   46
   References   47

Coronals and the Phonotactics of Nonadjacent Consonants in English   49
STUART DAVIS

1. Introduction   49
2. Distinguishing MSCs from SSCs   51
3. The Underspecification of Coronals in English   54
   References   60

Coronals, Consonant Clusters, and the Coda Condition   61
MOIRA YIP

1. Introduction   61
2. The Special Behavior of Coronals: English   63
3. The Special Behavior of Coronals: Menomini   64
4. The Cluster Condition: Diola Fogny   65
5. Coronals Again: The Cluster Condition in Attic Greek   67
6. The Coda Condition and Place Features: Japanese   68
7. A Mixed Case: Finnish   70
8. Issues in Underspecification   73
9. Conclusions   74
   References   77

Palatalization and Coronality   79
ADITI LAHIRI AND VINCENT EVERS

1. Introduction   79
2. Palatalization and the Representation of Coronal   80
3. An Alternative Solution   85
4. Palatalization and Secondary Articulation   89
5. Conclusion   98
   References   99

On the Relationship between Laterality and Coronality   101
KEREN RICE AND PETER AVERY

1. Introduction   101
2. Assumptions   103

3. The SV Hypothesis 107
4. The Coronal Properties 114
5. Conclusion 121
   References 122

Consonant Harmony Systems: The Special Status of Coronal Harmony
PATRICIA A. SHAW

125

1. Introduction 125
2. Cross-Linguistic Survey of Consonant Harmony 127
3. Theoretical Framework 129
4. Harmony Systems and the Scansion Parameter 132
5. Consonant Harmony across Place of Articulation 137
6. Chumash Coronal Harmony 140
7. Tahltan Coronal Harmony 144
8. Conclusions 152
   References 155

On the Universality of the Coronal Articulator
YOUNG-MEE YU CHO

159

1. Introduction 159
2. Two Theories for the Place Node 160
3. The Coronal Node in Sanskrit 165
4. Korean Place Assimilation 170
5. On the Universality of the Articulator Nodes 174
   References 177

The Underspecification of Coronals: Evidence from Language Acquisition and Performance Errors
JOSEPH PAUL STEMBERGER AND CAROL STOEL-GAMMON

181

1. Introduction 181
2. Something versus Nothing 183
3. Coronals in Speech Errors 185
4. Coronals in Child Phonology 188
5. Other Explanations 191
6. Discussion and Conclusions 194
   References 197

On the Special Status of Coronals in Aphasia
RENÉE BÉLAND AND YVES FAVREAU

On the Special Status of Coronals in Aphasia 201

1. Introduction   201
2. Method   203
3. Segmental Representation   204
4. Substitutions and Consonant Harmonies: Predictions   205
5. Consonant Epenthesis and Syncopation Processes   211
6. Coronal Transparency in Vowel Spreading   216
7. Conclusion   218
   References   220

Index   223

CONTRIBUTORS

Numbers in parentheses indicate the pages on which the authors' contributions begin.

PETER AVERY (101), *Department of Languages, Literatures and Linguistics, York University, North York, Ontario M3J 1P3, Canada*

RENÉE BÉLAND (201), *Laboratoire Théophile Alajouanine, Centre hospitalier Côte-des-Neiges, Montréal, Québec H3W 1W5, Canada*

YOUNG-MEE YU CHO (159), *Department of Asian Languages, Stanford University, Stanford, California 94305*

STUART DAVIS (49), *Department of Linguistics, Indiana University, Bloomington, Indiana 47405*

VINCENT EVERS (79), *Max Planck Institute for Psycholinguistics, 6525 XD Nijmegen, The Netherlands*

YVES FAVREAU (201), *Laboratoire Théophile Alajouanine, Centre hospitalier Côte-des-Neiges, Montréal, Québec H3W 1W5, Canada*

PATRICIA A. KEATING (29), *Department of Linguistics, University of California, Los Angeles, California 90024*

ADITI LAHIRI (79), *Max Planck Institute for Psycholinguistics, 6525 XD Nijmegen, The Netherlands*

CAROLE PARADIS (1), *Département de langues et linguistique, Université Laval, Québec, Québec G1K 7P4, Canada*

JEAN-FRANÇOIS PRUNET (1), *Département de linguistique, Université du Québec à Montréal, Montréal, Québec H3C 3P8, Canada*

KEREN RICE (101), *Department of Linguistics, University of Toronto, Toronto, Ontario M5S 1A1, Canada*

PATRICIA A. SHAW (125), *Department of Linguistics, University of British Columbia, Vancouver, British Columbia V6T 1W5, Canada*

JOSEPH PAUL STEMBERGER (181), *Department of Linguistics, University of Minnesota, Minneapolis, Minnesota 55455*

CAROL STOEL-GAMMON (181), *Department of Speech and Hearing Sciences, University of Washington, Seattle, Washington 98195*

MOIRA YIP (61), *Program in Linguistics and Cognitive Science/Center for Complex Systems, Brandeis University, Waltham, Massachusetts 02254*

FOREWORD

The studies collected in this volume investigate in depth an intuition shared by most phonologists: that dental (more generally coronal) is the unmarked consonantal point of articulation. This intuition is tested and corroborated by the study of phonological rules and constraints in an impressive variety of languages, as well as through results from phonetics, aphasia, and acquisition. Dentals are the most frequent choice in the construction of phonological inventories. In sound change they also stand out from the labials and velars because they are more liable to assimilate the point of articulation of a neighboring consonant and to appear as the product of neutralization in syllable codas. Dentals act like identity elements in escaping constraints on concatenation and are a favored linking consonant. And while labials and velars may erect a barrier to the spread of a vocalic feature, dentals are often permeable.

The contributors propose a variety of solutions to make sense of this special status of the dental/coronal consonants. Although no definitive answer emerges, most of them take as their point of departure a formalization of the traditional notion of "unmarked": Dentals are initially uncharacterized for point of articulation and acquire this specification through a default mechanism. In the course of defending, modifying, restricting, or rejecting this thesis, ideas are recruited from two of the most active lines of research in current linguistics: underspecification and feature theory. This volume is the first large-scale, systematic application of these theories to a well-defined research problem. It will interest the specialist as well as introduce the general reader to one of the liveliest areas in contemporary linguistics.

Michael Kenstowicz
Massachusetts Institute of Technology

PREFACE

Our book is intended for graduate students and scholars interested in phonology, phonetics, general linguistics, psycholinguistics, or language pathology. It contains a phonetic survey of coronal articulations and discusses many aspects of the phonological behavior of coronals as opposed to noncoronals. Assimilation, deletion, insertion, consonant harmony, palatalization, and morpheme structure constraints, among others, are treated as both internal and external evidence in favor of the unmarked status of coronals in child and adult language, as well as in speech errors in both normal and aphasic speech. All contributions to this volume use current nonlinear generative models of phonological representation.

This book is the result of a long process which began in 1988, when we noticed a renewal of interest in the behavior and representation of coronals in several papers (e.g., Avery and Rice, 1988, and Shaw, 1988, among others), due to advances in models of segmental structure. In the same year and the following year, we presented our own work on coronal transparency to different audiences: the 19th North Eastern Linguistic Society meeting at Cornell University, the annual meeting of the Canadian Linguistic Association at Université Laval, the Phonology Workshop at the University of Amsterdam, and lectures at Université de Nice, Université de Paris VII, the University of Ottawa, and Addis Ababa University.

Questions from these audiences made us realize that the specificity of coronals was too broad a subject to be discussed on the basis of isolated arguments. It was clear that to be conclusive, a study of the special status of coronals must be conducted on a wide empirical basis. The problem was that while several recent studies, as well as earlier work, assigned coronals a status fundamentally distinct from that of other consonants, there was no basic and reasonably thorough reference work available discussing the special properties that coronals were assumed to display. Indeed, one could say that in generative grammar, the claim that coronals are the unmarked consonants had become an orthodox position since Kean (1975), without ever being justified by more than a few passing comments. In addition to this lack of empirical coverage, much of the earlier literature on places of articulation was written in the framework of linear phonology. This approach, because it was essentially descriptive, made a large part of this research obsolete for theorists using the more recent nonlinear frameworks, which now allow us to define the questions differently and answer them in more principled and explanatory manners.

In view of the fact that problems of markedness are central to current phonological research (for instance, to underspecification theories and element-based theories), while little is known about the actual properties of consonants, we decided to bring together studies examining coronals from different points of view. We drew up an outline of what a balanced and extensive study of coronals ought to look like, and invited submissions by specialists who had either already made significant contributions to the literature on coronals or whose current research had important implications for the study of these consonants. The result of these efforts, ours and those of the contributors, is a volume in which coronals are treated in as systematic and coherent a manner as possible. We hope that this book will fulfill the need for a basic reference work on coronals and the distinctive properties which make these consonants special.

We are grateful to the contributors for the enthusiasm they immediately showed for this project, for their trust and patience, and for bearing with us in our numerous requests. We are particularly indebted to Harry van der Hulst for his advice and encouragement with the project. We extend our thanks to the colleagues who allowed us to present our work to various audiences: Jean-Pierre Angoujard at Université de Nice, Harry van der Hulst and Norval Smith at the University of Amsterdam, Georges Boulakia at Université de Paris VII, and Doug Pulleyblank at the University of Ottawa. We thank our colleagues and students at Université Laval and Université du Québec à Montréal (UQAM), especially Emmanuel Nikiema, for lending a critical ear to some theoretical and organizational issues. Jean Lowenstamm has been extremely generous in permitting part of the work for this book to be conducted at the African Linguistics Project at UQAM. Glyne Piggott, Keren Rice, and Doug Pulleyblank sent us detailed comments about the form and content of the introductory chapter. We are also indebted to Stephen Anderson and Patricia Keating for their efficient handling of the evaluation process for Academic Press.

Finally, we gratefully acknowledge SSHRC grant #410-89-1166, Fonds FCAR grant #90-NC-0383, SSHRC Canadian Research Fellowship #445-89-0103 awarded to Carole Paradis, and a postdoctoral fellowship from the I. W. Killam Memorial Fund for Advanced Studies awarded to Jean-François Prunet. We are also thankful for SSHRC grant #411-85-0012 and Fonds FCAR grant #90-EQ-2681 awarded to the African Linguistics Project at UQAM.

REFERENCES

Avery, P. and K. Rice (1988) "Underspecification Theory and the Coronal Node," *Toronto Working Papers in Linguistics* **9**, 101–121.

Kean, M.-L. (1975) *The Theory of Markedness in Generative Grammar*, Doctoral dissertation, MIT, Cambridge, Massachusetts. Distributed 1980, Indiana University Linguistics Club, Bloomington.

Shaw, P. (1988) "Feature Geometry and Coronality," Paper presented at the Annual Canadian Linguistic Association Meeting, University of Windsor, Windsor, Canada.

INTRODUCTION: ASYMMETRY AND VISIBILITY IN CONSONANT ARTICULATIONS

CAROLE PARADIS *
JEAN-FRANÇOIS PRUNET †

*Département de langues et linguistique
Université Laval
Québec, Québec GlK 7P4, Canada

†Département de linguistique
Université du Québec à Montréal
Montréal, Québec H3C 3P8, Canada

1. BACKGROUND

This book is dedicated to coronals, as opposed to labials, velars and so on, because coronals are often alleged to have properties shared by no other place of articulation.[1] It has long been known that coronals are the most frequent consonants in languages. Except for Hawaiian (see Maddieson, 1987:31), all languages possess at least one coronal stop. Out of 317 languages, 316 have the coronal dental or alveolar /n/, 299 the bilabial /m/, 167 the velar /ŋ/ (Maddieson, 1987:60). If a language has only one fricative, it will be the coronal /s/ 84% of the time (Maddieson 1987:52), and liquids are coronal in the overwhelming majority of the languages.[2] As mentioned by Keating (this volume), coronals are also special in that they include more contrasts of both place and manner than do other consonant classes. And acquisitional studies show that coronals with labials are the first consonants acquired by children (see Stoel-Gammon, 1985:509; Vihman, Ferguson, and Elbert, 1986:26).

These frequency and acquisition facts led Kean (1975) to conclude that coronals are the most neutral (unmarked) consonants. Since the early days of the gen-

1

erative paradigm, it has been customary to assume that some sounds are some-how simpler, less complex, or less marked than other sounds. Chomsky and Halle (1968:409) suggest that /a/ is the simplest of all vowels. However, in their classification of consonants, they assert that no specific consonant, and no spe-cific place of articulation, is less marked than the others. Kean (1975:48) pro-poses a universal markedness theory in which /t/ is the universally unmarked consonant and coronal the unmarked articulation (for an overview of markedness theory, see Moravcsik and Wirth, 1986). Indeed, the special status of coronals has become an accepted part of generative grammar, although one would be at a loss to identify any study in which this belief has been subjected to a thorough scrutiny. This volume aims at providing such scrutiny.

It has recently been argued by Kiparsky (1985:97–98) and Avery and Rice (1988, 1989b), among others, that, beside being more frequent, coronals are more prone to undergo assimilation processes than any other place of articula-tion. Conversely, coronals are the only consonants to be invisible to phonological processes such as deletion in Japanese (see Grignon, 1984:324). It has also been shown that, in some languages, coronals alone are transparent to vowels (see Paradis and Prunet, 1989a,b), and that consonant harmonies, to the exclusion of those involving laryngeal consonants, consist almost exclusively of coronal har-monies (Shaw, 1988). Puel, Nespoulous, Bonafé, and Rascol (1980:253) point out that coronals also pattern in a unique way in aphasic speech, thus providing external evidence for the claim that coronals have a special status. Knowing more about coronals is, consequently, indispensable to a complete understanding of the phonology of any language. The collection of articles in this volume supports and provides additional evidence, internal and external, for the hypothesis that coronals have a special status.

If the 1970s brought about a better understanding of suprasegmental phenom-ena, especially tone and, later, stress, one of the main advances of the 1980s was a better understanding of segmental structure. Linear phonology, as exemplified in Chomsky and Halle (1968) and related work, assumed that features were grouped into unordered matrices. Early autosegmental phonology (see Gold-smith, 1976, among others) showed that some features must be represented on autosegmental tiers on a language-specific basis. Significant progress in segmen-tal phonology was made possible with the idea that a universal structure exists that assigns a constituent structure to a segment, with features grouping into class nodes, which in turn group together to form segments (see Clements, 1985). This hierarchical view of segmental organization, or feature geometry, triggered a renewal of interest in segmental processes. If features are organized into nodes, then some natural classes of features must manifest themselves in phonological processes, whereas other groups of features that do not form a constituent are predicted never to be needed in phonological descriptions.

At the same time, models emerged that questioned the relative amount of information present in underlying representation (UR) and during derivations (e.g., Kiparsky, 1982; Archangeli, 1984). It is, for instance, a matter of debate whether some feature specifications needed for phonetic representations (e.g., the feature [+back] in the vowel [u]) are absent from UR. Both lines of questioning combined to offer new tools of analysis and new areas of phonological investigation that had hitherto remained unexplored. The facts gathered by the authors in this volume are a rich source of information on the content of URs and help define minimal adequacy criteria for phonological theories with respect to segmental structure, underspecification, and locality conditions. For most contributors here, the special status of coronals lies in the fact that they lack specifications for place features in UR. This volume is the first collection of studies to evaluate all traditional arguments in a modern perspective and to reevaluate the often summary evidence given for some properties of coronals. In addition, it introduces many new arguments that have not been considered before because of the absence of sufficiently developed theories of segmental representation.

Another novel aspect of this book is the appeal to both internal evidence (i.e., phonological evidence based on the usual derivational processes in the grammar of a given language) and external evidence (i.e., phonological evidence from other sources such as speech errors and language games). Speech errors in both aphasic and ordinary speech are examined with a view to comparing the behavior of coronals and other consonants (labials, velars, and laryngeals). While it can sometimes be argued that phonological processes in internal evidence reflect lexicalized morpheme alternations (although even lexicalized alternations must have been truly phonological at an earlier stage), external evidence is not subject to the same criticism. Indeed, spontaneous or test-induced errors committed in normal and aphasic speech often use processes that are not part of the phonology of the language. Speech errors are therefore a source of information regarding the phonological representation of segments that is largely free of morphological interference. Some test-induced errors used here as external evidence bear on the repetition of nonwords, that is, words that have no dictionary entry in the internalized grammar of the speaker. Errors involving words with no UR should not involve lexicalized morpheme alternations. Thus such errors provide a window on the phonology of the language and the segmental representations assigned to different sounds (see Singh, 1988, for a review of the issues involved in the use of internal and external evidence).

This article provides a general survey of the research presented in this volume, although the conclusions we draw do not necessarily represent the views of all contributors, an arguably impossible task. Our article is organized as follows. The main concepts and models used by most of the contributors in the volume are presented in Section 2, along with a review of the literature on coronals.

A more detailed discussion of the articles and prior research is given in Section 3. Section 4 is a review of the theoretical problems posed by the behavior of coronals and the overall conclusions that can be drawn from the body of research presented in the book. We conclude with a summary of these theoretical proposals in Section 5.

2. CENTRAL CONCEPTS

2.1. Segmental Structure

Most of the research reported in this book assumes a hierarchical model of feature organization. Features are the primitive units of segmental structure. A universal tree structure organizes features into class nodes and groups class nodes together, as shown in (1) (some irrelevant features are omitted).[3] All nodes, terminal or not, stand on their own autosegmental tier. It is assumed that, while features are usually binary, class nodes are unary. For instance, [+continuant] contrasts with [−continuant], whereas the presence of a class node contrasts with its absence.

(1)

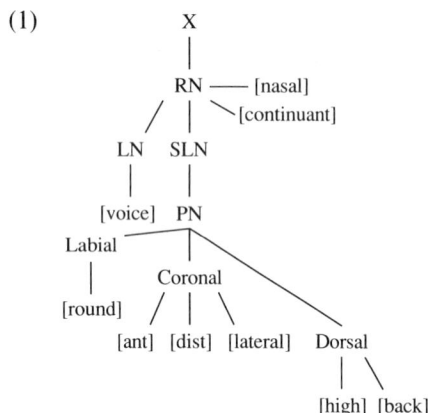

This model combines insights from Mascaró (1983), Clements (1985), Sagey (1986), Piggott (1987), and McCarthy (1988), among others. The highest level of segmental organization is the timing unit, which encodes segmental length. Several views on the nature of timing units prevail in current phonology (CV units, X-slots, moras), but a neutral term is sufficient here. The Root Node is quite similar to the traditional concept of "phoneme." Two class nodes separate features involving laryngeal articulation (the Laryngeal Node) and those features articulated above the larynx (the Supralaryngeal Node). The Laryngeal Node dominates features encoding contrasts such as voice, glottalization, and implosion. The Supralaryngeal Node dominates all place features. Manner features do not form a constituent and are scattered throughout the geometry. In the discussion below, a node or feature X immediately dominated by a node Y is said to be a dependent of node Y. Motivation for the feature geometry comes from rules repeatedly affecting some groups of features (see Clements, 1985).

The essential aspects of the feature geometry on which the present volume focuses are the articulators (Labial, Coronal, Dorsal), which encode place of articulation in both consonants and vowels, the features they dominate, and the feature [lateral]. All articulators are unary, so a labial consonant has a Labial articulator but neither a Coronal nor a Dorsal articulator. Labial consonants and round vowels use a Labial articulator, whereas coronals have a Coronal articulator. Velars and vowels share the Dorsal articulator. Glottals do not have a SLN (Supralaryngeal Node) and are represented solely under the LN (Laryngeal Node). Uvulars and pharyngeals are not directly relevant to the book.

2.2. Underspecification

Most current research assumes that some feature specifications are absent from URs and are filled in either during derivations or at a later stage (see Archangeli, 1988, and Mester and Itô, 1989, for an overview of the justification). Theories of underspecification diverge as to what feature specification is absent from UR, and as to when it is filled in. This section presents the basic underspecification concepts invoked in this volume.

Essentially, two types of theories of underspecification can be distinguished: radical and contrastive (for a thorough comparison of these theories and possible variants, see Archangeli, 1988; Mester and Itô, 1989; Mohanan, 1989). Radical underspecification is essentially a theory of markedness (e.g., see Kiparsky, 1982; Grignon, 1984; D. Pulleyblank, 1986), while contrastive specification is essentially a theory of redundancy (e.g., see Steriade, 1987a; Clements, 1988).

2.2.1. RADICAL UNDERSPECIFICATION

Radical underspecification holds that only one value of a feature, the unpredictable value, is present in UR (e.g., see Kiparsky, 1982:54; Archangeli and Pulleyblank, forthcoming). The other value, which is said to be predictable, is filled in by a redundancy rule during derivation or in the phonetic component. The predictability of values is usually determined by a universal theory of markedness, but it is a matter of debate whether, in some languages, an unpredictable value can correspond to the universally unmarked value (see Archangeli, 1984). Redundancy rules are formalized as follows.

(2) $[0F] \rightarrow [\alpha F]$, where α is either $+$ or $-$

If voicelessness in stops is predictable, then a voiceless labial stop like /p/ is [0voice] in UR, whereas, its voiced counterpart /b/ is specified as [+voice]; voiced stops are construed as more marked (less frequent) than their voiceless counterpart. So, if a language L has /p, b, g/ but no /k/, then /p/ is [0voice], whereas /b, g/ are [+voice]. On the basis of extensive and varied empirical evidence, summarized in Section 3, most contributors to this volume argue that the Coronal articulator is the unmarked (predictable) articulator. In other words, labials have a Labial articulator and velars a Dorsal articulator, but coronals have no Coronal articulator in UR, as shown below.

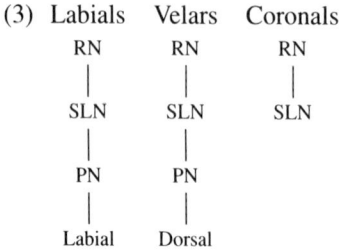

(3) Labials   Velars   Coronals
       RN   RN   RN
        | | |
       SLN   SLN   SLN
        | |
       PN   PN
        | |
      Labial   Dorsal

The following redundancy rule fills in the place features of coronals at a later stage.

(4)   [0Place] → Coronal

We will see in Section 3 that not only do coronals lack a Coronal articulator but also, for many authors in this volume, they lack a PN (Place Node), as shown in (3). Note that the feature geometry is such that if a consonant lacks a PN, it also lacks an articulator, since articulators are dominated by the PN.

If a language distinguishes several coronal subarticulations (such as dental, alveolar, retroflex, alveopalatal, palatal), these distinctions must be encoded by means of coronal features, such as [anterior] and [distributed]. Only one of the subarticulations can be exhaustively characterized as having the predictable value for each of the coronal features. It follows that only one of the subarticulations can be totally underspecified, that is, have no PN (presumably the dental articulation, or the alveolar articulation if there are no dentals), and thus have a special status in a given language. In the following discussion, we refer to the coronal subarticulation that is underlyingly absent when we refer to underspecified coronals. The thesis that [+anterior] coronals, and no other consonants (omitting, of course, glottals), lack place features is defended by most contributors to this volume. The differences between the proposals lie in which [+anterior] coronals are underspecified and on what arguments the underspecification thesis is based.

To conclude, note that it is generally assumed that [0F] and [αF] are nondistinct, so that only [−F] and [+F] can be distinguished by phonological rules (after Chomsky and Halle, 1968:336; see also Kiparsky, 1982:128; D. Pulleyblank, 1986:135). One could assume that this notion, called "distinctness," should be extended to articulators, which would mean that (5a) and (5b) below are nondistinct. In other words, a rule or a constraint involving articulators could not refer to the representation in (5b) to the exclusion of (5a), and vice versa.

(5) a. PN   b. PN
         |
         Labial

However, we will see in Section 4.3 that this notion of distinctness, which is implicit in many arguments, should not apply to monovalent (unary) phonological elements such as articulators.

2.2.2. CONTRASTIVE SPECIFICATION

In contrastive specification (e.g., see Steriade, 1987a; Clements, 1988), the content of URs is determined by examining contrasts in the phonemic inventory of the language. If two or more segments contrast with respect to a given feature, then the feature is said to be contrastive for that pair of segments. Both members of a contrasting pair are specified for the contrastive value but, if there is no contrast, neither value is present underlyingly. For instance, in language L, which has /p, b, g/ but no /k/, /p/ is [−voice], /b/ is [+voice], and /g/ is not specified for [voice] at all since there is no /k/.

Contrastive specification makes different predictions with respect to articulators. If a language has three stops /p, t, k/, radical underspecification can designate one articulator as predictable. For contrastive specification, /p/ contrasts with /t/ and both of them contrast with /k/. Consequently, all three should be specified with respect to place of articulation, that is, have an articulator in UR (see Clements, 1988:90). For instance, only in a system having one single nasal can this nasal be said to have no articulator in UR. It follows that, in a /p, t, k/ system, whatever empirical special status a given stop is found to have, this status could not be attributed to the absence of articulators. Therefore, contrastive specification seems unable to accommodate the claim that one class of consonants, namely [+anterior] coronals, has no PN.

2.2.3. MODIFIED CONTRASTIVE SPECIFICATION

The theory of contrastive specification presented in Avery and Rice (1988, 1989b) makes predictions different from those of Steriade (1987a) and Clements (1988), as it combines claims of both radical underspecification and contrastive specification. Avery and Rice (1988:103) suggest that features are underspecified according to a universal markedness theory, as in radical underspecification, unless a minimal phonemic contrast exists, in which case the marked value is specified. In such a case, however, the class node immediately dominating the contrastive feature must be present whatever the value of this contrastive feature (marked or unmarked). For instance, if language L has /p, b, g/, then /p/ is [0voice] and /b, g/ are [+voice], but all three have a specified Laryngeal Node, the node immediately dominating [voice].

Avery and Rice's model of contrastive specification differs from other versions of the theory in that it does designate a given articulator, namely, Coronal, as unmarked. Coronal is absent from coronals except for any coronal contrasting minimally with another coronal (for instance, /s/ and /ʃ/, where /s/ is [0anterior] and /ʃ/ [−anterior] both have a specified Coronal articulator). In a language where /p, t, k/ are the only stops, Avery and Rice's model predicts that only /t/ lacks an articulator. As a consequence, this model is compatible with at least some evidence for the underspecification of coronals, but its predictions are distinct from the predictions of radical underspecification: Only those consonants that do not contrast within the class of coronals must lack a Coronal articulator.

2.3. Syllable Structure

While few arguments presented in this volume hinge on a particular model of syllable structure, some references are made to specific syllabic nodes: Onset, Rhyme, Nucleus, and Coda (see the coda condition in Yip, this volume). These nodes are organized as follows.

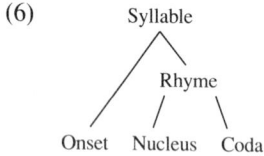

(6)

Terminal syllabic nodes immediately dominate the units of the timing tier, which in turn dominate Root Nodes.

2.4. Some Properties of Coronals

The phonological literature contains several arguments to the effect that coronals are essentially different from other consonants. In this section, we present some of these arguments.

2.4.1. ASSIMILATION

One of the immediate advantages of representing features autosegmentally is the elimination of much of the arbitrariness of phonological rules. In autosegmental phonology, there should be a transparent relationship between a process and the environment in which this process is observed. Thus, nasalization of a vowel when this vowel is preceded by a nasal consonant consists of adding an association line between the [+nasal] feature of the consonant and the following oral vowel, a process called spreading. Similarly, place assimilation must be expressed by spreading the place features of the assimilation trigger to the assimilation target.

Kiparsky (1985:97–98) observes that coronals are the consonants most likely to assimilate in place features. In his study of Catalan nasal assimilation, Kiparsky captures the fact that /n/ assimilates to all consonants (while /m/ only assimilates to labiodentals, and /ɲ, ŋ/ do not assimilate) by depriving coronals of place features in UR. This tendency to assimilate is expressed by the spreading of the place features of the following consonant to the unspecified consonant (the following is a reinterpretation of Kiparsky's proposal in terms of articulator theory).

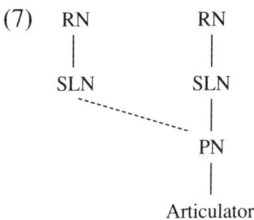

(7) RN   RN
     | |
    SLN   SLN
      ⸨⸩ |
                 PN
                 |
            Articulator

Assimilations targeting noncoronals, which are much less frequent and which usually also target coronals, are expressed by linking-and-delinking of place features in a feature-changing fashion. Assimilation-based arguments in favor of placeless coronals are also presented by Avery and Rice (1988, 1989a,b) and Cho (1988, also this volume).

Essentially the same reasoning is used for vowel harmony. These processes are viewed as the spreading of a specified (set of) feature(s) onto a vowel unspecified for this (set of) feature(s). Child phonology also exhibits consonant harmony, that is, consonants assimilating to a nonadjacent consonant, as shown in Stemberger and Stoel-Gammon (1989, also this volume). The same phenomenon is observed in speech errors by aphasics (Béland and Favreau, this volume). This type of consonant harmony is essentially a nonadjacent assimilation, that is, it operates across intervening segments. The important point is that coronals tend to be the assimilated segments in both adjacent and nonadjacent assimilations. This tendency is explained if coronals are underspecified for place features.

2.4.2. NEUTRALIZATION

The neutralizations that are sometimes observed in coda position provide another means of comparing the relative complexity of consonants. In coda position, it is common for several series to merge into the least complex one. Korean tensed and aspirated stops are neutralized to plain stops, and continuants to stops in coda position (see Cho, 1988:49). In the same way, of the three stop series (plain, glottalized, and aspirated), only plain consonants are found in coda position in Carrier, an Athapaskan language (see Cook, 1976:6). In Fula, prenasalized stops, which frequently occur in onset position, never show up in coda position (see Paradis, 1986).[4] One can conclude that the tendency is for complex segments to simplify in coda position. The Korean neutralization of palatals to dentals in coda position, which Cho (1988:49) reports, can then be seen as evidence that dentals are less complex than palatals. Other properties of the coda position and coronals are discussed in Yip (this volume) from the point of view of morpheme structure constraints.

2.4.3. TRANSPARENCY

One of the most persuasive arguments for underspecification lies in transparency effects, that is, cases where a segment allows a feature to spread across it. If coronals have no specified place features in UR, transparency effects ought to single out coronals, at least in some languages.

Paradis and Prunet (1989a–c, 1990) argue that such transparency effects are found in several West African languages where vowel spreading can take place across coronals but is blocked across noncoronals (and [−anterior] coronals). This difference can be accounted for if the process spreads the PN of the vowel: Coronals lack a PN and are transparent, whereas other consonants have a specified PN and necessarily act as blockers. The spreading vowel node must be the PN, as Dorsal Node spreading would treat all consonants as transparent. Similar coronal transparency effects with respect to vowel spreading in aphasic speech errors are observed by Béland and Favreau (this volume).

It should be noted that a model such as the tree structure in (1) allows for two types of vowel spreading: Dorsal Node spreading, to which all consonants (except velars) should be transparent, and PN spreading, to which at most one class of consonants (plus glottals) should be transparent, since only one class of consonants can lack a PN. Van der Hulst and Smith (1990) and Trigo (1988) argue that there exist cases of vowel spreading to which only velars are transparent. This is taken to be evidence for the underspecification of velars. In the absence of analyses that treat both coronal and velar transparency with the same assumptions, the possibility that two types of consonant transparency exist may require some parameterization in consonant underspecification, such as that expressed by complement rules in Archangeli (1984) and Archangeli and Pulleyblank (forthcoming). Obviously, this requirement would weaken the thesis that coronals have a special status. An alternative to parameterization is proposed in Paradis and Prunet (forthcoming).[5]

2.4.4. FREQUENCY

As mentioned at the beginning of the article, it is often claimed, in this volume and elsewhere, that coronals are the most frequent consonants and that this frequency is relevant to their unmarked status. In fact, what is meant by "fre-

quency" varies from author to author. For the sake of clarity, we propose the
following distinctions among frequency types.

(8) a. INVENTORY FREQUENCY: the number of coronals in the consonant in-
         ventory of a given language (in comparison with the number of other
         consonants in the same inventory).
     b. TYPOLOGICAL INVENTORY FREQUENCY: the number of coronals attested
         in a universal phonemic inventory (in comparison with all other attested
         consonants in the same inventory).
     c. OCCURRENCE FREQUENCY: the number of times coronals are produced
         in a representative speech corpus (in comparison with the number of
         times other consonants are produced in the same corpus).

Labial, dental–alveolar, and velar places of articulation are found in all languages, but the dental–alveolar series predominates in all frequency types (as
does the class of coronals as a whole). Let us review some evidence regarding
these three frequency types.

Consider first inventory frequency. For instance, English coronals are pho-
nemically more frequent than phonemes of any other place of articulation: Omitting glides, there are 13 coronals (out of which 7 are alveolars), 5 labials, and
2 velars (counting both voiceless and voiced segments). French shows similar
proportions: 5 labials, 9 coronals (out of which 7 are dentals), and 2 velars.

Consider next typological inventory frequency. In the International Phonetic
Alphabet, coronal sounds are over three times more numerous than either labial
or velar sounds. This predominance is also reflected in Maddieson (1987).
Maddieson notes (1987:40) that if a language has /p/ then it has /k/, and if it has
/k/ then it has /t/. Concerning fricatives, Maddieson (1987:41, and references
therein) notes that /s/ is the most common fricative. Out of 317 languages, /s/ is
attested in 266 languages, /ʃ/ in 146 languages, /f/ in 135 languages, and /x/ in
45 languages. As for nasals, we mentioned at the beginning of the article that 316
languages have /n/, while 299 languages have /m/, and 167 the velar /ŋ/.

Coronals also dominate in occurrence frequency. For instance, Fry (1947)
showed that the five most frequent consonants in a (Southern British) English
conversation corpus were all coronals (*n, t, d, s,* and *l,* in that order). Ferreres
(forthcoming) reports the following distribution in a conversational (Argentinian) Spanish corpus: 69% coronals, 18% labials, and 11% velars.

Frequency figures are important for any claims about the special status of coronals, because some of the asymmetrical behavior of coronals could be attributed to
their frequency. We mentioned in Section 2.4.1 that assimilations involving coronals are more common than assimilations involving noncoronals. This assimilation tendency is an argument for the special status of coronals since it is usually
coronals that assimilate *to* other consonants, rather than the opposite. We claim,
along with most of the contributors to this volume, that such a difference must be

explained in terms of absence versus presence of segmental content. If matters of substance were irrelevant, one would not expect asymmetrical behavior from coronals and noncoronals with regard to assimilation. It could be objected that coronals are more frequent than other consonants, so that they are more likely to be involved in any process. This objection can be discarded, however, if the analysis takes into account the inventory and the occurrence frequencies of coronals. In Section 3.4.2, we report on evidence from Béland and Favreau (this volume) that coronals still behave asymmetrically on a statistical basis.

3. ON THE SPECIAL STATUS OF CORONALS

The contributions in this volume fall into four categories: articles presenting a classification of coronals, articles bearing on coronals and phonological constraints, articles improving on the representation of coronals, and articles discussing the status of coronals in speech errors.

3.1. The Classification of Coronals

An in-depth investigation of the possible phonetic and phonological coronal articulations is presented in Keating (this volume). Coronals are those consonants that use the tongue blade. Keating notes that, from a phonetic point of view, the special status of coronals lies in the greater variety of places and manners of articulations that is available to them. There are as many traditional coronal articulations (dental, alveolar, palato-alveolar, retroflex, and palatal) as all noncoronal articulations put together (bilabial, labiodental, velar, uvular, and pharyngeal). As for manner, two classes, affricates and liquids, are almost invariably coronal. Keating evaluates traditional as well as recent feature classifications against a wide body of phonetic data (X-ray tracings).

One important proposal concerns the representation of palatals and alveopalatals. Keating shows that, from an articulatory point of view, these consonants can be viewed as coronals including a high front vowel, or as complex segments distinguished by means of a new feature, [Lower Incisors Contact] (see Halle, forthcoming, for this term). The postulation of a high front vowel in at least some coronals is to be related to Lahiri and Evers' (this volume) study of palatalization and van der Hulst and Smith's (1990) encoding of place features in terms of $|a|$, $|i|$, $|u|$ primitives, with $|i|$ being characteristic of coronal articulation.

3.2. Coronals and Morpheme Structure Constraints

Morpheme structure constraints (MSCs) are an important source of evidence for phonological representations because their domain of application is unambiguous: They apply to URs before any kind of rule. As underspecification theories are primarily theories of the content of URs, MSCs occupy a privileged position among the various types of phonological evidence.

In the recent literature on underspecification, several authors have referred to MSCs on coronals as evidence for the presence or absence of place features in UR. Let us review three of these arguments.

Clements (1988:86) points out the existence of an English MSC that prohibits adjacent [+strident, +coronal, +continuant] segments (such as [sz, zs]). The existence of this MSC presumably implies the presence of underlying Coronal articulators. In the same way, Greenberg (1950:162) and McCarthy (1989) discuss MSCs in Arabic that prohibit homorganic consonants in consonantal roots. (Homorganic consonants are possible in second and third position of roots if they are identical. However, these roots should be treated as biliteral; see McCarthy, 1981:396.) Significantly, these MSCs do not treat coronals as distinct from other places of articulation (see Greenberg, 1950:177). Mester and Itô (1989:265) point out that such MSCs, which are also attested in Javanese (Uhlenbeck, 1950; Kenstowicz, 1986; Mester, 1986), indicate that all articulators, including Coronal, are present in UR. It is therefore clear that the existence of MSCs prohibiting adjacent coronals poses a genuine challenge to the underspecification of coronals. Two articles in this volume deal with MSCs, to whose findings we now turn.

Davis (this volume) presents a detailed examination of an English MSC that prohibits homorganic consonants in *sCVC* words. This prohibition has been tested with a 20,000-word computerized dictionary. It has been found that this MSC rules out homorganic labials and velars (*spep, *skek) but permits homorganic coronals (*stet, state). Unlike the MSCs discussed above, this MSC does single out coronals as special: They are the only consonants exempt from the homorganicity restriction. The fact that coronals do not obey the MSC is explained if the MSC rules out identical homorganic articulators and coronals do not have an articulator. Davis concludes that the presence of a Coronal Node in UR is a parameterized option. He concludes that coronal stridents do have a PN, as evidenced by Clements' (1988) MSC against adjacent coronal stridents, but that at least /t/ (and possibly *n, l,* and *r,* though independent constraints make it difficult to test coronal sonorants) does not.

Yip (this volume) introduces two parameterized constraints belonging to Universal Grammar.

(9) MODIFIED CODA CONDITION
     Codas may not have Place features.
     CLUSTER CONDITION
     Adjacent consonants are limited at most to one Place specification.

These two constraints, combined with the assumption that coronals lack place features in UR, explain two recurrent generalizations on consonant distribution in a number of languages. The first constraint allows one to explain the appearance of only one class of consonants, namely, coronals, in syllable-final position and in suffixes. The second constraint explains why consonant clusters are frequently limited to geminates or clusters including a coronal. Both constraints can operate as well-formedness conditions on morphemes, that is, as MSCs. Thus, these MSCs treat coronals as distinct from other consonants because they lack place features. Yip concludes that the class of underspecified coronals is better defined by the premises of radical underspecification, which specify only one value of a contrastive feature.

3.3. The Structure of Coronals

The contributions that argue for a more adequate representation of coronals and of coronal features deal with the following aspects of coronals: the representation of high vowels as coronals (Lahiri and Evers), the representation of [lateral] and of other sonorant features (Rice and Avery), coronal harmonies (Shaw), and the status of the Coronal Node on a universal basis (Cho).

3.3.1. PALATALIZATION AND CORONALS

Lahiri and Evers (this volume), drawing on Bhat's (1978) typology of palatalization processes and on other sources, argue that current views of coronal structure do not permit adequate accounts of palatalization processes. Bhat (1978) showed that palatalization is typically caused by a high front vowel–glide, or sometimes by the class of front vowels, or even, in a few cases, by a back high vowel. Also typically, but not exclusively, palatalization targets are coronals. The affinity between high front vowels–glides and coronals suggests that palatalization is an assimilatory phenomenon (see also E. Pulleyblank, 1989). However, as Lahiri and Evers point out, current feature-geometric representations (and previous models, such as Chomsky and Halle, 1968) do not assign similar structures·to both coronals, represented by a Coronal articulator, and front vowels, represented by a Dorsal articulator. A recent attempt to unify consonant and vowel features, motivated by similar considerations, is found in Clements (1989), but Lahiri and Evers argue that it reintroduces two distinct sets of features by positing different PNs for consonants and vowels.

Lahiri and Evers propose a feature geometry that includes two new nodes dominated by the PN: Articulators, which dominate articulators (Labial, Coronal, Dorsal, Radical), and Tongue Position, which dominates height features ([high] and [low]). There is no feature [back]. Independent support for a node that groups height features is in Hyman (1988:269) and Odden (1989), who suggest, for different reasons, that height features form a constituent.

(10)

```
                        PN
                  /           \
          Articulators      Tongue Position
          /    |    \  \       /    \
      Labial Coronal Dorsal Radical [high] [low]
```

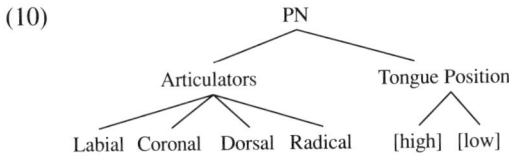

Both palatalized coronals and front vowels are [−anterior] and share a Coronal articulator, which explains their tendency to interact in assimilation processes. Three types of palatalization are documented: Coronal articulator spreading, [−anterior] spreading, and [+high] spreading.

Two aspects of this analysis treat coronals as essentially different from other consonants. First, palatalization of noncoronals (labials and velars) can only add a secondary articulation (for instance, [pʸ], [kʸ], whereas coronals can acquire a different articulation (from dental–alveolar /t/ to palato-alveolar [tʃ]). The second aspect lies in the nature of the off-glide typical of palatalized segments. This off-glide always takes the form of a high front glide, even when the trigger is not a high front vowel–glide. Lahiri and Evers suggest that high front glides appear because the default realization of a high glide is a coronal glide (not a labial glide) and point out that if a language has only one glide, it usually is [y] (see Maddieson, 1987:92).

3.3.2. CORONALS AND [LATERAL]

Rice and Avery (this volume) and Shaw (this volume) examine the feature geometry position of [lateral]. Some current research assumes that [lateral] is a Coronal dependent because laterals are almost always coronals (see Levin, 1988; McCarthy, 1988). Rice and Avery, and Shaw (see Section 3.3.3), argue that while it is true that laterals are normally coronal, it does not follow that [lateral] is a Coronal dependent. They argue instead that [lateral] is located higher up in the feature geometry of sonorant laterals (Rice and Avery) and of fricative laterals (Shaw). This issue is most important for coronal underspecification. If [lateral] is a Coronal dependent, then a segment specified for [lateral] must have a Coronal articulator in UR. If, on the other hand, [lateral] is above the PN, a segment specified for [lateral] can lack a Coronal Node in UR.

Rice and Avery assume the theory of underspecification proposed in Avery and Rice (1988, 1989b) and discussed in Section 2.2.3. In addition, they assume that all features (and nodes) are unary. One new node is proposed, Spontaneous Voice (SV), which is a daughter of the SLN and a sister of the PN (see also Piggott, forthcoming, on the SV Node). Sonorants normally have a SV Node and nonsonorants do not. The SV Node immediately dominates two sister nodes: [nasal] and [lateral]. It is further maintained that nasals are underlyingly unspecified for [nasal], on the assumption that nasals are the unmarked sonorants, that is, nasals only have a SV Node in UR. Laterals are marked sonorants and have both [lateral] and SV specifications in UR. The following is a partial sketch of the proposed geometry (nodes between parentheses are default nodes).

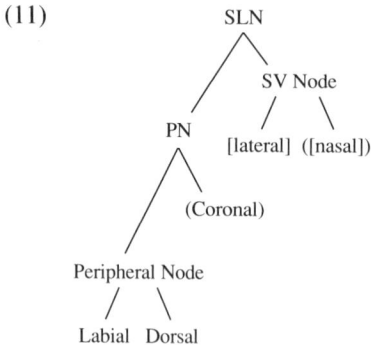

(11)

```
                    SLN
                    /\
                   /  \
                  /    SV Node
                 /    /  \
               PN  [lateral] ([nasal])
               /\
              /  \
             / (Coronal)
            /
    Peripheral Node
        /  \
       /    \
    Labial  Dorsal
```

The Coronal articulator is the default (i.e., unspecified) value for the PN. The structure of the PN also includes a Peripheral Node, which is invoked in their article and to which we later return.

In a model where [lateral] is a Coronal dependent, the reason why laterals are always coronals follows from the representation itself. This is not the case in a model like (11). According to Rice and Avery (this volume), laterals have no PN in UR because a complexity constraint imposes an upper limit on the underlying complexity (i.e., markedness) of consonants, based on a balance between the PN and the SV Node. If a segment has a specified PN, then it cannot have a specified SV Node. This explains why nasals, which have no specification under the SV Node, can have labial and velar articulations. But laterals have a marked [lateral] specification under the SV Node and, as a consequence, cannot have a specified PN. Laterals are phonetically realized as coronals because Coronal is the default articulation, as shown in (4). Arguments based on lateral assimilation, and on lateral transparency in Guere and in Mau (see Paradis and Prunet, 1989c), are adduced to show that laterals do not have a Coronal articulator in UR, a situation compatible with (11) but not with [lateral] as a Coronal dependent.

3.3.3. CORONAL HARMONIES

Shaw (this volume) examines phonological consonant harmony systems in a variety of languages. The term "phonological harmony" covers all phenomena of assimilation, dissimilation, or MSCs operating on nonadjacent consonants if the purpose of the harmony is not to indicate morphemic information. Shaw observes that some consonantal harmonies are well attested (laryngeal, labial, coronal) while others are not (dorsal, pharyngeal). It is assumed that proper feature geometry representations combined with underspecification ought to explain why vowel harmonies are more frequent than consonant harmonies, and why some consonant harmonies are unattested. Most important for this volume are the following questions. First, why are coronal harmonies much more frequent than other harmonies? Second, why is only a subset of coronals involved as trigger and target in coronal harmonies?

Shaw argues that coronal harmonies are more frequent than other consonant harmonies because, of the three articulators (Labial, Coronal, and Dorsal), Coronal is the only articulator that does not dominate vowel features. As vowels never appear under the Coronal articulator, it is easier for coronal harmonies to spread across intervening vowels. Shaw makes some proposals on how to reconcile the assumption that Coronal does not dominate vowel features with recent contradictory claims such as those of Lahiri and Evers (this volume) and van der Hulst and Smith (1990).

As for the second question, certain assumptions regarding what features and nodes are underspecified explain why some coronals are not targeted by coronal harmonies. Other harmonies, on the other hand, do not normally allow a subset of transparent segments with the same articulation as the trigger–target segments. This, argues Shaw, is due to the fact that Coronal is the unmarked articulation. Only (some) coronals lack a PN in UR and, as a consequence, are transparent to harmonies affecting other coronals. It follows that some coronals must lack place features in UR while other consonants (except, of course, laryngeals) cannot.

A detailed analysis of Tahltan, an Athapaskan language with five series of coronals, shows that in this language laterals belong to the set of transparent consonants. Shaw shows that [lateral] must be distinctive in Tahltan. Yet, the facts of Tahltan coronal harmony show that laterals lack a PN. It follows that [lateral] cannot be a Coronal dependent and that it must be above the PN. Like Rice and Avery (this volume), but for different reasons, this article shows that [lateral] is not a Coronal dependent.

There are two other important implications for feature geometry. First, Shaw argues that velars and vowels must share the same Dorsal articulator, contrary to Steriade's (1987b) distinction between Velar and Dorsal articulators. Second, this article demonstrates that current views on the levels of feature hierarchy scanned by harmonies must be revised. The minimal scansion parameter (see Archangeli and Pulleyblank, 1987) must be redefined to scan the tier of the spreading feature/node itself, not the tier immediately dominating it.

3.3.4. THE UNIVERSALITY OF THE CORONAL ARTICULATOR

Cho (this volume) questions the universality of articulators, with special reference to Coronal. Comparing two theories of place features, articulator theory

(AT), which uses unary articulators, and place of articulation theory (PT), which uses binary features such as [coronal] and [anterior], Cho argues that both theories are needed for different languages such as Sanskrit and Korean. As a consequence, AT and PT must be selected as different options of a parameter somewhat similar to the nonconfigurationality parameter in syntax (see Whitman, 1986).

PT defines two classes with respect to [coronal]: Coronals are [+coronal] and noncoronals are [−coronal]. AT, on the other hand, defines only one class: Coronals have a Coronal articulator but there is no single class including both labials and velars. Cho shows that there are processes (in Old Korean, Old English, and Hungarian) referring to noncoronals as a natural class and concludes that PT sometimes makes better predictions than AT.

Much of the evidence adduced by Cho is of an assimilatory nature. It is argued that coronals are the prime targets of assimilation because they lack a PN in UR (radical underspecification is assumed). One important contribution is the identification of gradient assimilations, that is, assimilations in which several (but not all) classes of consonants are place assimilation targets. In Korean, dentals assimilate to labials, palatals, and velars, but labials and palatals only assimilate to velars. Velars do not assimilate. A gradient complexity is proposed (dentals, labials–palatals, velars) where dentals are least specified, velars most specified, and labials and palatals are in the middle. Less complex segments assimilate only to more complex segments. Cho argues that AT cannot capture this complexity gradation because it assigns equal complexity to Labial and Dorsal.

We saw in (11) a proposal by Rice and Avery (this volume) to recognize a Peripheral Node dominating Labial and Dorsal only, which could provide an interesting alternative analysis for some of the problems pointed out by Cho. Avery and Rice (1989b:195) claim that the Peripheral Node can solve the problem of characterizing the class of noncoronals. It appears that their proposal can also assign different complexity values to Labial and Dorsal, and to the class of labials and velars in Korean.

3.4. Coronals and Speech Errors

Two articles draw on external evidence to shed light on consonant structure. Stemberger and Stoel-Gammon (this volume) examine errors produced by unimpaired English-speaking adults and children, both in spontaneous speech and in tests, whereas Béland and Favreau (this volume) examine similar errors in French-speaking aphasics. The consonant systems of English and French are similar enough to exhibit essentially the same contrasts. Both languages have only two clearly contrastive coronal classes: the [+anterior] s / z and the [−anterior] $\int$ / $ʒ$. While both articles conclude that only coronals (i.e., [+anterior] coronals) may lack place features, they disagree on the proper underspecification model. Stemberger and Stoel-Gammon see no difference in [+anterior] coronals and hence opt for radical underspecification. Béland and Favreau argue that *s* / *z* behave more like ʃ / ʒ than like other [+anterior] coronals and hence opt for Avery and Rice's contrastive specification.

3.4.1. NORMAL SPEECH

Stemberger and Stoel-Gammon (this volume) draw on adult and child speech errors to determine whether all places of articulation are equal. After concluding that coronals are systematically more vulnerable than other consonants, they compare several explanations: frequency, markedness without underspecification, and underspecification. They argue that only underspecification can account for the observed phenomena and that speakers use underspecified representation in on-line processing.

Coronals differ from other consonants in several respects.

1. Substitution: It appears that coronals are replaced more often by other consonants than other places of articulation.
2. Harmony: Harmony processes also indicate that coronals assimilate more to labials and velars than the reverse. Both of these tendencies are interpreted as a tendency toward specification (by insertion or by spreading).
3. Exchange: Consonants are exchanged more in a word when one of the two exchanged segments is a coronal.
4. Fusion: Fusion processes between consonants indicate that what usually remains in the output are the manner features of coronals and the place features of noncoronals. This is again easily explained if coronals lack place features.

Stemberger and Stoel-Gammon go on to compare three alternative explanations. First, an acquisition-based theory fails because coronals and labials are acquired at the same time. Thus, acquisition does not distinguish between labials and coronals. Second, a frequency-based theory ("frequency" here is of both the occurrence and typological inventory types) encounters difficulties because the observed tendency is toward *less* frequent segments (noncoronals) when coronals are in contact with other consonants, but the tendency is toward *more* frequent segments when labials are in contact with velars. Finally, a markedness-without-underspecification approach, such as that advocated by Mohanan (1989), fails to account for the presence of both marked and unmarked segment biases in the same language if it is assumed that less marked means more frequent. In other words, Mohanan's proposal has the same problem as the frequency-based explanation.

An important point addressed in their article is the necessity of referring to the absence of a node within a segmental structure, an unavailable option under some interpretations of distinctness (see Section 2.2.1). Stemberger and Stoel-Gammon maintain that, in spite of the absence of a Coronal articulator, speech error processes must see the difference between a coronal (nothing) and a non-coronal (something), a point to which we return in Section 4.3.

3.4.2. APHASIC SPEECH

Béland and Favreau (this volume) examine the behavior of consonant articulations in speech errors made by French-speaking aphasics. This study is based on a large corpus of data collected by the authors from a total of 31 aphasic subjects. Every aphasic subject is matched by a normal control subject with respect to age, sex, and educational level. Errors produced by both groups are identical qualitatively, the only difference being that aphasics make about six times more errors than normal subjects.

A major contribution of their article is that, for the first time, the statistics presented on occurrence frequencies of every phoneme take into account the inventory frequency bias toward coronals. Let us take a hypothetical statistical argument in favor of coronals to illustrate the importance of this point. One could argue that coronals are special because, say, coronals are epenthesized more often than other segments in French speech errors. The higher percentage alone is insufficient as evidence because French has more coronals than noncoronals. (French has five labials, seven [+anterior] coronals, two [−anterior] coronals, and two velars, omitting glides, the rare palatal nasal, and the dialectal [h].) So, even if the phonological properties of coronals were identical to those of noncoronals, random distribution would still yield at least as many coronal epentheses as noncoronal. This study argues that coronals still differ significantly from other consonants when statistics compensate for the built-in inventory frequency bias toward coronals.

Coronals differ with respect to the following processes.

1. Substitution: Coronals are more often replaced by noncoronals than any other class is replaced by its complement.
2. Harmony: Excluding fricatives, coronals are more often replaced by noncoronals present in the correct form than any other class is replaced by its complement. As in Stemberger and Stoel-Gammon (see Section 3.4.1), these biases are explained as tendencies toward specification (by insertion or by spreading).
3. Epenthesis: In initial and intervocalic positions, coronals (excluding fricatives) are inserted more often than noncoronals. In final position, the pattern differs slightly with the [+anterior] coronal fricatives (/s, z/) inserted more often than other consonants.
4. Deletion: In any position, coronals are more often deleted than noncoronals.

5. Transparency: Only coronals are transparent to vowel spreading(e.g., [ɔpete] instead of French [ɔpte] 'opted').

The facts of epenthesis contradict one of Mohanan's (1989) arguments against underspecification. Mohanan points out that if Coronal were the default articulation, one should find a number of languages with epenthetic coronals, whereas in fact epenthetic consonants are usually glides or glottal stops. However, coronal epenthesis does exist, for instance, in Gokana (see Hyman, 1985:65). Another example is *t*-epenthesis in Amharic (see Leslau, 1967:254, nn. 1–2; Broselow, 1984:22). In Amharic, the infinitive skeletal pattern is /mä-$C_1C_2VC_3$/, which yields *mälbäs* 'to dress' and *mäkfät* 'to open' for the triliteral roots /lbs/ and /kft/, respectively. When the root is biliteral, as is the case with /bl/ and /fǰ/, the final consonant slot of the infinitive pattern, C_3, is filled by an epenthetic [t]: *mäblat* 'to eat' and *mäffät* 'to consume'. Broselow (1984:22) shows that this epenthetic [t], which is demonstrably not part of the root, also appears in other skeletal patterns to fill in a consonant slot when the root does not have enough consonants. Moreover, Béland and Favreau's French data indicate that *r-l*-epentheses in particular are common in at least external evidence (see also Bagemihl, 1989:525), on *n*-epenthesis in a Fula language game). The frequency of glottal epenthesis is not necessarily a problem for coronal underspecification. Underspecified coronals lack a Coronal articulator, and probably also a PN (depending on one's assumptions), but have a SLN. This makes them more complex than glottals, which do not have a SLN. Thus, the prediction is that glottal epenthesis will be more frequent than coronal epenthesis, and coronal epenthesis more frequent than labial or velar epenthesis.

4. SOME THEORETICAL IMPLICATIONS

We now turn to some theoretical implications of the research on coronals presented in this volume and in the literature.

4.1. Markedness and Underspecification

Mohanan (1989), in an overview of underspecification theories, suggests that (at least some of) the phenomena attributed to underspecification could be handled by a theory of markedness using linking rules, as in Chomsky and Halle (1968), or by a theory of rule naturalness. It is not clear how such an approach would handle any of the various arguments presented here for the special status of coronals: the coda and cluster conditions, assimilation, neutralization, transparency, deletion, epenthesis, substitution, the frequency of coronal harmonies, etc. It is even less clear how it could connect all of these properties together.

Linear phonology has been criticized because it could operate any change irrespective of its context. Perhaps the major innovation of autosegmental phonology, and its central goal, has been the attempt to eliminate arbitrariness in phonological processes. An analysis is now considered arbitrary if it fails to relate a rule change to the context in which it occurs, for example, a vowel lowers before a pharyngeal because pharyngeals are [+low], but vowel lowering before [−low] consonants is unexpected. In other words, nonlinear phonology tries to relate alternations to phonological representations rather than relegate these alternations to rule typologies or to a nonstructural notion of rule naturalness. Relating the various properties of coronals to a structural characteristic, their lack of place features, represents another way to satisfy the central objective of nonlinear phonology. Explanations that are not based on underspecification are conceivable, but they would have to share this one advantage with underspecification theory: The special status of segments is encoded in phonological structures themselves. It is not clear how linking rules or a typology of natural rules could attain this goal.

Mohanan (1989) maintains that coronals also behave asymmetrically in the postlexical component, where it is possible that they already have been specified. This would imply that the special status of coronals is not due to the lack of place features but to some other property. Cases where it could be shown that coronals are already specified and yet behave asymmetrically would be problematic for the theoretical position of most contributors to this book. Further research is needed to determine if such cases can be positively identified, and how they could be analyzed.

4.2. Consonant and Vowel Features

It is sometimes suggested that the special status of coronals lies in their articulator (Coronal) having no vowel-feature dependents. Morris Halle and Michael Kenstowicz (personal communication, 1989) have pointed out to us that this proposal can account for the cases reported in Paradis and Prunet (1989a–c, 1990), where coronals alone are shown to be transparent to vowels. Shaw (this volume) makes a strong case for this being the reason why coronal harmonies are more frequent than other harmonies. However, this property alone is insufficient to explain lateral transparency to consonant harmonies, for which Shaw must also invoke coronal underspecification. The assumption that Coronal does not dominate vowel features (Shaw, this volume) or that it does (Lahiri and Evers, this volume) cannot account by itself for all the properties of coronals.

For instance, the dichotomy between consonant and vowel features seems to have no bearing on the coda and cluster conditions (Yip), the behavior of coronals in MSCs (Davis), the coronality of laterals (Rice and Avery, Shaw), the assimilation of coronals (Kiparsky, 1985:97–98; Avery and Rice, 1989a,b;

Cho, this volume), coronal substitutions, harmonies, epentheses and deletions (Stemberger and Stoel-Gammon, this volume; Béland and Favreau, this volume), coronal neutralization in coda position (Cho, 1988:49), and other coronal properties. It appears that only the hypothesis that coronals lack place features can account for and relate these asymmetries in the behavior of coronals and noncoronals. Besides, it is not clear that a complete dichotomy between vowels and coronals can explain the relation that seems to exist between palatalization and front vowels (see Lahiri and Evers, this volume).

4.3. Distinctness

To assume that coronals lack place features in UR, and to represent them as having gaps on the PN tier, is a necessary hypothesis, but it requires clarification with respect to the notion of distinctness presented below (see also Section 2.2.1). Consider the Arabic MSC against homorganic consonants in a root, which treats coronals and noncoronals alike (see Section 3.2). According to Mester and Itô (1989:265), this constraint indicates that Arabic coronals are specified in UR, otherwise they would be invisible to MSCs. However, one can alternatively argue that this coronal visibility indicates instead that two incomplete structures are perceived as identical, and distinct from other consonant types. For instance, it is clear from Béland and Favreau (this volume) and Stemberger and Stoel-Gammon (this volume) that a PN gap must be distinguished from a PN specification to account for speech errors (see Section 3.4). The possibility of referring to a gap was hinted at by Kiparsky (1985:98–99), but some current positions such as that of Mester and Itô (1989) do not consider that incomplete structures can be referred to by MSCs. Their argumentation is based indirectly on the notion of distinctness.

This notion is related to the ternariness debate, that is, to the desire to prevent binary features from creating ternary contrasts (see Dresher, 1985; Archangeli, 1988:184; for recent overviews). For this purpose, D. Pulleyblank (1986:135) resorts to the following distinctness constraints, due to Archangeli (1984).

(12) a. A rule must not refer to [αF] in its structural description before a default rule assigns [αF].

  b. A rule must not refer to the fact that a slot is *not* linked to a value on tier *n* for purposes of affecting a feature value on tier *m*.

Reference to [0F] creates potential ternary distinctions only if [F] is a binary feature (i.e., if [+F], [−F], and [0F] are all available at the same stage in a derivation). However, class nodes, such as articulators or PNs, are unary. Yip (1989: 370) points out that with unary nodes, distinguishing a gap and a specification does not create the same problems as with binary features since only presence or absence of a given node is available.[6] Actually, D. Pulleyblank (1986:70, 147) proposes structure-changing rules that refer to nothing (a gap) when nothing is the absence of an autosegmental link (a floating tone or a floating segment), that is, the absence of a monovalent phonological element. Monovalent elements are theoretically unproblematic with respect to ternariness. It is not surprising then that processes involved in speech errors are sensitive to the absence of an articulator, as argued by Stemberger and Stoel-Gammon. If articulator gaps can be perceived, the Arabic MSC on homorganic consonants discussed by Mester and Itô (1989) does not necessarily entail that coronals are specified in UR.[7]

5. CONCLUSION

In summary, the feature geometry coming out from a partial synthesis of the various proposals presented here is the following.[8]

(13)

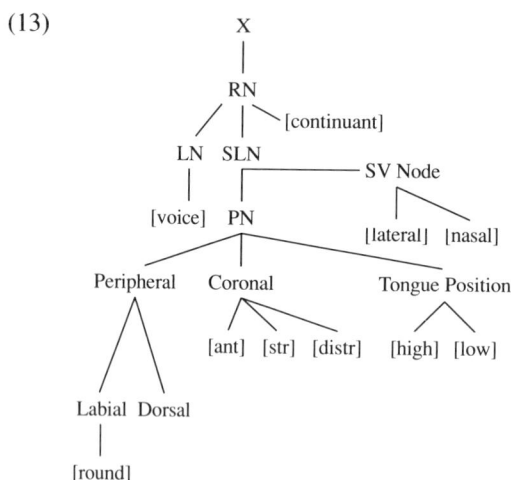

This model places [lateral] above the PN rather than as a Coronal dependent (see Rice and Avery, Shaw). Whether [lateral] is attached to the RN (as proposed by Shaw) or to the SV Node (as proposed by Rice and Avery) is still a question of debate. What matters here is that both proposals agree that [lateral] is not a Coronal dependent. This model also includes a Peripheral Node (see Rice and Avery, Cho) and a Tongue Position Node (see Lahiri and Evers). The identity of several terminal features remains a topic for further research.

The underspecification of coronals is needed for most empirical problems addressed here and in the literature, although it appears that none of the present underspecification theories can account for the full range of the properties identified as constituting the special status of coronals. This volume attempts to clearly outline areas of consensus as well as points of disagreement. Most importantly, it dispels some of the myths associated with coronals and defines adequacy criteria with respect to segmental structure, underspecification, and locality conditions, which any theory of phonology, present or future, must meet.

ACKNOWLEDGMENTS

We are very grateful to the contributors to this volume for their patience and perseverance. We are also thankful to Glyne Piggott, Doug Pulleyblank, Keren Rice, and Emmanuel Nikiema for their meticulous comments on this article, and to Harry van der Hulst for his advice and encouragement in the early stages of the book. Of course, we are solely responsible for any mistakes or misinterpretation. C. Paradis acknowledges SSHRC Grants 410-89-1166, 410-90-0575, FCAR 90-NC-0383, and SSHRC Canadian Research Fellowship 455–89–0103. J.-F. Prunet acknowledges grants CRSH 411-85-0012 and FCAR 88-EQ-2681 to the Groupe de recherche en linguistique africaniste, Université du Québec à Montréal.

NOTES

[1] There is an extensive literature on the need to recognize a class of coronals and what consonants must be included in this class (see Jakobson, Fant, and Halle, 1952; Chomsky and Halle, 1968:304; Hyman, 1973; Vago, 1976; Becker, 1978; Odden, 1978; Keating, 1988; Lahiri and Blumstein, 1984; among others). In this volume, the term "coronal" covers the articulatory area ranging from interdental to palatal, including both of the extremities (see Keating, this volume, for a precise phonetic definition).

[2] Maddieson (1987:52) reports that, "of the 37 languages with only one fricative, 31 have some kind of /*s/," which means 84% of these languages. Note that /*s/ stands for dental or alveolar. His UPSID (University of California, Los Angeles, Phonological Segment Inventory Data Base) sample includes 317 languages.

[3] In (1), X = timing unit, RN = Root Node, SLN = Supralaryngeal Node, PN = Place Node, LN = Laryngeal Node, ant = anterior, and dist = distributed.

[4] Prenasalized stops can be found at the end of stems (e.g., jam^mb-el 'little ax') but never at the end of words (see Paradis, 1986:327ff.).

[5] Trigo (1988:90–100) reports on two languages, Chinook and Choctaw, where velars appear to be transparent to vowel spreading. The Chinook case always involves the spreading of a round vowel. In Paradis and Prunet (forthcoming), we argue that this case in fact involves two operations unrelated to velar transparency: formation of a labialized consonant and spreading of a round feature from the labialized consonant to the preceding vowel. We show that a similar phenomenon is found in Ennemor, and reanalyze the Choctaw case.

[6] The creation of a ternary value also follows from a rule-based conception of phonology in which structural descriptions can vary without limit and where rules can be extrinsically ordered. Alternative conceptions are available that minimize the use of rules. Such approaches make constraint or parameter descriptions the trigger of rules (see Kaye, Lowenstamm, and Vergnaud, 1985; Piggott, 1987; Paradis, 1988; Yip, 1988; among

others) and avoid extrinsic orderings (see Archangeli, 1988:185). It is not clear that the
notion of distinctness is still relevant in these frameworks.

[7] The MSC documented by Davis (this volume), which prohibits identical specifications
in labials and velars, should also prohibit two gaps (i.e., two coronals), but it does not.
Two solutions are available. First, one can follow Davis and say that coronal underspecification is a parameterized option. Second, one could say, as we suggest, that Arabic
and English MSCs disallow $*\alpha\ \alpha$ and that the value of α is parameterized with the Arabic
setting comprising gaps and specifications, and the English setting comprising specifications only.

[8] In (13), str = strident; see n. 3 for other abbreviations.

REFERENCES

Archangeli, D. (1984) *Underspecification and Yawelmani Phonology and Morphology,* Doctoral dis-
    sertation, MIT, Cambridge, Massachusetts. Published 1988, Garland, New York.
Archangeli, D. (1988) "Aspects of Underspecification Theory," *Phonology* 5.2, 183–207.
Archangeli, D. and D. Pulleyblank (1987) "Maximal and Minimal Rules: Effects of Tier Scansion,"
    Proceedings of NELS 17, 16–35.
Archangeli, D. and D. Pulleyblank (forthcoming) *The Content and Structure of Phonological Repre-
    sentations,* MIT Press, Cambridge, Massachusetts.
Avery, P. and K. Rice (1988) "Underspecification Theory and the Coronal Node," *Toronto Working
    Papers in Linguistics* 9, 101–121.
Avery, P. and K. Rice (1989a) "Constraining Underspecification," *Proceedings of NELS* 19, 1–15.
Avery, P. and K. Rice (1989b) "Segment Structure and Coronal Underspecification," *Phonology*
    6.2, 179–200.
Bagemihl, B. (1989) "The Crossing Constraint and 'Backwards Languages'," *Natural Language
    and Linguistic Theory* 7.4, 481–549.
Becker, L. (1978) "The Feature(s) [grave]," *Journal of Phonetics* 6, 319–326.
Bhat, D. N. S. (1978) "A General Study of Palatalization," in J. Greenberg, C. Ferguson, and E.
    Moravcsik, eds., *Universals of Language,* Vol. 2: *Phonology,* pp. 47–92. Stanford University
    Press, Stanford, California.
Broselow, E. (1984) "Default Consonants in Amharic Morphology," *MIT Working Papers in Lin-
    guistics* 7, 15–31.
Cho, Y.-M. (1988) "Korean Assimilation," *Proceedings of WCCFL* 7, 41–52.
Chomsky, N. and M. Halle (1968) *The Sound Pattern of English,* Harper & Row, New York.
Clements, N. (1985) "The Geometry of Phonological Features," *Phonology* 2, 225–252.
Clements, N. (1988) "Towards a Substantive Theory of Feature Specifications," *Proceedings of
    NELS* 18, 79–93.
Clements, N. (1989) "A Unified Set of Features for Consonants and Vowels," ms., Cornell Univer-
    sity, Ithaca, New York.
Cook, E. (1976) "Central Carrier Phonology," Report to the Royal British Columbia Museum, Vic-
    toria, British Columbia.
Dresher, E. (1985) "Constraints on Empty Positions in Tiered Phonology," *Cahiers Linguistiques
    d'Ottawa* 14, 1–51.
Ferreres, A. (forthcoming) "Phonematic Alterations in Anarthric and Broca Aphasic Patients Speak-
    ing Argentinian Spanish," *Journal of Neurolinguistics.*

Fry, D. (1947) "The Frequency of Occurrence of Speech Sounds in Southern English," *Archives Néerlandaises de Phonétique Expérimentale* 20.

Gamkrelidze, T. (1975) "Correlations of Stops and Fricatives in a Phonological System," *Lingua* 35, 231–261.

Goldsmith, J. (1976) *Augosegmental Phonology,* Doctoral dissertation, MIT, Cambridge, Massachusetts. Published 1979, Garland, New York.

Greenberg, J. (1950) "The Patterning of Root Morphemes in Semitic," *Word* 6.2, 162–181.

Grignon, A.-M. (1984) *Phonologie lexicale tri-dimensionnelle du japonais,* Doctoral dissertation, Université de Montréal.

Halle, M. (forthcoming) "Features," in W. Bright, ed., *Oxford International Encyclopedia of Linguistics,* Oxford University Press, Oxford.

Hyman, L. (1973) "The Feature [grave] in Phonological Theory," *Journal of Phonetics* 1, 329–337.

Hyman, L. (1985) *A Theory of Phonological Weight,* Publications in Language Sciences 19, Foris Publications, Dordrecht.

Hyman, L. (1988) "Underspecification and Vowel Height Transfer in Esimbi," *Phonology* 5.2, 255–273.

Jakobson, R., G. Fant, and M. Halle (1952) *Preliminaries to Speech Analysis,* MIT Press, Cambridge, Massachusetts.

Kaye, J., J. Lowenstamm, and J.-R. Vergnaud (1985) "The Internal Structure of Phonological Elements: A Theory of Charm and Government," *Phonology* 2, 305–328.

Kean, M.-L. (1975) *The Theory of Markedness in Generative Grammar,* Doctoral dissertation, MIT, Cambridge, Massachusetts. Distributed 1980, Indiana University Linguistics Club, Bloomington.

Keating, P. (1988) "Palatals as Complex Segments: X-ray Evidence," *UCLA Working Papers in Phonetics* 69, 77–91.

Kenstowicz, M. (1986) "Multiple Linking in Javanese," *Proceedings of NELS* 16, 230–248.

Kiparsky, P. (1982) "Lexical Morphology and Phonology," in I.-S. Yang, ed., *Linguistics in the Morning Calm,* pp. 3–91. Hanshin, Seoul, Korea.

Kiparsky, P. (1985) "Some Consequences of Lexical Phonology," *Phonology* 2, 85–138.

Lahiri, A. and S. Blumstein (1984) "A Re-Evaluation of the Feature Coronal," *Journal of Phonetics* 12, 133–145.

Leslau, W. (1967) *Amharic Textbook,* Otto Harrassowitz, Wiesbaden.

Levin, J. (1988) "A Place for Lateral in the Feature Geometry," ms., University of Texas, Austin.

Maddieson, I. (1987) *Patterns of Sounds,* Cambridge Studies in Speech Science and Communication, Cambridge University Press, Cambridge, England.

Mascaró, J. (1983) "Phonological Levels and Assimilatory Processes," Paper presented at the GLOW colloquium, York.

McCarthy, J. (1981) "A Prosodic Theory of Nonconcatenative Morphology," *Linguistic Inquiry* 12, 373–418.

McCarthy, J. (1988) "Feature Geometry and Dependency," *Phonetica* 43, 84–108.

McCarthy, J. (1989) "Guttural Phonology," ms., University of Massachusetts, Amherst.

Mester, R.-A. (1986) *Studies in Tier Structure,* Doctoral dissertation, University of Massachusetts, Amherst. Published 1988, Garland, New York.

Mester, R.-A. and J. Itô (1989) "Feature Predictability and Underspecification: Palatal Prosody in Japanese Mimetics," *Language* 65.2, 258–293.

Mohanan, K. P. (1989) "On the Bases of Underspecification," ms., Stanford University, Stanford, California.

Moravcsik, E. and J. Wirth (1986) "Markedness: An Overview," in F. Eckman, E. Moravcsik, and J. Wirth, eds., *Markedness,* pp. 1–11. Plenum, New York.

Odden, D. (1978) "Further Evidence for the feature [grave]," *Linguistic Inquiry* 9, 141–144.

Odden, D. (1989) "Vowel Geometry," ms., Ohio State University, Columbus.

Paradis, C. (1986) *Phonologie et morphologie lexicales: les classes nominales en peul (Fula)*, Doctoral dissertation, Université de Montréal. (University Microfilms International, Ann Arbor, Michigan)

Paradis, C. (1988) "On Constraints and Repair Strategies," *Linguistic Review* 6.1, 71–97.

Paradis, C. and J.-F. Prunet (1989a) "Markedness and Coronal Structure," *Proceedings of NELS* 19, 330–344.

Paradis, C. and J.-F. Prunet (1989b) "On Coronal Transparency," *Phonology* 6.2, 317–348.

Paradis, C. and J.-F. Prunet (1989c) "Vowel Fusion and Antigemination in Guere and in Mau," *Toronto Working Papers in Linguistics* 10, 1–20.

Paradis, C. and J.-F. Prunet (1990) "On Explaining Some OCP Violations," *Linguistic Inquiry* 21.3, 456–466.

Paradis, C. and J.-F. Prunet (forthcoming) "Velar or Coronal Placeless Consonants?" *Proceedings of WCCFL* 9.

Piggott, G. (1987) "On the Autonomy of the Feature Nasal," *Proceedings of CLS* 23, 223–238.

Piggott, G. (forthcoming) "Variability in Feature Dependency: The Case of Nasality," *Natural Language and Linguistic Theory*.

Puel, M., J.-L. Nespoulous, A. Bonafé, and A. Rascol (1980) "Étude neurolinguistique d'un cas d'anarthrie pure," *Grammatica VII* 1, 239–291.

Pulleyblank, D. (1986) *Tone in Lexical Phonology*, Studies in Natural Language and Linguistic Theory, Kluwer, Dordrecht.

Pulleyblank, E. (1989) "The Role of Coronal in Articulation Based Features," *Proceedings of CLS*.

Sagey, B. (1986) *The Representation of Features and Relations in Non-Linear Phonology*, Doctoral Dissertation, MIT, Cambridge, Massachusetts.

Shaw, P. (1988) "On the Phonological Representation of Laterals and Affricates," Paper presented at the LSA, New Orleans, Louisiana.

Singh, R. (1988) "In Defense of External Evidence," in R. Singh (ed.),Special Issue: Linguistic Theory and External Evidence. *Canadian Journal of Linguistics* 33.4, 329–343.

Stemberger, J. and C. Stoel-Gammon (1989) "Consonant Harmony and Underspecification," ms., University of Minnesota, Minneapolis.

Steriade, D. (1987a) "Redundant Values," *Proceedings of CLS* 23, 339–362.

Steriade, D. (1987b) "Locality Conditions and Feature Geometry," *Proceedings of NELS* 17, 595–617.

Stoel-Gammon, C. (1985) "Phonetic Inventories, 15-24 months: A Longitudinal Study," *Journal of Speech and Hearing Research* 28, 505–512.

Trigo, L. (1988) *On the Phonological Derivation and Behavior of Nasal Glides*, Doctoral dissertation, MIT, Cambridge, Massachusetts.

Uhlenbeck, E. (1950) "The Structure of the Javanese Morpheme," *Lingua* 2, 239–270.

Vago, R. (1976) "More Evidence for the Feature [grave]," *Linguistic Inquiry* 7, 671–674.

van der Hulst, H. and N. Smith (1990) "Components for Vowels and Consonants," ms., University of Leiden and University of Amsterdam.

Vihman, M., C. Ferguson, and M. Elbert (1986) "Phonological Development from Babbling to Speech: Common Tendencies and Individual Differences," *Applied Psycholinguistics* 7, 3–40.

Whitman, J. (1986) "Configurationality Parameters," in T. Imai and M. Saito, eds., *Issues in Japanese Linguistics*, Foris Publications, Dordrecht.

Yip, M. (1988) "The Obligatory Contour Principle and Phonological Rules: A Loss of Identity," *Linguistic Inquiry* 19.1, 65–100.

Yip, M. (1989) "Feature Geometry and Cooccurrence Restrictions," *Phonology* 6.2, 349–374.

CORONAL PLACES OF ARTICULATION

PATRICIA A. KEATING

Department of Linguistics
University of California
Los Angeles, California 90024

1. INTRODUCTION

Coronal consonants are probably universal in the world's languages. Maddieson's (1984) statistical sample contains no languages without at least some coronal consonant, and only one language without coronal obstruents.[1] A number of typological observations support the special status of coronal consonants. First, coronals include more contrasts of both place and manner than do other consonant classes. For example, with respect to manner, affricates and liquids are most often coronal. With respect to place, Maddieson's survey recognizes five primary places of articulation that are commonly classified as coronal (dental, alveolar, palato-alveolar, retroflex, and palatal), and only five other primary places (bilabial, labiodental, velar, uvular, and pharyngeal), so that coronals account for half of the primary places of articulation.

Second, coronals account for a high proportion of consonants in languages. For example, of the 20 consonants in Maddieson's modal inventory, 10 are coronal. Also, Maddieson found that across the languages in the sample, the preferred inventory of stops and affricates contains three stop places of articulation (dental or alveolar, labial, and velar), plus one affricate place of articulation (palato-alveolar). Thus, two of these four stop–affricate place categories are coronal. Further, if a language has four (rather than three) stop places, then again two of the four are usually coronal.[2]

29

Thus, there are more coronal consonant types, and languages use them more. Put simply, coronals are special phonologically because there are so many of them. Presumably, this sheer preponderance of coronal consonants is a factor in the status of coronals as the usual unmarked or unspecified place of articulation: If half of the consonants in a language are coronal, then any given consonant is more likely to be coronal than any other place class. In phonetic terms, coronals are special because they can be made in so many ways. The tongue blade seems to lend itself to a greater variety of articulations than do other speech articulators.

In this article, the variety of possible coronal places of articulation is examined. We consider traditional place of articulation distinctions plus some manner distinctions that are generally used to make fine place distinctions. Some of the other manner distinctions found among coronals, such as lateralization, stridency, trill–tap, gradations of stricture, various release types, and certain secondary articulations, are not discussed here. The article is organized as follows. In Section 2, some necessary terminology is reviewed, and anatomical definitions are discussed. In Section 3, various coronal places of articulation are described. Features that have been used to characterize these places are considered in Section 4. Section 5 provides a summary discussion.

2. TERMINOLOGY

2.1. Tongue

Coronals can be defined as segments produced with the blade (including the tip) of the tongue. It was noted above that among the generally recognized coronal places of articulation are dental, alveolar, palato-alveolar, retroflex, and palatal. (Palato-alveolar refers to the place of English [š] (IPA [ʃ]), while palatal refers to the place of the front glide [y] (IPA [j]). American usage of "palatal" often encompasses both of these.) The IPA also includes another place using the tongue blade, alveolo-palatal. Ladefoged and Maddieson (1986) add two less-common coronal places, linguolabial and interdental. These places of articulation lie from front to back in the mouth, from the upper lip (linguolabials) to the hard palate (palatals), that is, virtually the entire span that can be touched or approached by the tip or blade of the tongue.

What part of the tongue counts as the blade? Different sources give different answers to this question. Catford (1977: 143) notes that there are two traditions: one from British phonetics, which he adopts, in which the blade is "the part that lies opposite the teeth and alveolar ridge when the tongue is at rest," that is, just the tip plus 10–15 mm; and one from American speech science (see Daniloff,

1973:173) in which that part is called the tip, while the blade lies further back. Ladefoged (1982:4) defines the tip and blade as "the most mobile parts" of the tongue, and Ladefoged (1989) defines the blade as the part not attached to the floor of the mouth, roughly corresponding to the part below the alveolar ridge. Ladefoged considers the blade to be a bit shorter than Catford suggests, no more than a centimeter long.

However, linguistically speaking the blade must be taken to extend somewhat further back than Catford or Ladefoged suggest. A sense of the extent of the blade in its linguistic uses can be gleaned from the following point. Alveolar stops and fricatives can be produced with the tongue tip down behind the lower teeth and a part of the tongue further back forming the constriction at the alveolar ridge. The phonological notion "coronal" surely depends on such articulations being made with the blade of the tongue, yet they are formed more than 1 cm behind the tip. Dart's (1988) linguograms agree with this observation. In my own case this suggests a blade length on the order of 15–20 mm. The part of the tongue 1 cm behind the tip reaches only to the upper teeth.

This is a minimum estimate of the extent of the tongue involved in producing coronal consonants, since it is based only on anterior coronals. How much further back on the tongue nonanterior coronals are produced is a circular issue, since it depends on the status of certain articulations as coronal or dorsal. In any event, the maximum estimate for blade length is that part of the tongue in front of the part used to produce velars, that is, some 3 or 4 cm.

To some degree such differences of definition may be a function of the extension of the tongue. The blade can be moved quasi-independently of the rest of the tongue (e.g., protruded, curled, wiggled). If the tongue is at rest in the mouth, this movable part will appear quite small; but if the tongue is extended out of the mouth or stretched in any other way, it will appear quite large because it is stretched. Thus, if one considers the blade to be the part of the tongue that can be grasped in one's hand, and if one protrudes one's tongue to grasp it, then the blade will appear to be much longer than 10–15 mm. Perhaps in articulations with the tongue tip down, the tongue blade similarly stretches itself.

The definition of tongue tip also requires mention. Catford (1977) distinguishes between the very "apex" itself, and the "rim" around it. However, it seems just as valid to follow Ladefoged (1989) in considering the tip to include both of these at once, since in practice it is nearly impossible to use the very tip of the tongue without also involving a couple of adjacent millimeters.

Thus, we will consider the blade of the tongue to be, conservatively, the movable part extending from 1 to 2 cm behind the tip, and we will consider the tip to include a small rim around the edge of the tongue. Articulations with the tip are called apical; those with the blade are called laminal. Articulations made with both at once can be called apicolaminal. Traditionally, laminal refers only to the

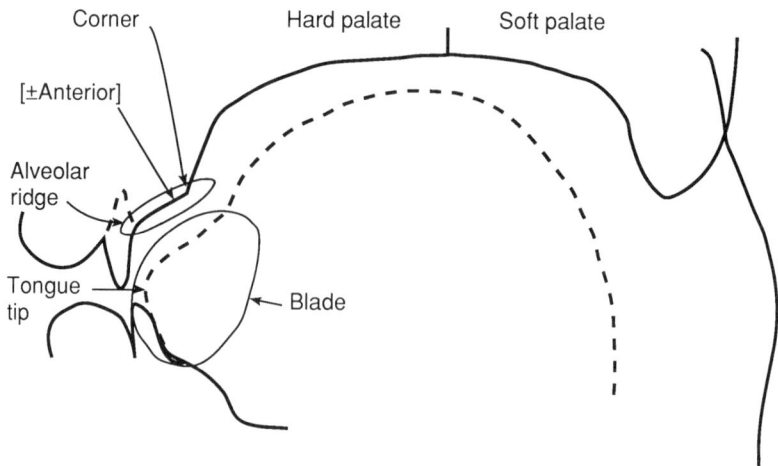

Figure 1. Overview of relevant anatomical distinctions: tongue tip and blade; alveolar ridge, corner, hard palate, soft palate; dividing point between [+anterior] and [−anterior].

top surface of the blade, while sublaminal refers to the lower surface. These points are summarized in Figure 1.

Apical versus laminal is sometimes equated with another descriptive parameter, the position of the tongue tip as "up" or "down." The tip is said to be up when it is raised above the lower teeth, so that the view of the tongue from outside the mouth is of the lower surface of the tongue. The tip is said to be down when it is behind or below the lower teeth, so that the view from outside is of the upper surface of the tongue. Individual speakers of English differ especially in whether /s/ is tip up or tip down.

2.2. Palate

As noted earlier, coronal articulations extend from the upper lip to the hard palate. Key divisions along the palate are represented in Figure 1. Behind the upper teeth is the alveolar ridge, a source of some confusion in articulatory descriptions. For phonetic purposes, the alveolar ridge is the entire area from the upper teeth back to the prominence at which the palate starts angling upward toward the roof of the mouth. This prominence is sometimes called the "ridge" but can also be referred to as the "edge," "center," "corner," "turning point," or "protuberance" of the ridge. The alveolar ridge is this whole area, not just the prominence. Catford (1988:86–87) has a helpful discussion of this point.

Given such definitions, we can now proceed to consider the variety of coronal places of articulation available to languages.

3. DESCRIPTIONS OF CORONALS

In this section, the articulations of some of the coronal consonants are discussed. The observations are based on discussions in the literature and on review of published physiological data, especially X-ray tracings but also palatography.

3.1. Anterior Coronals

Coronals that are [+anterior] have their contact or constriction on the front part of the alveolar ridge, on the upper teeth, or, in the case of linguolabials, the upper lip. Linguolabials, interdentals, dentals, and alveolars are variably apical or laminal. Still, one might view linguolabials and interdentals as variants of a basic sound type, sharing an extension and protrusion of the blade, and differing largely in terms of apicality. Linguolabials would be primarily apical, in the sense that the tip is aimed at the upper lip, though it sometimes overshoots. Interdentals would be primarily laminal, in the sense that the blade contacts the teeth, but sometimes the tip does not quite protrude.

Figure 2 shows a dental and an alveolar. Dart (forthcoming) provides details about dental and alveolar articulations, particularly about cross-speaker variability in apicality. In both French and English, speakers vary in the place and the manner of their dentals and alveolars. For example, Dart presents data that refute the claim by Ladefoged and Maddieson (1986:78) that dental sibilants are always apical: 6 of the 14 dentals in her sibilant sample were laminal. See Ladefoged and Maddieson for further discussion of a variety of anterior coronals, especially strident versus nonstrident fricatives.

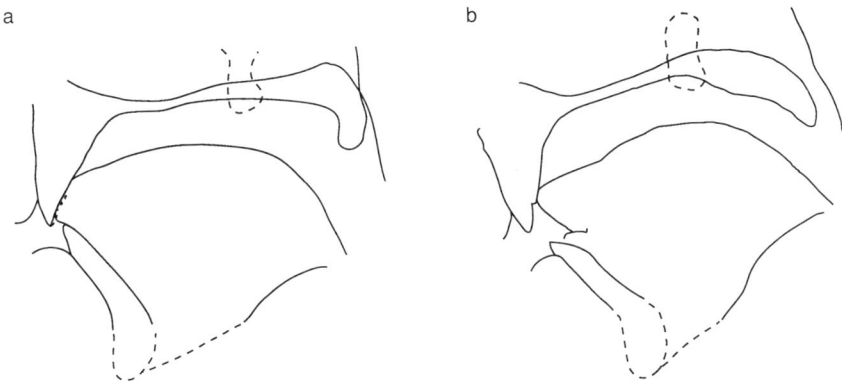

Figure 2.   Dental (denti-alveolar) stop (a) and alveolar nasal (b) in French, after Simon (1967). Both are tip up, but the first is apicolaminal while the second is apical.

3.2. Palato-alveolars

Palato-alveolar constrictions (for English [ʃ], see Figure 3) are at or near the corner of the alveolar ridge. The tip may approach the ridge in front of the corner, while the blade approaches the corner; thus, the blade runs parallel to the ridge. In these cases the articulation is both apical and laminal at once, and so the constriction is fairly long (and thus should be counted as primarily laminal rather than apical). However, for speakers with a prominent corner, coming nearly to a point, a laminal constriction can be quite short. Palato-alveolar articulation is most often laminal, sometimes apical. However, even the laminal articulation can have the tip up, that is, raised above the lower teeth. Basically the tip lies behind the upper teeth, but far enough away from them that no dental constriction is formed. The tip is above the lower teeth so that a cavity can occur behind them, under the tongue. Catford (1977:158) shows an articulation of this sort. Palato-alveolars are also reported with a tip-down articulation. However, it seems unlikely that this could ever mean that the tip contacts the lower teeth, since no cavity would be formed under the tongue. More likely, the tip-down palato-alveolars have the tip just below the upper teeth, but free of the lower teeth.

Palato-alveolars also have a somewhat "domed" or convex tongue behind the constriction, which Ladefoged and Maddieson (1986) characterize as a slight degree of palatalization.

3.3. Retroflexes

Figure 4 shows two kinds of retroflexes. Many apical and sublaminal retroflexes (Figure 4a) involve curling back the tongue blade so that its tip or underside forms a constriction along the palate. With just a slight curl, the very tip can touch the rear part of the alveolar ridge, in front of the corner. However, more commonly the constriction is behind the corner; the further back it is, then the more curled and stretched the tongue, the more the underside of the blade is used, and the longer the constriction. Ladefoged and Maddieson (1986) note that

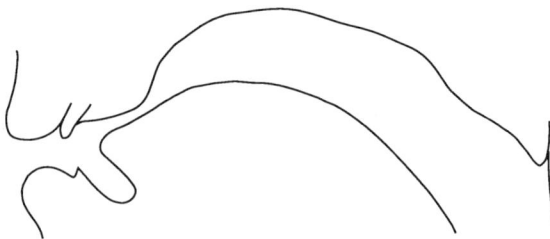

Figure 3. Palato-alveolar fricative in English, after Ladefoged and Maddieson (1986).

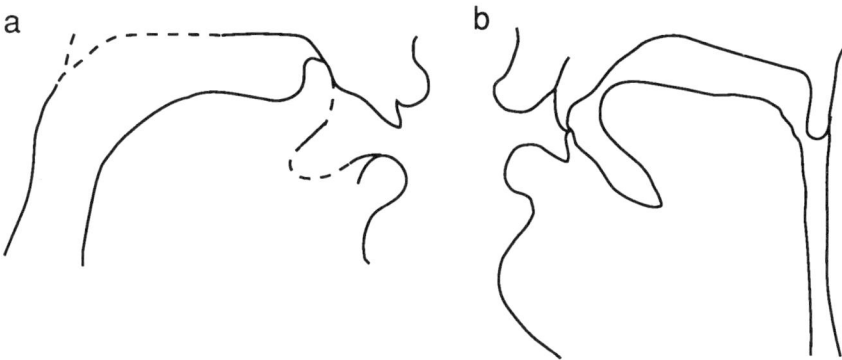

Figure 4. Retroflexes: (a) sublaminal stop in Tamil, after Ladefoged and Maddieson (1986); (b) flat apical fricative in Serbian, after Miletič (1960).

this description applies most clearly to stops; the retroflex fricatives in the languages of India are not as well documented, but they seem not to involve the same kind of curling of the tongue. They have the same place of articulation on the palate as the stops, but the blade is not extended out from the body of the tongue. This makes it difficult to distinguish the tip from the rest of the blade in X-ray tracings. However, it should be noted that several tracings of Russian /š/ and /ž/ (e.g., Oliverius, 1974; Dem'janeko, 1966) are clearly retroflexes of the expected type: apical with the tongue curled back.

A somewhat different kind of retroflex fricative (Figure 4b) is also described by Ladefoged and Maddieson (based on earlier work). These sounds are found in Mandarin Chinese and in Slavic languages, where they are often transcribed as palato-alveolars, though they sound more like other retroflexes.[3] Relative to palato-alveolars, or to the tongue at rest, the entire blade is moved up and back and is positioned just behind the corner of the alveolar ridge. The tip is up, and the tongue is flat from front to back, not domed. Ladefoged and Maddieson categorize them as (laminal) flat postalveolar sibilants, with a sublingual cavity. They describe the constriction as like that of [ʃ], but at the center of the alveolar ridge. They also note an articulatory difference between the versions found in Polish versus Chinese: The former are rounded while the latter have a larger sublingual cavity. (These fricatives are both said to differ from the retroflex fricative of Tamil, which is further back, possibly apical, and has a larger sublingual cavity.)

Although Ladefoged and Maddieson characterize these retroflexes as laminal, data sources show greater variability. The active articulator for affricates is relatively easy to determine from available data. The retroflex affricates in the X-ray tracings of Ladefoged and Wu (1984) are either apical or laminal, though in either case with the tip up. Linguograms and palatograms, along with X-ray tracings, are available for the fricatives and corresponding affricates of Polish

(Wierzchowska, 1965, 1967, 1980) and Serbian (Miletič, 1960). In these records, the stop portions of the affricates are clearly apical, possibly partly sublaminal. The fricatives also appear to be apical, in the sense that the linguograms show no narrowing anywhere along the blade. Since the palatograms show that there is indeed a constriction, it must be the tip forming it. The difference between Slavic and Dravidian fricatives, then, would appear to be in the location (backness) of the constriction, and thus in the size of the sublingual cavity.

3.4. Alveopalatals

Figure 5 shows three kinds of alveopalatals. Alveopalatals, or "prepalatals," probably occur most commonly as nasals and laterals, where they are generally confused with palatals. (For example, Maddieson, 1984, collapses these catego-

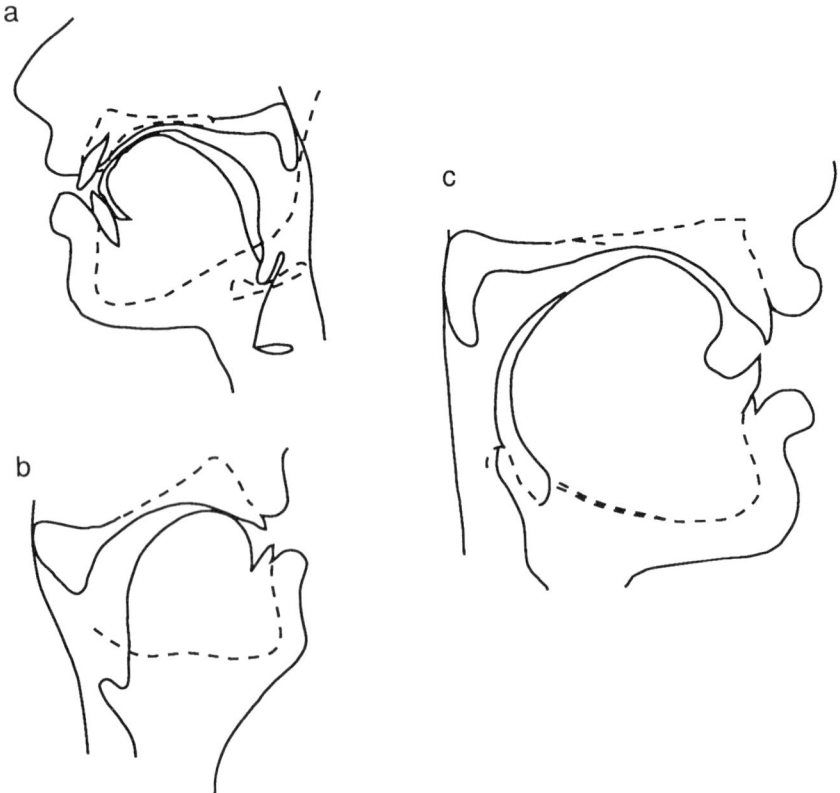

Figure 5. Alveopalatals: (a) Polish fricative, after Wierzchowska (1967, 1980); (b) Polish affricate, from same source; (c) Mandarin fricative, after Ohnesorg and Śvarný (1955).

ries.) They also occur as fricatives and affricates, for example, in Polish and Mandarin [ç], where they sound like sharpened palato-alveolars or strident palatals. They most commonly involve the blade approaching the corner of the alveolar ridge. The tip is usually down, pointing to the lower teeth, but often does not touch them; however, tip-up examples can also be found (e.g., Ladefoged and Wu, 1984). In either case there may or may not be a cavity under the tongue. The front of the tongue is raised behind the constriction. Available X-rays of alveopalatals (in Mandarin and Polish) show quite a bit of variation, even within languages.

Figure 5a shows a fricative from Wierzchowska (1967, 1980), with a long constriction, the tip behind the lower teeth, and a small sublingual cavity. Figure 5b shows another tracing from the same author, this time of the stop component of an affricate just before the release. Here, the requirement of complete occlusion leads to a raising of the blade, with the tip also raised, resulting in a slightly larger sublingual cavity. Figure 5c shows a Mandarin alveopalatal fricative with an even larger sublingual cavity, one as large as for other nonanterior coronals.

Since alveolopalatals are generally articulated at the corner of the alveolar ridge, they are [−anterior]. Chomsky and Halle (1968) and Halle (1988) give somewhat different descriptions of the Polish alveopalatals, classifying them as [+anterior]. These descriptions are based on figures from Wierzchowska that are not, in fact, alveopalatals. This error is corrected in Halle and Stevens (1989), where the alveopalatals are defined as [−anterior].

See Recasens (in press) for further data and discussion on alveopalatals.

3.5. Palatals

In Chomsky and Halle (1968), hereafter referred to as *SPE*, palatals (such as [j] and [ç]) were considered to involve tongue-body articulations, and so were [−coronal], but they were later reclassified as coronals on phonological grounds (see Keating, 1988b, among others, for a summary). Halle and Stevens (1979) proposed a redefinition of coronal to mean the blade or front of the tongue so as to include the palatals. However, this move seems unnecessary, as palatals generally do involve the blade proper, in addition to the front of the tongue.

Figure 6 shows a palatal stop. The key component of palatals seems to be their articulation near a large part of the hard palate, between the alveolar ridge and the roof of the mouth (Keating, 1988a). The tongue is both raised and fronted from its position for [i] vowels so that parts of the blade and the front form a very long constriction. The tip, and the front part of the blade nearest the tip, are not involved and are usually low in the mouth so that there is no sublingual cavity. Palatograms show that the occlusion for stops is about the length of a velar constriction, but quite front; the blade touches just behind the alveolar ridge. Thus, the stop occlusion itself is coronal and nonanterior. At the same time, there is

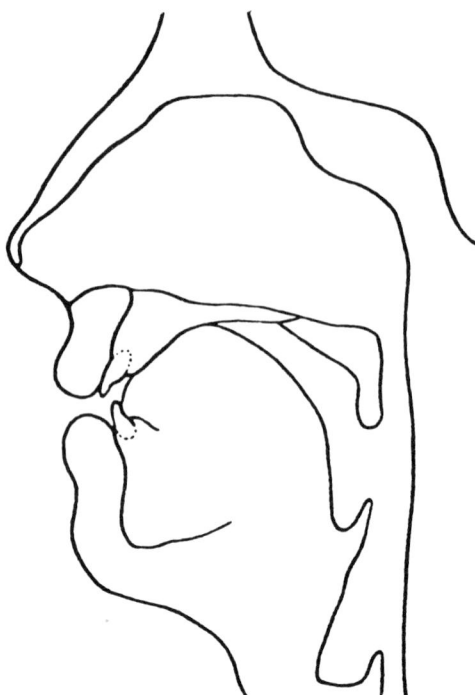

Figure 6.   Palatal nasal stop in Czech, after Hála (1962).

extensive side-to-side and front-to-back lateral contact as for [j], and the entire front of the tongue is extremely close to the palate. Nonstops have more open constrictions covering about the same area. See Recasens (in press) for additional data on and discussion of palatals.

One basic observation here is that palatals have a very large constriction area, probably the largest of any outside the pharynx. A second basic observation is that palatals are articulated much further forward in the mouth, and on the tongue, than has often been assumed. Although the palatal place of articulation is "next to" the velar place, these are very far apart in practice. Palatals are even further forward along the palate than velars fronted in a front-vowel context. There is room along the roof of the mouth for three different places of articulation, with fronted velars in between palatals and velars. In Keating (1988a) I proposed that the SPE tongue-body feature values assigned to palatals be used instead for fronted velars. In particular, the value [−back] would refer to a tongue-body articulation on the hard, rather than the soft, palate; thus fronted velars would be [−back] while nonfronted velars would be [+back]. The representation of palatals is discussed below.

3.6. Palatalized Coronals

Thorough coverage of all the secondary articulations that can affect coronals is beyond the scope of this article. However, in the case of palatalization, the secondary articulation can effect a change in the primary place and/or manner of articulation and thus needs to be considered here. As a technical phonetic term, palatalization refers to the superposition of a high front tongue-body position on a separate primary articulation, such as a primary articulation with the tongue blade. However, Bhat (1978) emphasizes that "palatalization" is used as a cover term for any combination of three independent articulatory components: tongue fronting, tongue raising, and spirantization. He points out that the term palatalization, in its wider use, more often refers to restricted changes in certain primary places of articulation, as when velars palatalize to palato-alveolars. It less often refers to a general secondary articulation across all the primary places in a language, as in Russian, where labials, coronals, and velars can all come in surface contrasting pairs of palatalized versus nonpalatalized.

3.6.1. ANTERIOR CORONALS

Russian has surface contrasts of plain versus palatalized anterior coronals. Bhat shows that, across languages, anterior coronals are more likely to undergo tongue raising than either tongue fronting or spirantization. Tongue raising of coronals usually results in retracted and laminal articulations. The X-rays of Russian coronals in Oliverius (1974) show this effect quite clearly.

Polish alveopalatals, which are [−anterior], pattern phonologically as palatalized variants of dentals, which are [+anterior]. However, a change in anteriority under palatalization is in accord with the cross-language observations of Bhat (1978).

3.6.2. NONANTERIOR CORONALS

Secondary articulations involving the tongue are very rare with [−anterior] places of articulation. However, surface contrasts do occur; in Russian, between retroflex and palatalized retroflex fricatives, and in Polish, between palatalized retroflex, retroflex, and alveopalatal fricatives. The Russian palatalized retroflex looks straightforwardly like a palatalized version of the plain (curled) retroflex. However, X-rays of Abkhaz reproduced by Ladefoged and Maddieson (1986:77) show that in that language, the alveopalatal looks like a palatalized version of the retroflex, which is of the flat-tongued, apical type. Ladefoged and Maddieson therefore analyze it as such. Furthermore, the palatalized retroflex of Polish shown in Wierzchowska (1965) looks very much like the alveopalatal of Abkhaz, supporting Ladefoged and Maddieson's analysis. By this account, there is no

TABLE 1

TONGUE PROFILE BEHIND CONSTRICTION

Language	Flat	Raised	Palatalized
Polish	š	š′	ç
Abkhaz	š	ç	

separate *place* of articulation for alveopalatals; they are collapsed with the retroflexes, and only the palatalization distinguishes the two (see Halle and Stevens,
1989, on equating Russian /š′/ with Polish /ç/). The change from apical retroflex
to laminal palato-alveolar would be a natural concomitant of palatalization. The
problem, however, is the fact that Polish also has an alveopalatal, contrasting with
its palatalized retroflex. Since the alveopalatal then cannot be just a palatalized
retroflex, how are these to be analyzed? Tokens vary, but overall the three Polish
fricatives lie on a continuum of tongue-body raising. The retroflexes have a flat
tongue, the alveopalatals have a very raised and fronted tongue, and the palatalized
retroflexes fall in between. Since the Abkhaz alveopalatal looks somewhat like
the Polish palatalized retroflex, the Polish alveopalatal represents a more extreme
palatalization. These relations are summarized in Table 1. It might be possible to
vary the feature values used to represent the palatalization so as to distinguish
these two Polish types, for example, whether both Back and High are used.

It is not clear that palato-alveolars are ever palatalized. Reported cases, as in
Slavic, instead seem to involve retroflexes.

4. FEATURES PROPOSED FOR CORONALS

Coronal segments have as their active articulator the tongue blade and therefore can be specified with a positive value for the Coronal feature.[4] To distinguish
the various coronal places of articulation, further features are needed. Though
the issue is not addressed here, these features must also be capable of expressing
the natural class relations among coronals. We consider first some of the standard
SPE features (for further related discussion, see Keating, 1988b) and then some
others.

4.1. Anterior

The feature Anterior describes the place of articulation, not the active articulator. It divides coronals into more-front and more-back categories, determined
by their place of articulation along, for example, the roof of the mouth. The

operational definition provided in *SPE* is that alveolars are [+anterior] while palato-alveolars are [−anterior]. The phonetic basis of this division has scarcely been discussed in the literature and has not received a precise articulatory description. It is often described in terms of the alveolar ridge: [−anterior] segments are formed behind the alveolar ridge, or, more exactly, behind the corner of the alveolar ridge. Alveolars are said to be articulated in front of this point and palato-alveolars behind it (e.g., Ladefoged, 1989:48). For speakers with prominent alveolar ridges this would be a clear articulatory distinction and thus a clear boundary between the values of Anterior.

However, examination of X-ray data shows that this characterization is incorrect. Both values of Anterior can be found in front of the corner. Alveolars are articulated on the frontmost part of the ridge. Palato-alveolars are generally articulated at about the corner, either centered there or extending into the part of the ridge in front of the corner (see Ladefoged and Maddieson, 1986:65–67). Some English readers can feel this for themselves by saying *chop*—the stop component of the affricate is not made behind the corner but instead at a point just behind where the /t/ in *top* is made. Both palato-alveolars and retroflexes can be made at or just in front of the corner of the alveolar ridge, so that they are only minimally different in place from alveolars. Thus, palato-alveolars look like alveolars, but with the whole tongue moved back and up just a little; retroflexes can also look like alveolars, but with the blade curled back just a little more. (Sublaminal retroflexes can also be made well behind the corner, of course.) Thus, the true dividing point between the values of the feature Anterior appears to be the midpoint of the part of the alveolar ridge between the upper teeth and the corner. This point is summarized in Figure 1.

Considered only in terms of millimeters of difference between constriction locations, the difference between [+anterior] and [−anterior] can be incredibly subtle. However, the corner of the alveolar ridge provides a more definitive landmark to which the tongue may orient itself for the [−anterior] articulations.

4.2. Distributed

The feature Distributed uses a description of length of the consonant constriction (i.e., a manner property) to represent differences in place of articulation. In *SPE* Chomsky and Halle proposed that this feature subsumes the traditional apical–laminal distinction, with apical articulations having shorter ([−distributed]) constrictions and laminal articulations having longer ([+distributed]) ones. (Sometimes the name apical–laminal is used instead of Distributed, e.g., Clements, 1989.) Chomsky and Halle make clear that there is no intended a priori correspondance between the values of Distributed and place of articulation, for example, both dentals and alveolars can be distributed or nondistributed, and it is left to the low-level phonetic rules in a language to specify the exact place of articulation of any coronal segment. It is even possible that in some particular case a laminal articulation might be shorter than an apical one (e.g., if a speaker with a very sharp corner of the alveolar ridge made a laminal palato-alveolar, but an apical retroflex with sublaminal contact). In this case, the usual correspondance between Distributed and apical–laminal would be reversed.

In general, dentals and alveolars do differ in other ways besides their place, and apicality is one of the differences observed. With stops, as Ladefoged (1989) discusses, dentals are more likely to be laminal, and alveolars to be apical, and thus Distributed can usually be used to distinguish these places.[5] Ladefoged and Maddieson (1986) report only one case of anterior coronals contrasting in place but not in apicality or any other feature, namely, apical fricatives in certain Amerindian languages. Dart (1988, forthcoming) studied the dental–alveolar stop contrast in Papago, where both places are said to be apical. However, all of the speakers who made any contrast used at least moderately different articulators: Either the only difference was in apicality, or apicality varied along with place (the dentals were tip-down laminals or tip-up apicolaminals). Furthermore, the "alveolar" stops were usually actually postalveolar, so that only the dentals are in fact [+anterior]. That is, the Papago case turns out to support Chomsky and Halle's claim that place alone never distinguishes anterior coronals.

The same result holds of another case presented by Ladefoged and Maddieson. They note that the two apical laterals of Albanian differ not only in place but also in tongue-body backness. However, it appears from their figure that they would also differ in their values for Anterior, as happened in Papago.

In general, the use of the tip versus the blade is often not consistent enough to rely on as the basis of phonological distinctions. It is important to note that while this is a highly salient aspect of coronal articulations, it is largely a matter of speaker choice, not definition of sound types. Dentals, alveolars, and palato-alveolars can be made either apically or laminally, and retroflexes can be made either apically or sublaminally. Dart (1988, forthcoming) shows that French and English, languages without a contrast in apicality, permit great speaker variability in dental or alveolar stops and fricatives. Neither the place nor the apicality is invariant across speakers within a language. However, as Catford (1977) points out, an apical versus a laminal articulation will have acoustic effects within the "same" place of articulation category. In particular, the size of any sublingual cavity will vary with the position of the tongue blade, and this in turn will affect the resonance frequencies of obstruent noise.

In its original form, where Distributed describes constriction length quite generally, it is equally well used for other constriction types. Chomsky and Halle employ it to distinguish alveopalatals from other places of articulation in Polish. Alveopalatals have the tongue front raised up behind the blade and so may have longer constrictions than otherwise similar laminal coronals. Since Chomsky and Halle considered alveopalatals to be [+anterior], they used Distributed to distinguish them from the dentals.[6] With alveopalatals as [−anterior], Distributed would instead distinguish them from the Polish retroflexes.

It is useful to ask how much the coronal articulations actually differ in constriction length, that is, whether the phonetic definition of Distributed in its SPE usage is supported empirically. Chomsky and Halle, after all, rely on very little data in this regard. I therefore measured the length of contacts or constrictions from tracings of a wide set of coronals. To allow comparison across speakers, these were compared with velars where possible. Alveopalatals and especially palatals usually have quite long constrictions, longer than those of velars. Retroflex stops have constrictions about as long as those of velars—longer than expected, given their usual classification as [−distributed]. Beyond this, no clear differences emerge. Though laminal constrictions are longer than the shortest apical constrictions, apicals can also be long. Palato-alveolars can sometimes have among the shortest constrictions, in speakers with sharply defined alveolar ridges. Thus, there appears to be little available physiological support for this phonetic definition of Distributed. This finding supports limiting the feature Distributed (by this or some other name) to the apical–laminal distinction.

4.3. Sublingual Cavity

Stevens and colleagues (Perkell, Boyce, and Stevens, 1979) have called attention to the importance of the presence of a cavity under the tongue blade during the articulation of palato-alveolars, because of its lowering effect on acoustic resonances. The same is true for retroflexes. At first glance, then, the sublingual cavity would seem to be a correlate of [−anterior] segments. However, some [−anterior] coronals lack it. In particular, the absence of a sublingual cavity is a consistent and key characteristic of palatals. Also, Ladefoged and Maddieson (1986) discuss a rare sibilant fricative in Abkhaz, described by Catford, which is palato-alveolar but has the tip down and no sublingual cavity ("hissing-hushing"). The [−anterior] coronals can be arranged in order of increasing size of sublingual cavity, from the palatal and hissing-hushing, to the alveopalatal, the palato-alveolar, the apical retroflex, to the sublaminal retroflex. Halle and Stevens (1989) discuss the acoustic consequences of such a sublingual cavity in Polish retroflex and alveopalatal fricatives. They estimate the resonance of the cavity at 3,200–3,500 Hz.

Halle (1988) proposes a new tongue feature, Lower Incisors Contact, to encode this property, with this contact implying no sublingual cavity. Halle thus distinguishes alveopalatal from dental–alveolar (all as [+anterior]) and palatal from palato-alveolar (all as [−anterior]). We have already noted that phonetically alveopalatals are in fact [−anterior]. Thus Lower Incisors Contact plays no contrastive role among the true [+anterior] places (dental and alveolar). Furthermore, most X-rays of Polish alveopalatals show at least a small sublingual cavity, implying no contact between tongue and teeth (see Figure 5). In most alveopalatals, the tongue tip points at, but does not touch, the lower teeth. If anything, then, the presence of Lower Incisors Contact distinguishes most alveopalatals from palatals, taking both as [−anterior] and [+distributed].

Halle's name for this sublingual cavity feature, Lower Incisors Contact, suggests a correspondance with another traditional phonetic descriptive dimension for coronals, referred to earlier as tip up versus tip down. When there is Lower Incisors Contact, clearly the tip is down. (However, for interdentals, the tip rests on the lower teeth, blocking off any sublingual cavity; yet it might be considered "up.") In contrast, to guarantee a cavity large enough to affect the acoustic output substantially, the tip is best raised above the lower teeth; this is what is observed for most palato-alveolars and retroflexes. In these two cases, then, Lower Incisors Contact correlates well with tip position. The only question is whether there are cases where the tip is down but does not make lower incisors contact. We have suggested that this is the case with some palato-alveolars: They are reported as tip down but nonetheless have a sublingual cavity. Therefore, the feature Lower Incisors Contact, or sublingual cavity, is not exactly equivalent to tip up or down, unless by tip "up" we mean any position above the base of the lower teeth.

Ladefoged and Maddieson (1986) instead equate tip position with apical–laminal: Tip up is apical, while tip down is laminal. However, a similar discrepancy is met here. Tip position does correlate with apicality if the tip is down, for then the articulation must be laminal. But the reverse is not necessarily true. The tip may be raised only to the level of the upper teeth, and so be "up," while the constriction is formed laminally on the palate. Palato-alveolars are an example of this. (The flat retroflexes described as laminal by Ladefoged and Maddieson, 1986, would also be examples, but it was suggested above that these are in fact apical.) Therefore, apical or laminal is not exactly equivalent to tip up or down, unless by tip "down" we mean any position below the base of the upper teeth. In sum, then, none of these descriptive parameters—sublingual cavity, apicality, tip position—quite covaries.

4.4. Tongue Shape Features

Ladefoged and Maddieson (1986) offer additional descriptive parameters for coronals, which provide phonetic detail that is redundant rather than contrastive in nature. One of these is constriction width (from side to side); a narrow constriction, as found for [s] sounds, involves grooving the tongue blade. Another parameter is pitting of the tongue behind the grooved constriction, again found for [s] sounds. That is, as Ladefoged and Maddieson point out, the grooving and pitting of the tongue in the formation of [s] sounds are important components of their articulation; feature descriptions in terms of Anterior and Distributed (or Laminal) alone do not give a complete phonetic description. The redundant detail is necessary to say exactly how the [s] sound is to be made. I would suggest that these parameters might be related to the feature Strident (or Sibilant): Particular blade and body configurations, appropriate to the given place of articulation, are needed to produce the right kind of airstream jet for stridency. Thus, instead of being features, they are phonetic parameters that are marshaled to help effect (or enhance) a phonological feature value such as [+strident].

Ladefoged and Maddieson also use a new feature, flat versus domed tongue shape, to distinguish retroflex from palato-alveolar fricatives. Both are "post-alveolar" in place, and both are laminal by Ladefoged and Maddieson's account. The problem with using this phonetic parameter as a phonological feature is that the retroflex stops that correspond to the fricatives are domed, not flat, and thus the stops are grouped with the wrong set of fricatives. Instead, as I suggested above, the retroflex fricatives should be considered apical, like the corresponding stops.

Tongue shape features can also enter into the description of palatals. In Keating (1988a) I proposed that palatals are complex segments involving both coronal and tongue-body articulations, with values for the tongue-body features equivalent to palatalization. This complex representation makes the structure of palatals parallel to that of labial-velars, which also combine two major articulations. It also represents the direct articulatory relation between palatals and front vowels. However, another option in the representation of palatals is to treat them as simple coronals, and to introduce at least one additional feature to distinguish them from the other [−anterior] coronals. This in effect is what Halle (1988) does with his new feature Lower Incisors Contact. Actually, both options should be exercised for more complete descriptive coverage. We have already seen that alveopalatals as well as palatals might be viewed as palatalized, or complex, segments with a high-front vowel component. As discussed above, phonetically speaking both are [−anterior] and [+distributed], so some further feature is needed to distinguish them. Halle's cavity feature can be used in this way, with the palatals as [+lower incisors contact], and the alveopalatals as [−lower incisors contact]. However, it must be noted that in the end, phonological evidence is needed to support the natural classes entailed by such proposals about features.

By using tongue-body features, the proposal here is that palatals, and probably alveopalatals, are treated as palatalized segments. We might ask, palatalized versions of what? We already discussed the palatalization relation between alveopalatals and retroflexes. Palatals, by their feature values, would correspond to the

Abkhaz hissing-hushing category. Both are [−anterior] and have the tongue tip behind the lower teeth with no sublingual cavity. The tongue lowering seen in the hissing-hushing fricative is replaced with extreme tongue fronting and raising in palatals.

5. DISCUSSION

The main points of this article can be summarized by showing how the features discussed above characterize the coronal phonetic categories. Several ambiguities or inadequacies have been found.

Linguolabials and interdentals are both anterior. It was proposed that they differ in tip orientation, with linguolabials apical and tip up, and interdentals laminal and probably tip down.

Dentals and alveolars are also both anterior. When not in contrast with each other, they vary rather freely in apicality and tip position–sublingual cavity. When in contrast, they may be distinguished by apicality, stridency, or a secondary articulation.

Three types of retroflexes were discussed, all [−anterior] and all tip up with a sublingual cavity. The sublaminal retroflexes, attested most clearly for stops, would count as laminal (or [+distributed]) in most feature systems. The other two types of retroflexes are apical, occurring with either domed or flat tongue shapes. This distinction (which is never contrastive) poses a problem for current systems of phonetic description. A possible alternative description would use tongue-body features such as Back.

Palato-alveolars are [−anterior] but vary in tip position and apicality. Most commonly, they are tip up but laminal. It seems likely that all apical palato-alveolars are at the same time also laminal (i.e., apicolaminal), but none having the tip down to the point of lower incisors contact. The laminality distinguishes palato-alveolars from retroflexes.

A secondary articulation of palatalization was invoked to describe the palatals and alveopalatals. These are both [−anterior] and laminal–distributed. They differ (though not always reliably) in tip position and presence of a sublingual cavity. The phonetic distinction here is problematic because of variability in the available data.

It can be seen that feature systems must be developed further to account for all of the possible coronal places of articulation. The problems of representation presented here, however, only serve to underline the great variety of coronals encountered in languages.

ACKNOWLEDGMENT

This work was supported in part by NSF Grant BNS-8418580.

NOTES

[1] Maddieson (1984) does not use the term or category "coronal." The observations here are based on his findings but are couched in other terms. It should be noted that labial and velar categories are also almost universal (see Maddieson, 1984:31–32, with Wichita, Hupa, and Aleut in this sample lacking bilabial stops, and Hupa and Kirghiz lacking velar stops).

[2] Maddieson describes the same data differently because he classifies palatals and palato-alveolars as tongue-body articulations. However, both of these are now standardly considered coronal by phonologists.

[3] Contrasts between retroflexes and palato-alveolars are rare.

[4] In *SPE* this meant a [+coronal] feature value; in more recent feature hierarchies, it means the presence of a Coronal articulator node.

[5] Surprisingly, Chomsky and Halle (1968:314) describe dentals as most usually [−distributed], but I believe this is not common usage.

[6] Thus Distributed can be seen to be a relative property in *SPE:* When dentals form a phonological contrast with alveolars, they might be [+distributed], but when they contrast with alveopalatals, they are [−distributed].

REFERENCES

Bhat, D. N. (1978) "A General Study of Palatalization," in J. S. Greenberg, ed., *Universals of Human Language*, Vol. 2: *Phonology*, pp. 47–92, Stanford University Press, Stanford, California.

Catford, J. C. (1977) *Fundamental Problems in Phonetics*, Indiana University Press, Bloomington.

Catford, J. C. (1988) *A Practical Introduction to Phonetics*, Clarendon Press, Oxford.

Chomsky, N. and M. Halle (1968) *The Sound Pattern of English*, Harper & Row, New York.

Clements, G. N. (1989) "A Unified Set of Features for Consonants and Vowels," ms., Cornell University, Ithaca, New York.

Daniloff, R. G. (1973) "Normal Articulation Processes," in F. D. Minifie, T. J. Hixon, and F. Williams, eds., *Normal Aspects of Speech, Hearing, and Language*, Prentice-Hall, Englewood Cliffs, New Jersey.

Dart, S. (1988) "Acoustic Correlates of Apical and Laminal Articulations," *Journal of the Acoustical Society of America* 84, Suppl. 1, S112.

Dart, S. (forthcoming) *Articulatory and Acoustic Properties of Apical and Laminal Articulations*, Doctoral dissertation, University of California at Los Angeles.

48 Patricia A. Keating

Dem'janenko, M. J. (1966) *Vstupnyi Fonetyko-Hrafichnyi Kurs Francuz'koi Movi*, Laboratorii Eksperimental'noi Fonetiki.

Hála, B. (1962) *Uvedení do fonetiky češtiny: Na obecně fonetickém základě*, Nakladatelství Československé Akademie Věd, Prague.

Halle, M. (1988) "Features," to appear in W. Bright, ed., *Oxford International Encyclopedia of Linguistics*, Oxford University Press, Oxford.

Halle, M. and K. N. Stevens (1979) "Some Reflections on the Theoretical Bases of Phonetics," in B. Lindblom and S. Ohman, eds., *Frontiers of Speech Communication Research*, Academic Press, London.

Halle, M. and K. N. Stevens (1989) "The Postalveolar Fricatives of Polish," ms., MIT, Cambridge, Massachusetts.

Keating, P. (1988a) "Palatals as Complex Segments: X-ray Evidence," *UCLA Working Papers in Phonetics* 69, 77–91.

Keating, P. (1988b) *A Survey of Phonological Features*, Indiana University Linguistics Club, Bloomington.

Ladefoged, P. (1982) *A Course in Phonetics*, 2nd ed., Harcourt Brace Jovanovich, New York.

Ladefoged, P. (1989) "Representing Phonetic Structure," *UCLA Working Papers in Phonetics* 73, 1–79.

Ladefoged, P. and M. Halle (1988) "Some Major Features of the International Phonetic Alphabet," *Language* 64, 577–583.

Ladefoged, P. and I. Maddieson (1986) "Some of the Sounds of the World's Languages" (preliminary version), *UCLA Working Papers in Phonetics* 64, 1–137.

Ladefoged, P. and Z. Wu (1984) "Places of Articulation: An Investigation of Pekingese Fricatives and Affricates," *Journal of Phonetics* 12, 267–278.

Maddieson, I. (1984) *Patterns of Sounds*, Cambridge University Press, Cambridge, England.

Miletič, R. (1960) *Osnovi Fonetike Srpskog Jezika*, Naučna Kniga, Belgrade.

Ohnesorg, K. and O. Švarný (1955) *Études Experimentales des Articulations Chinoises*, *Rozpravy*, Vol. 65, No. 5, Československé Akademie Věd, Prague.

Oliverius, Z. F. (1974) *Fonetika Russkogo Jazyka*, Státní Pedagogické Nakladatelství, Prague.

Perkell, J., S. Boyce, and K. N. Stevens (1979) "Articulatory and Acoustic Correlates of the [s-š] Distinction," in J. J. Wolf and D. K. Klatt, eds., *Speech Communication Papers Presented at the 97th Meeting of the Acoustical Society of America*, Acoustical Society of America, New York.

Recasens, D. (in press) "The Articulatory Characteristics of Palatal Consonants," *Journal of Phonetics* 18, 267–280.

Simon, P. (1967) *Les consonnes françaises*, Bibliothèque française et romane, Série A, No. 14, Klincksieck, Paris.

Wierzchowska, B. (1965) *Wymowa polska*, Pánstwowe Zaklady Wydawnictw Szkolnych, Warsaw.

Wierzchowska, B. (1967) *Opis Fonetyczny Języka Polskiego*, Pánstwowe Wydawnictwo Naukowe, Warsaw.

Wierzchowska, B. (1980) *Fonetyka i Fonologia Języka Polskiego*, Ossolineum, Warsaw.

CORONALS AND THE PHONOTACTICS
OF NONADJACENT CONSONANTS IN ENGLISH

STUART DAVIS

Department of Linguistics
Indiana University
Bloomington, Indiana 47405

1. INTRODUCTION

Much recent work on underspecification has focused on the status of coronal consonants. One question this work addresses is whether or not coronal consonants lack the Place Node. (I assume here a theory of feature geometry like that proposed in Sagey, 1986, in which the Place Node dominates the articulator nodes Labial, Coronal, and Dorsal.) The conclusions reached about the status of coronals are quite varied. Some researchers such as Paradis and Prunet (1989a,b) have concluded that ([+anterior]) coronal consonants are different from labials and dorsals in that as a principle of grammar they lack the Place Node. Other researchers, such as Avery and Rice (1989), contend that whether or not coronal consonants in a language lack the Place Node depends on the phonemic inventory of that language, while still other researchers such as Clements (1988) and Mester and Itô (1989) give no special status to coronals with respect to underspecification.

The major reason why these researchers have reached different conclusions is that they have used competing criteria in determining what is underspecified in underlying representation. For example, Avery and Rice (1989) assume that phonemic inventories (and not phonological rules) are relevant for determining what is underspecified. Thus, in their view, the Coronal Node is present in the underlying representation of any two phonemes (in an inventory) that differ only in a

Phonetics and Phonology, Volume 2
The Special Status of Coronals

feature that is dominated by the Coronal Node (such as [anterior]). Thus, in a language like English that has an anteriority contrast between /s/ and /š/, the Coronal Node would be present underlyingly in both sounds, whereas /t/ would not have a Coronal Node since /t/ does not contrast with a corresponding non-anterior coronal stop.

In more radical versions of underspecification (e.g., Archangeli, 1988; Paradis and Prunet, 1989b) at least some coronal consonants could lack the Coronal Node in underlying representation in spite of a (minimal) contrast with another coronal phoneme. For example, Paradis and Prunet (1989b) contend that Fula coronal consonants that have the feature [+anterior] completely lack the Coronal Node, while the corresponding coronal consonants with the feature [−anterior] possess the Coronal Node in underlying representation. Paradis and Prunet base their contention on the fact that vowel spreading and assimilation between non-adjacent vowels occur in Fula only if the intervening consonant is an anterior coronal. They argue that such consonants must lack the Place Node completely (and consequently the Coronal Node) or else they would not be transparent to vowel spreading and assimilation. Paradis and Prunet show that similar cases of coronal transparency are found in Guere and Mau. However, in languages where coronals are opaque to vowel spreading and assimilation, they propose that there is early coronal specification. Thus, they are able to maintain that ([+anterior]) coronals always lack the Place Node in underlying representation.

In more restrictive views of underspecification (e.g., Clements, 1988; Mester and Itô, 1989) coronal consonants are not necessarily viewed as having any special status, regardless of the nature of the phonemic inventory. For example, Mester and Itô argue that the Coronal Node must be present underlyingly in all coronal consonants in Japanese (except /r/), even though there are no (phonemic) contrasts between anterior and nonanterior coronals. Their argument for lack of underspecification of coronals is based on palatal prosody in Japanese. This is a process whereby palatalization of certain consonants in the base form of a word adds to the meaning of the word a sense of "uncontrolledness." They contend that which consonants become palatalized is quite predictable: Essentially the rightmost coronal consonant of the base (excluding /r/) becomes palatalized, or, in the absence of a coronal consonant, the first consonant of the word becomes palatalized. They argue that this process assumes that coronal consonants cannot be unspecified for place of articulation in underlying representation or else coronal consonants could not be singled out.

Moreover, Yip (1989), Clements (1988), and Mester and Itô (1989) have all employed (to different degrees) an argument against coronal consonants being underspecified based on morpheme structure constraints (MSCs). As Yip (1989) has pointed out, MSCs pertain to underlying representations, and therefore they should have access to underlying specifications only. These authors contend that coronals (especially coronal obstruents) are not treated differently than other consonants (i.e., labial or dorsal) by MSCs. That is, MSCs do not seem to treat coronal consonants as if they were unspecified. This finding has led Mester and Itô to conclude that the coronal place of articulation has no special status, and the finding is also probably a motivating factor behind Clements' proposal that articulator nodes of consonants are always present in underlying representation.

Thus, we see that various researchers have reached different conclusions about the underspecification of coronals because they have examined different types of criteria for determining what features (or Nodes) are unspecified. Of these, it is only MSCs that do not seem to treat coronals as special. In this article I focus on the MSC argument for (under)specification. I contend, contrary to Clements (1988) and Mester and Itô (1989), that MSCs can and do treat coronal consonants as special. The evidence discussed in this article comes from English MSCs that pertain to nonadjacent consonants. These MSCs can only be understood if at least some coronals lack the Place Node in underlying representation. This finding, taken together with different MSCs that occur in other languages, provides evidence for a view in which the presence of the Place Node for coronals is a parameterized option.

The organization of this article is as follows. In Section 2 I show that the need for MSCs cannot be obviated completely as has been argued by Hooper (1975), who contends that MSCs are always reducible to, and thus expressible as, syllable structure constraints (SSCs). It is shown that MSCs are required and that they can be distinguished from SSCs. In Section 3 I show that the English MSCs holding between nonadjacent consonants treat coronals differently than noncoronals. It is subsequently argued that this finding provides support for a view of underspecification in which the presence of the Place Node for coronals is a parameterized option.

2. DISTINGUISHING MSCs FROM SSCs

Before discussing MSCs that hold between nonadjacent consonants in English, it is important to show that MSCs can be distinguished from SSCs in light of the work of Hooper (1975). Hooper argues against the existence of MSCs altogether. Basically, Hooper contends that all MSCs are expressible as, and so reducible to, syllable structure constraints. Hooper's argument for replacing MSCs with SSCs comes largely from Spanish data. She notes that in Spanish there seem to be no constraints on morpheme-final clusters, since final clusters that are impossible in isolated syllables do occur morpheme-finally. Examples of such clusters include *bl* and *pr*, which occur in final position in the morphemes *abl* 'speak' and *kompr* 'buy', respectively. In syllable-final position, on the other hand, there are strong constraints on what consonants (and consonant clusters) can occur.

Hooper contends that such constraints are missed in an analysis incorporating (only) MSCs. Hooper's example from Spanish, though, does not really argue against MSCs, rather it provides evidence for the necessity of SSCs. That is, there are certain constraints that are best expressed in terms of the syllable.

Hooper does consider the possibility that there are both SSCs and MSCs. She ends up rejecting completely MSCs. One reason that she rejects MSCs is that there would be different MSCs for stems and for suffixes (in Spanish). For example, the sequence *nd* is a possible initial sequence of a suffix (as in the progressive morpheme *ndo*), but it is not a possible stem-initial sequence. However, this potential reason for rejecting the existence of MSCs would probably not be relevant if inflectional morphemes (such as the progressive *ndo* in Spanish) were not represented in the lexicon in the first place. Such a view of inflectional morphemes is argued for by Anderson (1982), Janda (1983), and others who work within the item-and-process view of morphology. Anderson, for example, argues that since inflectional morphology is integrated into the syntax, inflectional morphemes could not be listed in the lexicon. Instead, they are introduced by inflectional rules. Consequently, they may not necessarily display the same sound sequence constraints as the other morphemes of the language.

Hooper does consider one potential MSC for English but rejects it as being accidental. This is the constraint that rules out morphemes that end in two voiced obstruents. While it is certainly the case that English syllables can end in two voiced obstruents (e.g., *nabbed, pigs*), monomorphemes do not—ignoring the uncommon words *adze* and *ides*. In order to defend her position against the necessity of MSCs, Hooper contends that the existence of this constraint is the result of a historical accident and so does not reflect the morpheme structure of English. On the other hand, Kahn (1976:40) has maintained that the constraint really does reflect a MSC. He notes that English nonsense words like [nEgz] are always interpreted as having two morphemes, and, moreover, English has other possible syllable-final sequences that are not possible morpheme-final sequences (e.g., [ksθs] as in *sixths*). Thus Hooper's contention about the accidental nature of a constraint against English morphemes ending in two voiced obstruents cannot be maintained.

What Kahn (1976) has actually pointed out is one way in which to determine that a constraint is a MSC rather than a SSC. Specifically, if there are no occurrences of a particular type of monomorphemic monosyllable (e.g., those ending in two voiced obstruents), but there are occurrences of such monosyllables that are bimorphemic, then the restriction being dealt with is one pertaining to morphemes and not to syllables.

Another way of determining whether a constraint is a MSC rather than a SSC is by examining polysyllabic monomorphemic words. For example, if a constraint is posited between two segments based on monosyllabic monomorphemic words (where the two segments would be members of the same syllable), and that constraint is also relevant for the same segments in polysyllabic mono-morphemic words (in which the two segments would be members of different syllables), then that constraint is a MSC rather than a SSC. If, on the other hand, the constraint is not relevant for the same segments in polysyllabic mono-morphemes (i.e., the constraint holds between two sounds in the same syllable but not when they are in different syllables), then the constraint reflects a SSC. An example that can help elucidate this contrast comes from the MSCs that hold among root consonants in Arabic, of which Hooper (1975) seems unaware. Arabic has restrictions on which consonants can co-occur in a root. Greenberg (1950) notes restrictions such as the following: Two postvelars cannot occur in the same root, and the first two root consonants cannot be homorganic obstruents. The syllable plays no role in such constraints. This is because root consonants in a word can all be in one syllable, or in two syllables, or even in three different syllables. Thus the constraints on root consonants in Arabic are not syllable sen-sitive, rather they reflect MSCs. Examples like Arabic clearly show that, despite Hooper's (1975) contention, MSCs cannot always be reduced to SSCs.

Another way of determining whether a constraint is a MSC or a SSC concerns instances where position within the word is the main factor in whether or not two sounds co-occur. If the two sounds can co-occur in a word only if they are hetero-syllabic, then the restriction that prevents them from occurring within the same syllable of the word is a reflection of a SSC. A good example of such an instance is the restriction in English on *tl* and *dl*. In English no morphemes begin with *tl*. However, sequences of *tl* do occur when they are heterosyllabic, as in words like *atlas* and *Atlantic* (or even in morpheme-final position as in the name *Aristotle* where the stress pattern—primary stress on the first syllable—indicates that the final *l* is not underlyingly syllabic). The restriction on English *tl* (as well as on *dl*) thus reflects a SSC that prohibits such sequences in syllable onsets.

Based on our discussion so far, it can be concluded that languages can have both MSCs and SSCs and that there are means for determining whether a given constraint is a MSC or a SSC. Besides applying over different domains (mor-pheme versus syllable), MSCs and SSCs differ from one another in another im-portant way. MSCs pertain to underlying representation whereas SSCs come into play at the point in the derivation in which syllable formation rules apply. We assume here a rule-based account of syllabification along the lines of Steriade (1982). Because MSCs and SSCs are relevant at different points in the deriva-tion, they may assume different representations for the same phoneme. For ex-ample, if the feature (or node) [coronal] is unspecified in underlying representa-tion, it would be predicted that MSCs could not refer to the feature (or node) [coronal] but SSCs could refer to [coronal] as long as specification of [coronal] occurs before the application of the syllable formation rules. In the following section we consider the case of English, where it is shown that MSCs treat some coronals such as /t/ as lacking the Place Node. As noted above, English SSCs do not necessarily treat /t/ as lacking it.

In summary, in this section we have seen that despite Hooper's (1975) contention, MSCs are not always reducible to SSCs. Moreover, we have pointed out various ways to determine whether a restriction holding between two segments reflects a MSC or a SSC. Finally, it has been suggested that MSCs reflect the nature of underlying representations, while SSCs reflect the nature of representations at the point in the derivation where syllable formation rules apply.

3. THE UNDERSPECIFICATION OF CORONALS IN ENGLISH

Most of the recent work examining what is underspecified in English has not used MSCs as a criterion—with the notable exception of Clements (1988). As mentioned earlier, Avery and Rice (1989) base what is specified on the nature of the phonemic inventory. They contend that for English the anterior coronals /t/ and /n/ are underspecified for place of articulation since these phonemes do not contrast with nonanterior coronals. On the other hand, /s/ would be specified for place of articulation (i.e., it has the Coronal Node) since it does contrast with the nonanterior coronal /š/. Avery and Rice find support for their view of English underspecification from phonological rules that seem to treat /t/ and /n/ as if they do not possess the Place Node. The specific rules that Avery and Rice mention are a rule that turns (syllable-final) /t/ into [ʔ] in such words as *button* and *cotton* and a rule that optionally assimilates word-final /n/ to the place of articulation of the following word-initial consonant. However, it can be maintained that the former rule really does not show that /t/ is underspecified for place-of-articulation features. This is because the rule affects syllable-final /t/, which means that rules of syllabification (and resyllabification) have already applied before the /t/-to-[ʔ] rule. Since syllabification has already applied, then SSCs have also already taken effect. Because English has a SSC that specifically refers to the Coronal Node of /t/ and /d/ (i.e., the one prohibiting syllable-initial /tl/ and /dl/ sequences), the Coronal Node must be present at the time the /t/-to-[ʔ] rule applies. Consequently, this rule should be interpreted as simple delinking of the Supralaryngeal Node of /t/, and it would not constitute evidence that /t/ is unspecified for the Place Node in underlying representation. Moreover, Avery and Rice's contention that specification of the Coronal Node can be determined by the presence of an anterior–nonanterior contrast is called into question by Paradis and Prunet's (1989b) work on Fula. They argue that in Fula, a language that contrasts both anterior and nonanterior coronals, the anterior coronals lack the Place Node altogether since they are the only consonants that are transparent to a process of vowel spreading. They conclude that all ([+anterior]) coronals lack the Place Node as a principle of grammar.

In this section, we consider MSCs as a criterion for determining what features (or nodes) are unspecified in underlying representation. If we use MSCs as criteria for determining underspecification, rather than phonological rules or the nature of phonological inventories, it becomes more readily apparent what features (and nodes) are present in underlying representation. This is because MSCs hold on underlying representations prior to phonological or morphological processes. The specific question addressed in this section is whether or not MSCs treat coronals as "special." By special, I mean that coronals (or, at least, some coronals) are treated as if their Place Node is absent in underlying representation. I show that despite claims to the contrary by Mester and Itô (1989) MSCs can treat coronals as special. Specifically, I show that English MSCs treat coronal stops as special.

Recently, it has been argued explicitly by Mester and Itô (1989) (and implicitly by Clements, 1988) that MSCs do not treat coronals as special even in languages where there is no contrast between anterior and nonanterior coronals. For example, in Classical Arabic (Greenberg, 1950; McCarthy, 1988), which has no contrast between anterior coronal stops and nonanterior coronal stops, there is a constraint that rules out homorganic consonants (or, more accurately, obstruents made with the same articulator) from occurring in the same root morpheme. This MSC holds for all places of articulation including coronal. Coronal consonants are not ignored by this constraint. Because Arabic coronal obstruents are subject to a MSC that prevents them from occurring with other coronal obstruents in the same root, the Coronal Node must be present in the underlying representation. Consequently, MSCs, like those in Arabic involving place of articulation, argue against a specific place of articulation (like coronal) being completely unspecified in underlying representation. This is pointed out by Mester and Itô (1989: 265), who note that with such morpheme structure conditions "no special status is accorded to the unmarked place, whatever it may be."

If special status were accorded to an unmarked place (i.e., coronal), it would be expected that MSCs that pertain to homorganic consonants would not hold for consonants of the unmarked place. So, for example, if in some hypothetical language it is posited that a coronal consonant such as /t/ has no Place Node, and if that language possesses MSCs of the sort found in Arabic, then it would be predicted that, in general, morphemes would not contain homorganic consonants. However, this prediction would not hold for /t/ since it would not be represented with the Place Node. The existence of such a hypothetical language would lead to the conclusion that because of the type of MSCs found in a language like Arabic, it is a parameterized option whether or not a language can have the Place Node completely absent in underlying representation. We now consider a type of MSC found in English that shows that English is our hypothetical language.

Fudge (1969), Clements and Keyser (1983), and Davis (1984) have all observed a number of constraints restricting the type of consonant that flanks both sides of a vowel in *sCVC* sequences. One of the strongest of these constraints is that in *sCVC* monosyllables, the same noncoronal consonant cannot flank both sides of the vowel. Hence, there are no English words like *spap, spep,* and *skik.* On the other hand, monosyllables with the same coronal flanking both sides of the vowel in a *sCVC* word do occur (e.g., *state, stout, stoat*).

Fudge (1969), Clements and Keyser (1983), and Davis (1984) express the *sCVC* constraint as a SSC. However, it will be shown here that this constraint is not a condition on syllables but rather a reflection of a MSC. Afterward, it will be shown that the condition pertains to homorganic consonants flanking both sides of the vowel, rather than just to identical consonants.

If the constraint on *sCVC* sequences were a reflection of a SSC, one would expect to find English words containing the sequence *sCVCV,* since the postvocalic C would not be part of the initial syllable. So, for example, one might expect that there would be words like *spapoon* and *skikanda* in which the first postvocalic consonant is not part of the initial syllable. If, as argued here, the constraint against *sCVC* sequences is a reflection of a MSC, then possible monomorphemic forms like *spapoon* and *skikanda* would never occur (or at least would be extremely rare). In order to determine whether such English monomorphemes occur, a search was conducted on a computerized lexicon containing nearly 20,000 words from *Webster's Pocket Dictionary.* The only word in this lexicon in which the sequence *sCVC* was found (where the C's are identical noncoronal consonants) was the word *dyspepsia,* where the sequence *spep* occurs. However, the sequence *spep* in this word spans a morpheme boundary since the initial *s* is part of the morpheme *dys,* which also occurs in words like *dysfunction* and *dystrophy.* Thus no monomorphemic *sCVC* sequences were found in which the two C's were identical noncoronal consonants. Consequently, the constraint on *sCVC* sequences in English seems truly a reflection of a MSC. Moreover, this MSC is indeed restricted to noncoronals because in addition to the monosyllabic morphemes mentioned above, like *state, stout,* and *stoat,* where the coronal /t/ flanks both sides of the vowel, there are monomorphemic *stVt* sequences in such words as *astute, statistics, status, stutter,* and *substitute.*

For the sake of completeness, we note that morphemes having the sequence *sCVC,* where the two C's are different noncoronals, are common. A search through the 20,000-word lexicon gives us such words as *speak, skip, spaghetti, scaffold, scuba, Eskimo,* and *episcopal.* Also, morphemes having the sequence *sCVC,* where the first C is coronal and the second C noncoronal, are common. Such forms include *stake, stop, stable,* and *stagger.* Thus, with the data discussed so far, it can be concluded that the constraint on *sCVC* sequences is a reflection of a MSC holding between identical noncoronal consonants.

The MSC pertaining to *sCVC* sequences on further investigation turns out to be a more general constraint in that it rules out morphemes where the two C's are homorganic, not merely identical. That is, there are virtually no mono-morphemic forms in English that have the sequence *sCVC* where the two C's are either both labial or both velar. The only word in the 20,000-word lexicon that was found to violate this constraint is *skunk* (on the assumption that English has underlying velar nasals).[1] That this constraint really does involve identical places of articulation is made evident when we consider the situation where the two C's in a *sCVC* sequence are not homorganic. A search through the 20,000-word computerized lexicon revealed that no constraint whatsoever held when the two C's were made at different locations in the vocal tract. For example, the sequence *skV* was followed by a labial consonant in 58 entries (e.g., *skip, scuba*), an alveolar consonant in 151 entries (e.g., *skit, skate*), and a palato-alveolar conso-nant in 25 entries (e.g., *scotch, sketch*). The fact that there are virtually no words with a velar consonant following a *skV* sequence is of interest. Moreover, the sequence *spV* was followed by a velar consonant in 56 entries (e.g., *spike, spook*), an alveolar consonant in 196 entries (e.g., *spit, speed*), and a palato-alveolar consonant in 20 entries (e.g., *speech, special*); there are virtually no words where a labial consonant followed a *spV* sequence.

Finally, while the constraint on *sCVC* sequences holds for homorganic non-coronals, it clearly does not hold for /t/. Many morphemes have the sequence *stVC* where the postvocalic C is a coronal. There are over 100 entries in which the coronal was an obstruent and over 200 entries in which the coronal was a sonorant. Typical examples include *stud, study, astound, stadium, stash, stitch*, and *stone*. Furthermore, there were over 100 entries in which the postvocalic C was a labial (*stable, stop*) and over 100 entries in which it was a velar (*stock, plastic*). Thus, English has a MSC that prevents homorganic noncoronals from flanking both sides of the vowel in *sCVC* sequences.

Consequently, it is concluded that, contrary to what Mester and Itô (1989) contend, MSCs can treat coronal consonants as special. The English MSC dis-cussed in this article can only be understood if /t/ in English lacks the Place Node but labial and dorsal consonants do not.[2] For it is only /t/ that is not subject to the MSC that prevents homorganic consonants from flanking both sides of the vowel in *sCVC* sequences.[3]

Although we have so far argued that /t/ lacks the Place Node in English, we have yet to focus on other coronal consonants. It is briefly noted here that the evidence from other MSCs in English is compatible with a view that coronal sonorants (/n/, /l/, and /r/) lack the Place Node in underlying representation, whereas coronal stridents do not.

The MSC evidence relevant for coronal sonorants is inconclusive regarding whether these sounds lack the Place Node. Consider, first, the coronal nasal /n/. English has a MSC that prohibits *sNVN* sequences (where *N* = any nasal). The coronal nasal is not exceptional to this constraint. There are no sequences like *snan* in English monomorphemes. This MSC, though, only implies that all nasal consonants in English must have the feature [+nasal] in underlying representation. But this does not at all imply the presence of the Place Node for /n/ (at least under a view of feature geometry in which [nasal] is located immediately under the Root Node or the Supralaryngeal Node). As for /l/ and /r/, English has a MSC that prohibits identical liquids from occurring in CLVL sequences (where L = liquid). Thus potential sequences like *plil* or *bror* do not occur in English monomorphemes. The only exception is *slalom* (although *flail* would also be exceptional if it were pronounced with a single vowel). This MSC, though, only implies the presence of the feature [lateral] in underlying representation for the phonemes /l/ and /r/. It does not, however, imply the presence of the Coronal Node.[4] Thus English MSCs relating to coronal sonorants are not incompatible with a view that these sonorants lack the Place Node.

The evidence that coronal stridents require the Place Node in underlying representation comes from a MSC discussed by Clements (1988). He notes that English roots do not contain adjacent coronal stridents that are both [+continuant].[5] This MSC assumes the presence of the Coronal Node (and, consequently, the Place Node) in the underlying representation of stridents.

In conclusion, based on the evidence from the English MSCs discussed in this section, /t/ (and presumably /d/) lack the Place Node in underlying representation, but coronal stridents do not. The MSC evidence is inconclusive concerning the lack of the Place Node in coronal sonorants.[6] Nonetheless, we have found in this article that MSCs can and do treat coronals as special. This finding shows that the contention of Mester and Itô (1989:265) that "homorganicity restrictions hold for ALL places of articulation, and no special status is accorded to the unmarked place" cannot be maintained.

Moreover, our finding argues against the view of underspecification advanced by Clements (1988) in which the Place Node must be present in underlying representation. The English MSC forbidding homorganic noncoronals in *sCVC* sequences is best understood only if /t/ is represented without the Place Node in underlying representation.

However, our finding for English is basically compatible with either contrastive theories of underspecification (e.g., Avery and Rice, 1989) or more radical theories of underspecification (e.g., Archangeli, 1988) since [+anterior] coronal stridents, which would differentiate the two types of theories, are never involved in *sCVC* sequences. Coronal stridents are the only coronal consonants in English that are contrastive for the feature [anterior] (ignoring the problem of how English affricates—which are coronal stridents—should be represented).

In contrast to our specific finding for English, the MSCs on homorganicity of root consonants in Arabic discussed earlier seem incompatible with both types of theories. This is because in Arabic there is no contrast between the voiceless anterior coronal stop /t/ and a corresponding nonanterior coronal. So both contrastive and radical theories of underspecification would apparently posit that the

Arabic /t/ should be represented without the Coronal Node in underlying representation. But because Arabic /t/ is subject to a MSC that prevents it from occurring with other coronal obstruents in the same root, the Coronal Node must be present in the underlying representation of /t/. Consequently, the different realizations of MSCs that are found in languages like English and Arabic provide support for a theory of underspecification in which the presence of the Place Node for coronals is a parameterized option. At least some English coronal consonants lack the Place Node whereas Arabic coronal consonants do not.

ACKNOWLEDGMENTS

I thank Diana Archangeli, Nick Clements, Mike Hammond, Carole Paradis, Jean-François Prunet, Doug Pulleyblank, and Moira Yip for their comments on earlier versions of this article. I am also grateful to Sue Steele, who first suggested to me that the topic of phonotactics between nonadjacent consonants was worth investigating. I alone am responsible for any mistakes in this paper. The research for this paper was supported by an NIH Training Grant NS-7134-09 to Indiana University.

NOTES

[1] There is a handful of other words that violate the constraint but do not appear in the computerized lexicon. These include *spam, spumoni, spoof,* and *spiffy.* It may be that the MSC preventing two homorganic noncoronal consonants from occurring in *sCVC* sequences is "tighter" if the two consonants are both oral stops.

[2] It is also possible to conclude that English /t/ does not lack the Place Node, rather it lacks the articulator node Coronal. While I am unaware of evidence from English MSCs that would help determine this, I am assuming that it is the Place Node that is lacking. This is the case for other languages such as Fula, where Paradis and Prunet (1989b) show that for ([+anterior]) coronals it must be the Place Node that is lacking (and not just the articulator node) in order for such consonants to be completely transparent to vowel spreading.

[3] It is interesting to note that while English has a MSC on *sCVC* sequences, there appear to be no systematic constraints on CVC sequences. Such monosyllables as *pipe, kick, tight, pub, cog,* and *toad,* with homorganic consonants flanking both sides of the vowel, occur in CVC sequences. I repress the temptation to speculate on why the MSC only holds for *sCVC* sequences, but I note that the constraint is not idiosyncratic. MSCs on the homorganicity of other consonants are found in other languages such as Arabic (McCarthy, 1988), Javanese (Mester, 1986), and Cambodian (Yip, 1989).

[4] Levin (1988) has argued that the feature [lateral] is dominated by the Coronal Node, so that the presence of the feature [lateral] implies the presence of the Coronal Node. However, here we follow the position of Shaw (1988) in which it is argued that [lateral] cannot be dominated by the Coronal Node but instead is located higher up in the feature geometry tree.

[5]The MSC holds on a sequence of two strident fricatives, a sequence of a strident affricate and a strident fricative, but not on a sequence of a strident fricative followed by a strident affricate (e.g., *sš* and *čs* do not occur, but *sč* does occur as in *eschew*). This constraint can be taken as evidence that affricates have the feature values [−continuant] and [+continuant] and that these features are sequentially ordered.

[6]The interdental phonemes /θ/ and /ð/ are not dealt with here because of their low frequency of occurrence.

REFERENCES

Anderson, S. (1982) "Where's Morphology?" *Linguistic Inquiry* 13, 571–612.

Archangeli, D. (1988) "Aspects of Underspecification Theory," *Phonology* 5.2, 183–207.

Avery, P. and K. Rice (1989) "Segment Structure and Coronal Underspecification," *Phonology* 6.2, 179–200.

Clements, G. (1988) "Towards a Substantive Theory of Feature Specification," *Proceedings of NELS* 18, 79–93.

Clements, G. and S. Keyser (1983) *CV Phonology*, MIT Press, Cambridge, Massachusetts.

Davis, S. (1984) "Some Implications of Onset-Coda Constraints for Syllable Phonology," *Proceedings of CLS* 20, 46–51.

Fudge, E. (1969) "Syllables," *Journal of Linguistics* 5, 253–287.

Greenberg, J. (1950) "The Patterning of Root Morphemes in Semitic," *Word* 6, 162–181.

Hooper, J. (1975) "The Archi-segment in Natural Generative Phonology," *Language* 51, 536–560.

Janda, R. (1983) "Morphemes Aren't Something That Grows on Trees: Morphology as More the Phonology than the Syntax of Words," *Proceedings of CLS* 19 (Parasession), 79–95.

Kahn, D. (1976) *Syllable-Based Generalizations in English Phonology*, Doctoral dissertation, MIT, Cambridge, Massachusetts. Distributed by the Indiana University Linguistics Club, Bloomington.

Levin, J. (1988) "A Place for Lateral in the Feature Geometry," ms., Department of Linguistics, University of Texas, Austin.

McCarthy, J. (1988) "Feature Geometry and Dependency," *Phonetica* 45, 84–108.

Mester, R. (1986) *Studies in Tier Structure*, Doctoral dissertation, University of Massachusetts, Amherst.

Mester, R. and J. Itô (1989) "Feature Predictability and Underspecification: Palatal Prosody in Japanese Mimetics," *Language* 65, 258–293.

Paradis, C. and J.-F. Prunet (1989a) "Markedness and Coronal Structure," *Proceedings of NELS* 19, 330–344.

Paradis, C. and J.-F. Prunet (1989b) "On Coronal Transparency," *Phonology* 6.2, 317–348.

Sagey, E. (1986) *The Representations of Features and Relations in Nonlinear Phonology*, Doctoral dissertation, MIT, Cambridge, Massachusetts.

Shaw, P. (1988) "The Locus of Lateral in Feature Geometry," Paper presented at the annual meeting of the Linguistic Society of America, Dec. 27–30, New Orleans, Louisiana.

Steriade, D. (1982) *Greek Prosodies and the Nature of Syllabification*, Doctoral dissertation, MIT, Cambridge, Massachusetts.

Yip, M. (1989) "Feature Geometry and Co-Occurrence Restrictions," *Phonology* 6.2, 349–374.

CORONALS, CONSONANT CLUSTERS, AND THE CODA CONDITION

MOIRA YIP

Program in Linguistics and Cognitive Science/
Center for Complex Systems
Brandeis University
Waltham, Massachusetts 02254

1. INTRODUCTION

It has often been observed (e.g., Clements, 1988:33, and references therein) that coronal consonants can occur in positions in syllables where consonants with other places of articulation cannot occur.[1] Geminates and homorganic nasal-stop clusters also enjoy unusual freedom of occurrence. This article argues for the fundamental claim given in (1):

(1) Freedom of occurrence of coronals, geminates, and homorganic clusters has a common explanation: their lack of Place features.

A secondary claim is given in (2):

(2) Restrictions on Place specifications may hold for specific syllable positions, particularly codas, or for any consonant cluster.

It is argued that geminates and sequences of consonants that include a coronal have in common the fact that only one set of Place features is needed for the cluster. In the case of geminates these features are shared; in the case of a cluster containing a coronal, the noncoronal has Place features and the coronal does not.

61

Languages may observe one of the conditions in (3) and (4), discussed in detail below:

(3) MODIFIED CODA CONDITION
     Codas may not have Place features.

(4) CLUSTER CONDITION
     Adjacent consonants are limited to at most one Place specification.[2]

I call (3) the *modified* coda condition in order to make clear my debt to the coda condition of Steriade (1982) and Itô (1986:21), given in (5):

(5) CODA CONDITION
     An obstruent can be syllabified as a coda only if it is segmentally linked to
         the following C.

Unlike (5), however, (3) makes explicit the relationship between the special behavior of coronals and that of linked structures like geminates and homorganic clusters. Empirically, it licenses coronals, but no other consonants, as codas that are not doubly linked to an adjacent consonant. This situation is illustrated below for Japanese and Finnish.[3]

   Given that the modified coda condition and the cluster condition are stated in terms of Place features, the argument presented here is also an argument that coronals lack Place features in some languages, a point made cogently by other articles in this volume.[4]

   Sections 2 and 3 of this article discuss the special privileges of occurrence held by coronals in English and Menomini. The fourth and fifth sections discuss two languages, Diola Fogny and Attic Greek, where the cluster condition holds, and the sixth section discusses a language, Japanese, where the coda condition holds. The seventh section deals with an ambiguous case, Finnish, and the eighth section deals with issues in underspecification theory.

   Before beginning the discussion of coronals, let me make explicit my assumptions about feature geometry and underspecification. I assume a model of feature geometry along the lines of Clements (1985) and a model of Place features along the lines of Sagey (1986), in which there is a Place Node dominating the three articulator nodes Labial, Coronal, and Dorsal. Other researchers have extended this model in ways not relevant to the discussion (see particularly McCarthy, 1989, on articulator nodes). I assume that underlying representations are not fully specified (Archangeli, 1984; Steriade, 1987) and argue particularly that coronal consonants may not have any underlying Coronal Node. A discussion of the implications for different models of underspecification is in Section 8. I also assume that surface representations are normally fully specified for Place features, the missing values being inserted by default rules. However, some data from Finnish in Section 7 suggest that this may not always be the case, and that even surface representations can remain underspecified.

2. THE SPECIAL BEHAVIOR OF CORONALS: ENGLISH

In monomorphemic words, English clusters never include more than one non-coronal. In (6) I show the range of possibilities for medial and final clusters. The data are from Clements (1988:35), but I have made many additions.[5]

(6) a. stop-stop $C_2 = t, d$ *chapter, factor, abdomen*
     b. stop-fricative $C_2 = s, z$ *capsule, axle, adze*
     c. fricative-stop $C_1 = s,$ *whisper, whisker, clasp, brisk*
                            or $C_2 = t, d$ *often, lift*
     d. nasal-stop   homorganic   *whimper, winter, wrinkle*
     e. stop-nasal $C_2 = n$[6]   *signify, open*
     f. liquid-stop   all OK   *alder, garden, help, elk*
     g. stop-liquid   all OK   *atlas, poplar, topple, wicker*
     h. fricative-fricative $C_1 = s$ *asphalt, aesthetic* (rare)
     i. nasal-fricative $C_1 = n$ *answer, panther, anvil, tense,*
                                                     plinth
     j. fricative-nasal   very rare   *prism*
     k. liquid-fricative   all OK   *wealth, hearth, elf, scarf,*
                                                     harsh
     l. fricative-liquid   all OK   *Teflon, whiffle, wither, usher*

Clements (1988:36) formulates the principle in (7), which says that since *t* is simpler than *k*, *pt* is simpler than *pk*.

(7) SEQUENTIAL MARKEDNESS PRINCIPLE
     For any two segments A and B and any given context X_____Y, if A is
     simpler than B, then XAY is simpler than XBY.

As I later claim, the insight that markedness is relevant here is captured by the underspecification of coronals for Place features, and English clusters observe the cluster condition, given again in (8):

(8) CLUSTER CONDITION
     Adjacent consonants are limited to at most one Place specification.

Further, the Place features show up predictably, in accordance with the rule given in (9):[7]

(9)   ASSOCIATION RULE FOR PLACE IN ENGLISH
       Associate Place with leftmost [−continuant] consonant; if there is no [−continuant], associate Place with rightmost consonant.

The effect of (9) is that if the cluster includes a stop, as in (6a–g), the leftmost stop will be the only noncoronal. If the cluster does not include a stop, as in (6h–j), the rightmost nonliquid will be the only noncoronal. Nasal-stop clusters spread Place features to create a homorganic cluster.

Finally, note that onset clusters also conform to the cluster condition. In (10) I give the positive conditions on onsets from Clements and Keyser (1983:42–47). The condition in (10a) produces *Cl, Cr* clusters, and that in (10b) produces *sC* clusters. The conjunction of the two gives *sCl* and *sCr*. Only the single consonant shown here by C can be a noncoronal. The association rule in (9) works correctly here too.

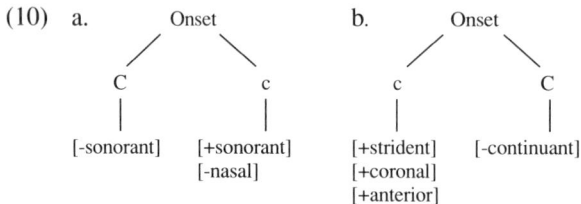

(10)   a.   Onset   b.   Onset

              C   c   c   C

         [-sonorant]   [+sonorant]   [+strident]   [-continuant]
                          [-nasal]   [+coronal]
                                               [+anterior]

I conclude that, in English, initial, medial, and final clusters all obey the cluster condition.[8] I emphasize that there is no obvious way to analyze these facts by means of a single statement that refers to syllabic constituents, such as onset or coda. This is because it may be the first or second consonant, coda or onset, that is required to be coronal. Cluster conditions must thus be part of the armory of Universal Grammar.[9]

3. THE SPECIAL BEHAVIOR OF CORONALS: MENOMINI

Bloomfield (1962) gives the following phoneme inventory for Menomini:

(11)   p   t   c   k
                 s
       m   n
       w   y   h   ʔ

where t = postdental, c = palatal affricate, and s = alveolar palatal.

Syllables are maximally CVC, where the onset may be any nonlaryngeal. There are no initial clusters (except [kw]). Intervocalically all C occur freely. The coda may also be any single consonant: *napo:p* 'broth', *apec* 'to that degree', *mE?tek* 'tree'. The only coda clusters are *?c* and *?s*, such as *ko:?c* 'fearing to' and *namE:?s* 'fish', restricted to particles and a very few nouns.

Given these facts, one might expect medial clusters to be any coda-onset sequence, but in fact only those in (12) are found. C_1 is always *c, s, h,* or *?*.

(12) *cp*   *ck*
      hp   *ht*   *hc*   *hk*   *hn*   *hs*
             ?t   *?c*   *?k*   *?n*   *?s*
      sp   *sk*

If *c, s,* along with *h, ?*, lack Place features, then Menomini, like English, can be said to observe the cluster condition. The single set of Place features links to the rightmost consonant, and there is no double linking. Since *t* and *n*, unlike *c* and *s*, do not cluster freely, it must be assumed, rather surprisingly, that the [+anterior] postdental *t* and *n* have Place features, and that the palatal [−anterior] *c* and *s* do not. I return to this point in Section 8.

Interesting confirmation of the link between coronals, laryngeals, and geminates comes from the historical evidence. Bloomfield (1946:88) gives charts showing correspondences between different Algonquian languages. One chart is partially reproduced in (13):[10]

(13)   Fox   Cree   Menomini   Ojibwa
       k   *hk*   *hk*   *nk*
       hk   *hk*   *hk*   *kk*
       hk   *sk*   *hk*   *kk*
       š   *hk*   *hk*   *sk*
       hk   *sk*   *č*   *šk*

The correspondences show that coronals, laryngeals, and geminates bear a close relationship to one another, and I argue that this relationship stems from a common lack of Place features.[11, 12]

4. THE CLUSTER CONDITION: DIOLA FOGNY

I have argued that English and Menomini observe the cluster condition, and that this accounts for the special freedom enjoyed by coronals. I now turn to a language in which coronals do not have special privileges, but the language shows an array of linked structures: geminates and homorganic clusters. As analyzed by Steriade (1982:282) and Itô (1986:61), the West African language Diola Fogny observes the coda condition. I argue instead that it observes the cluster condition. The purpose of this section is thus to emphasize the need for conditions on clusters in addition to conditions on positions in the syllable, especially codas, and to show that at least one supposed case of a coda condition is more illuminatingly analyzed as a cluster condition after all.

In Diola Fogny (Sapir, 1965) any consonant may close the word, but clusters, initial, medial, and final, must be homorganic or geminate.[13] Examples are given in (14). Note that the initial nasals in (14a) are realized as syllabic.

(14)   a. *mba*   'or'   b. *famb´*   'annoy'
          ndaw   'man's name'   *bunt*   'lie'
                                             kaŋg   'be furthest away'
                                             mañj   'know'
       c. *ekumbay* 'the pig'   d. *ninennen*   'I placed'
          jensu   'undershirt'   *niñaññañ*   'I rub arms'
          kaŋkan   'made'   *nimammaŋ*   'I want'
                                             niŋaŋŋan   'I cried'
       e. *salte*   'be dirty'   f. *kuñilak*   'the children'
          ạrtị   'negative'   *ijaut*   'I did not come'
                                             nikObOb   'I waited'

Diola Fogny has a maximally CVVC syllable plus an extra word-final consonant, as shown in (14b). Codas are unrestricted, as shown in (14f). However, all clusters, irrespective of syllable position, are subject to the cluster condition, and Diola Fogny, unlike English, has pervasive double linking, so that the clusters surface as geminate or homorganic. This is true even for liquids, which are found only before homorganic coronal *t* (Sapir, 1965:8). Note that the final extrametrical consonant must also observe the cluster condition.[14]

It is necessary here to contrast this with a coda condition analysis. Itô (1986) formulates the condition in (15):[15]

(15)   DIOLA CODA CONDITION
           *   C]$_\sigma$
                    |
           [+consonantal]

Doubly linked structures evade this condition because of the linking condition (Hayes, 1986), giving the acceptable codas in (14b–d). Since single word-final consonants are acceptable, as in *kuñilak* of (14f), they must be appendixes, not codas.

This analysis has the somewhat odd consequence that a coda is not allowed word-finally unless an appendix is also present to license it. Given that an appendix (i.e., extrametrical consonant) is something that can be added to any well-formed syllable at word edges, this consequence is undesirable. Note also a technical problem: The coda condition must also apply to the initial nasal-stop clusters in (14a), even though the usual analysis of a syllabic nasal would be that it fills the nucleus position but not the coda position. The condition in (15), as stated, will correctly apply to these cases too, but then it is not a condition on codas at all, but simply on syllable-final consonants, and should be renamed the rhyme condition (J.-F. Prunet and C. Paradis, personal communication, 1989).[16]

However, my major criticism of the coda condition analysis is that it obscures the fact that these restrictions hold on all consonant clusters in the language, irrespective of syllable structure. If anything is diagnostic of a cluster condition, this is it, and unless we wish to exclude cluster conditions on universal grounds (which I argued is impossible, in Section 2 on English), Diola Fogny must be analyzed as a clear instance of a language that obeys the cluster condition.

5. CORONALS AGAIN: THE CLUSTER CONDITION IN ATTIC GREEK

Steriade (1982:175ff.) gives a detailed and masterful discussion of Attic Greek syllable structure, invoking the coda condition. Here I sketch out another way of thinking about the Attic Greek facts in which the restrictions are restrictions on clusters, not on codas, and in which the special status of coronals is attributed to their lack of Place features.

Steriade observes (1982:215) that "there are no obstruent clusters the second member of which is not a coronal": *tp, *tk, *pk, *kp. In fact, it is striking that clusters never contain more than one noncoronal, and this holds true of onsets, codas (both maximally CC), intervocalic clusters, and clusters formed by the addition of extrametrical consonants at word edges. The exceptions to this, as Steriade notes, are geminates and homorganic clusters, which of course share Place features.[17] The clusters of Attic Greek are given in (16):

(16) a. Onsets (Steriade, 1982:208, 213)
          voiceless stops + *n, l* or *r*
          voiced stops + *r*, or *l* (except *dl*)
      b. Word-initially: Extrametrical slot available
          s   + any of onset clusters in (16a)
          p, k   + *t, s, d* (one or other may be aspirated)
          g, d, m + *n*
      c. Word-finally: Extrametrical *s*-slot available
          C   :*s, n, r*
          CC   :*n, l* + *s*
                 p, k + *s*
          CCC:homorganic nasal-stop cluster + *s*, e.g., *mps*
      d. Intervocalically
          CC   :i. any onset cluster
                 ii. homorganic nasal-stop cluster: *ŋg, mb*
                     geminates: *pp, tt, kk^h, pp^h, tt^h*

iii. *s, r, l* before any C

any stop if C_2 is coronal: *kt, kʰtʰ, gn, gl, ps, pt, pʰtʰ, bd, dn*

CCC: *r, l,* or homorganic nasal + acceptable stop-initial CC sequence

What we see here is the by now familiar array of clusters in all syllabic environments limited to one noncoronal per cluster, with the exception of doubly linked structures such as geminates and homorganic nasal-stop clusters. I suggest, then, that Attic Greek obeys the cluster condition, and that in the absence of double linking for Place features the unspecified consonant surfaces as coronal.[18]

Steriade's analysis is coda-based and says that stop codas are not allowed unless segmentally linked to a following slot (1982:175). In order to account for the intervocalic clusters like *kt,* she argues that they are doubly linked by laryngeal features, thus evading, by virtue of the linking condition (Hayes, 1986), the negative coda condition disallowing stops in coda position. This analysis has two problems. First, the negative coda condition must now include a Laryngeal Node in order for the linking condition to care about Laryngeal linkings. This is done explicitly by Itô (1986:108):

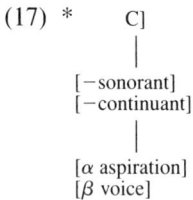

(17) *   C]
                |
         [−sonorant]
         [−continuant]
                |
         [α aspiration]
         [β voice]

There is no other motivation for inclusion of the Laryngeal Node complex [a aspiration, b voice] in the statement of the condition. Second, the laryngeal assimilation rule must be triggered only by coronals (Steriade, 1986:232). Otherwise it would wrongly license clusters whose second member is a noncoronal, such as *kp,* whereas in fact they are impossible and the first consonant deletes (making it impossible to ascertain whether laryngeal assimilation did in fact take place!). A cluster condition analysis suffers from none of these problems, and I conclude that Attic Greek provides another example of the privileged status of coronals, and of a restriction on clusters, not codas.

6. THE CODA CONDITION AND PLACE FEATURES: JAPANESE

Diola Fogny and Attic Greek offer examples of languages that observe a condition on consonant clusters. Japanese, by contrast, has a coda condition, as argued by Itô (1986:32), but I depart from Itô in arguing that the coda condition must be stated in terms of Place features.[19]

Unlike most of the languages discussed above, Japanese does not allow just any single C to close the word. Instead, only a single nasal is allowed, as shown in (18a). Medially, however, the familiar homorganic and geminate clusters are found, as shown in (18b–c). There are no initial or final clusters:

(18) a. *sekken*   'soap'
         zen   'goodness'
         hon   'book'
      b. *sensee*   'teacher'
         kampai   'cheers'
      c. *gakkoo*   'school'
         kappa   'legendary being'
         tossa   'impulsively'
         tootte   'passing'
         minna   'everyone'
         amma   'masseur'

The phonetic realization of the final nasal in (18a) is parasitic on its surroundings, as shown clearly by the phonetic data usefully summarized in Vance (1987:35 ff.) from a variety of sources in the phonetic literature. I follow Vance in denoting this "mora nasal" with N. Details are given in (19). In all cases the morpheme *hon* 'book' is used as an example.

(19) a. Pre-pausally, N is unreleased, either velar or uvular, and the oral closure may not be complete. Some authorities describe the tongue as in its "neutral state"; others call it a "nasalized spirant."
      b. Before consonants, as in *ho[n] ka* 'book?', it is an ordinary homorganic nasal.
      c. Before vowels and glides, it is a nasalized high version of the following vowels:
         ĩ before *i, e, y*   *ho[ĩ]*   *iru*   'need book'
         ũ before *o*   *ho[ũ]*   *o*   'book (dir obj)'
         ɨ̃ before *a, u, w*   *ho[ɨ̃]*   *aru*   'book exists'

N shows no signs of having Place features of its own. With no following context, its realization is indeterminate. With a following context it borrows its Place features entirely from that context. I conclude that it lacks Place features. If this is so, Japanese can then be seen to observe the modified coda condition (3), restated in (20) for convenience:

(20) MODIFIED CODA CONDITION
      Codas may not have Place features.

Japanese has pervasive double linking, giving homorganic clusters and geminates, and in the absence of a following context N surfaces by default as a variably articulated nasal.[20]

Itô (1986:32) gives the following coda condition for Japanese:

(21) * C]$_\sigma$
            |
        [−nasal]

This wrongly predicts the possibility of contrasting final *n, m, N,* and also non-homorganic medial nasal-stop clusters. It is therefore clear that Place is the relevant feature (see condition [20]), not [nasal], but I follow Itô in attributing the Japanese facts to a coda condition, not a cluster condition.[21]

7. A MIXED CASE: FINNISH

Finnish is interesting because it allows only coronals word-finally, suggesting that the modified coda condition may be at work. On the other hand, clusters never include more than one noncoronal, but the noncoronal may be an onset (*tk*) or a coda (*ps*). This fact suggests the cluster condition is involved. In either case note that the same parallels between freedom of occurrence of coronals, geminates, and homorganic clusters are found in Finnish as in the other languages we have looked at, reinforcing the point that what is special about coronals is their lack of Place features.

The data in this section are drawn from Harms (1964), Prince (1984), Itô (1986), Collinder (1957), Keyser and Kiparsky (1984), and Clements and Keyser (1983).

Finnish has the following phonemes:[22]

(22) p   t   k
          d
      v   s
      m   n
          l
          r

There are no initial or final clusters, and final consonants can be any of the coronals except *r:*

(23) *sammal* 'moss'   *vieras* 'guest'
      talot   'house (nom pl)'   *talon*   'house (gen sg)'

Medially, clusters are always geminate, homorganic, or contain only one noncoronal:

(24) CC geminate   *tt, pp, kk*   *loppu*   'end'
      sC   *st, sk, *sp* *ruskea* 'brown'

Cs	*ps, ts, ks*	*lapsi*	'child (nom)'
tC	*tk, *tp*	*matka*	'trip (nom)'
lC	*lp, lt, lk*	*külke*	'side'
rC	*rp, rt, rk*	*mörkö*	'bogeyman'
NC	*mp, ŋk, nt*	*kampa*	'comb'
		keŋkä	'shoe'

Three-consonant clusters have $C_2 = s$, or the first half of a geminate, and $C_1 = $ [+sonorant], although *t* may be possible:

(25) *salskea* 'slender'   *konsti* 'trick'
    yätski 'ice-cream (coll)'   *tarkka* 'exact'

There is a special constraint that disallows obstruent clusters that end in *p* (except geminate *pp*): **sp*, **tp*. However, *mp*, *lp*, and *rp* are acceptable. Prince (1984:239) formulates this as a melodic constraint *[−sonorant]*p*, and this correctly allows geminate *pp*, since on the melodic level there is only one /p/.

The first point to make is that word-final codas, which are always coronal, observe the modified coda condition.[23] Word-medial codas, however, do not, since we find clusters like *ps* and *ks*, in which the first consonant is clearly a coda but not a coronal. Harms (1964:61) is explicit that only the final consonant of a cluster is syllabified as the onset of the following vowel, so *ps* cannot be a complex onset:

(26) *yäts.ki* 'ice-cream'   *an.toi* 'he gave'
    rus.ke.a 'brown'   *it.ke.ä* 'to cry'
    si.joil.la 'pigs (adess)'

I return to this point below.

The second point to make is that all clusters do, however, observe the cluster condition, having no more than one set of Place features (i.e., one noncoronal) per cluster. For example, if the first consonant is a stop, the second must be *s*. If both are stops, the first is always *t*. In the case of geminates and homorganic clusters the Place features are doubly linked. Note also, as Prince observes (1984:236), that the overwhelming majority of suffixes have coronals, thus allowing them to cluster freely with the stem-final consonant. The cluster condition alone, however, fails to explain why word-final consonants are limited to coronals, so I conclude that it cannot be the relevant condition in Finnish.

Let us then return to the modified coda condition. Can the cluster restrictions be made to fall out from this alone? I conclude that they can, but that the modified coda condition holds only at the surface, not during the phonology.[24]

Inspection of the possible clusters shows that the non-final (i.e., coda) consonant(s) of the cluster are coronal or doubly linked (i.e., lack Place features in observation of the modified coda condition) in the majority of cases. The exceptions are the medial clusters *ps* and *ks*. In order to maintain the modified coda condition, it is thus necessary to argue that the *p* and *k* are not codas at all, but onsets. One fact suggests that this is a possibility. Harms (1964:66) says that there is "weak gemination (i.e., overlapping of the syllable boundary) of stops in stop plus *s* clusters."

(27)   *ük.^{k}si*   'one'
       mEt.^{t}sä   'forest'
       lap.^{p}si   'child'

Suppose this is actually resyllabification out of coda position; the modified coda condition would then hold without exceptions at the surface. Is there any other evidence that tells us whether *p* and *k* are codas or onsets in these clusters?[25]

If *p* and *k* are not codas, the previous syllable is open. There are two ways of telling whether a syllable is open or closed in Finnish: stress and gradation. In what follows I am indebted to Harms's careful description. Main stress in Finnish is always initial, but secondary stress depends on syllable weight. The relevant fact is this: Counting from the beginning of the word, secondary stress goes on the leftmost nonfinal heavy syllable (but never on the second syllable). Some examples are given in (28a). Examples in (28b) show that short vowels preceding *ks* clusters count as heavy for stress purposes, showing that they are closed by the *k*.[26]

(28)   a. *huó.maa.màt.to.mas.ti*   'unnoticeably'
          ún.ka.ri.lài.seen.kin   'also a Hungarian (ill sg)'
          pé.rus.te.le.màt.to.mal.ta   'unfounded'
          sór.mus.ti.mèl.li.nen   'a thimbleful'
       b. *hár.ras.tùk.sel.li.nen*   'relating to a hobby'

The second source of evidence on whether a syllable is closed comes from whether or not it provides the environment for gradation. Consonants that are prevocalic, and after vowels or voiced consonants, undergo gradation. Geminates shorten, and single stops weaken by voicing. The relevant fact is that gradation only happens in the onset of a short closed syllable (Keyser and Kiparsky, 1984:16), as shown in (29a). It appears that all clusters, including *ks,* close the syllable for the purposes of gradation, showing again that *k* is a coda in these clusters. The data are given in (29b):

(29)   a. *akka*   *akan*   'old woman (nom/gen)'
       b. *takki*   *takiksi*   'coat (nom/transl)'
          sukka   *sukaksi*   'sock (nom/transl)'

I conclude, then, that *p* and *k* are codas, and that the modified coda condition does not hold at all levels in Finnish. However, the phonetic data in (26) suggest the hypothesis that it is active as a condition on surface syllabification. Violations are allowed during the lexical phonology, and at that stage *p* and *k* are codas. At the postlexical level, however, they must be resyllabified into the onset by a special rule that allows [−continuant] *s* onsets. To put it another way, the presence of the *s* licenses the noncoronal coda by making eventual syllabification possible. The resyllabification is shown schematically in (30):

(30)

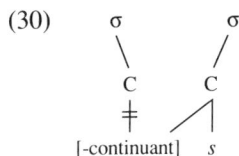

I have shown the process as one that creates an affricate-like structure, rather than licensing a true complex onset. Nothing of importance hangs on this decision here. Note that in other circumstances, when this rule cannot apply, unsyllabifiable consonants delete. Suppose the coda would have to contain a [−continuant] *s* cluster like *ps*. What happens is that the syllabifiable *s* remains, but the unsyllabifiable *p* deletes (Harms, 1964:57–58):[27]

(31) *lapsi laps-ten* [lasten] 'child (nom sg/gen pl)'

I conclude, somewhat tentatively, that Finnish observes the modified coda condition as a condition on surface syllabification, but that at earlier stages in the derivation noncoronal codas are permitted.

Before closing this section, let me briefly comment on previous analyses of Finnish consonant clusters. Prince (1984) views the constraints as cluster constraints, whereas Itô (1986:42) talks in terms of coda restrictions. Although I conclude that the modified coda condition is at work, in essence this analysis is closer in spirit to Prince than to Itô in paying primary attention to Place features. Prince (1984:243) remarks that "there cannot be two Place specifications in a row." In any case Itô deals only with the requirement that the medial consonant in triconsonantal clusters must be *s,* so a full comparison of the analyses cannot be made.

8. ISSUES IN UNDERSPECIFICATION

Kiparsky (1985:98, 135) suggests that coronals have no Place features. However, we also know that some coronals must be specified underlyingly. For example, they participate in co-occurrence restrictions caused by the OCP (obligatory contour principle) (Yip, 1989). The prediction of this article is that it is the unmarked coronals that will have special freedom of occurrence, or in fact the unmarked segments, whatever they may be—laryngeals, and possibly velars (Trigo, 1988), being other candidates. It is thus instructive to look at recent work on coronal underspecification that tries to predict under what circumstances coronals will be unspecified for Place, and to see how good the fit is with one of the cases examined in this article, English.

Avery and Rice (1988) propose a modified version of the restrictive theory of underspecification laid out in Steriade (1987), in which something is specified only if it is distinctive. For Avery and Rice (1988) coronals are specified only if contrasts among coronals exist. Now consider English. The fricatives *θ, s, š* must have Coronal Nodes, since they contrast in the dependent features [anterior] and [distributed]. The stops and nasals lack such contrasts and would be unspecified. This approach fails for the data given here, since the coronals that exhibit special freedom of occurrence include the fricative *s* as well as the stops and sonorants *t, n, l,* and *r.* If my arguments are valid, these must all lack Place features, contra Avery and Rice (1988).

Paradis and Prunet (1989) take a different position. They note that in Fula, alveolars lack Place Nodes but alveopalatals do not. The evidence comes from a rule of Place spread, to which only alveolars are transparent. In their theory, then, one class of coronals may lack Place features, while the others may have them. This of course is just what is needed for the English data. The [+anterior, −distributed] alveolars lack Place Nodes, but the interdentals and palatals have them. The alveolars will then show special freedom of occurrence but the other coronals will not. This is correct: *θ, š,* and *č* behave like the noncoronals in this regard.

I should note that there does not seem to be anything universal about the alveolars as unmarked. In Menomini the palatals are unmarked and the postdentals are marked, for example.

9. CONCLUSIONS

The special freedom of occurrence enjoyed by coronal consonants in many languages has been argued to result from their lack of Place features. Languages restrict the occurrence of Place features, and the result is that unspecified consonants occur more freely, surfacing as geminate or homorganic if doubly linked, or as default coronals or laryngeals otherwise.

Languages may place these restrictions on codas (Japanese and Finnish) or on clusters (English, Menomini, Diola Fogny, and Ponapean). The coda conditions discussed by Steriade and Itô, while descriptively correct, are derived from a more fundamental restriction.

ACKNOWLEDGMENTS

An earlier version of this article was given at the Brandeis University research seminar and the MIT Linguistics Colloquium; I thank the audiences at both presentations for their helpful comments.

The article has also benefited greatly from discussions (vocal and electronic) with Morris Halle, Paul Kiparsky, Alan Prince, Joseph Stemberger, Donca Steriade, and especially the editors of this volume, Carole Paradis and Jean-François Prunet. I want to make clear that this article relies heavily on two outstanding pieces of research: the dissertations of Steriade (1982) and Itô (1986). I reexamine many of the cases they have discussed and often reach different conclusions, but in every instance the groundwork is theirs, and I owe them a debt of gratitude. All errors and omissions are, of course, my own.

NOTES

[1] The following abbreviations are used in this article: dir obj = direct object, sg = singular, pl = plural, coll = colloquial, nom = nominative, gen = genitive, adess = adessive, ill = illative, and transl = translative.

[2] See also Prince (1984:243).

[3] To be more precise, the modified coda condition licenses any consonant unmarked for Place. In addition to coronals this may include laryngeals, and perhaps velars in some languages (see Trigo, 1988), including possibly Japanese.

[4] I do not wish to take a position here on whether coronals lack just Coronal Nodes, or Place Nodes too. "Unmarked for Place" should be understood as covering both possibilities. See Avery and Rice (1988) on the distinction.

[5] I am assuming that syllabic consonants form clusters too, so that words like *wicker* and *ripple* end in clusters. Note also that place words provide many exceptions to these generalizations. These and other exceptions are plausibly bimorphemic. See Clements (1988) for examples.

[6] The Greek vocabulary includes *atmosphere, sigma,* and *enigma,* where $C_2 = m$.

[7] I assume that [+sonorant] are unmarked for [continuant], and also that liquids cannot receive Place features, since arguably they are universally coronal, the default specification. This is certainly the case in the languages discussed here. The *ft* clusters obey the cluster principle but do not conform to the association rule. Note that this association rule is an instantiation of edge-in association (Yip, 1988) and has the property of defaulting to the opposite end of the domain argued for in Hewitt and Prince (1988). Specifically, a single value, Place, first tries one edge (the leftmost) and if blocked from attaching there, associates automatically to the other edge (the rightmost).

[8] It does seem that the impossibility of *tl and *dl onsets suggests the need for Coronal specifications on these segments. However, the existence of medial and final *atlas* and *whittle* suggests that this is not a cluster fact.

[9] It is noticeable that appendixes and suffixes are limited to coronals in many languages, including English. Under the account advocated here, this constraint follows from the fact that both suffixes and appendixes form clusters. If a language obeys the cluster condition, noncoronal suffixes will create ill-formed clusters (absent any kind of fix-up strategy like epenthesis). To put it another way, the cluster condition has as one consequence a prohibition on adding Place features.

[10] The Ojibwa *kk* clusters are phonetically fortis, but Piggott (1980) shows that they are phonologically geminate.

[11] Spanish has a well-known $s \rightarrow h$ rule (see Harris, 1983, for details). The rule is also in Finnish (Keyser and Kiparsky, 1984:30) and Ancient Greek.

[12] Outstanding problems are (1) that the other coronals t and n do not have the same freedom of occurrence, and (2) that there are restrictions on clusters of two coronals, since *ct, cn, cs, st, sn,* and *sc* are not found. These would most naturally be couched as OCP effects on the Coronal (or Place) Node, an impossibility if c and s have no Place features. However, Bloomfield (1946) shows that most of these gaps have a historical origin. For example, the failure of n to start a cluster results from a general rule turning nasals to h before another consonant. Where Ojibwa has *mp, nk,* and *nt,* Menomini has *hp, hk,* and *ht.* Similarly, Proto-Algonquian seems to have lacked all clusters of two coronals except *št,* and the reflex of this in Menomini is left blank by Bloomfield.

[13] Geminates are limited to sonorants and are found medially only. The initial nasal-stop clusters are very rare: four lexical items only, according to Sapir (1965).

[14] The absence of final geminates may be attributable to sonority restrictions. See Selkirk (1988) on this point. Note also that Ponapean, which has almost identical restrictions, does have final geminates.

[15] In her discussion of similar restrictions in Ponapean, Itô (1989:224, 226) states the condition in terms of Place features but does not discuss the change from her 1986 formulation.

[16] In principle, one could tell whether single word-final consonants are codas or extrametrical from the stress facts, but Sapir's (1965:9) description makes no mention of quantity sensitivity, and stress seems to be governed entirely by the morphology, falling mainly on the first syllable of the root. This is confirmed for a different dialect, Carabane Diola, by Wintz (1909:3), who says that "tonic accent falls on a syllable of the root, most commonly on the penult of the word." No mention of syllable weight is given, and the only example does not settle the matter, since the root is monosyllabic, with a long vowel.

[17] There is a small group of clusters of the form Cm that are counterexamples to the claim I am advancing here. These are k, k^h, ^+m onsets, and gm intervocalic clusters. Many are polymorphemic, but *agmos* 'broken cliff' is a tautomorphemic example. At present I have nothing to say about them.

[18] Note that there is also some sort of limitation on single final codas, which are limited to the coronal *s, n,* and *r.* However, word-final coda clusters such as *ps* and *ks* may have Place features, so the modified coda condition cannot be operating here (unlike in Finnish, see Section 5).

[19] Itô (1989:224) revises the Japanese coda condition to make reference to Place features, but without comment. Here I give arguments to support this change.

[20] In order to account for geminate obstruents there must be a [−sonorant] unspecified for Place as well. This "mora obstruent" may be realized as [ʔ] word-finally. See Vance (1987:39ff.) for discussion. Note also that N must be distinguished from /n/, which has an underlying Coronal Node. Trigo (1988) argues that N is actually an unspecified velar; what matters here is that it is unspecified, not whether it is coronal or velar.

[21] Durand (1988) discusses some remarkably similar facts in Southern French. The main difference seems to be that prevocalically, where Japanese has nasalized vowels, Southern French introduces a coronal nasal. Prepausally both languages have a velar nasal. Durand assumes that the coronal nasal is the result of default specification, and

that the velar nasal results from a sort of phonetic realization rule for remaining unspecified nasals. If correct, a similar tack could be taken for Japanese, and this might solve the mystery of why the "default" consonant, although generally coronal, *appears* to be velar in Japanese.

[22] Of the voiced stops, only *d* is found in the native vocabulary, and only intervocalically and after *h*. The stops *b* and *g* are only found in loans.

[23] Alan Prince has drawn to my attention a historical change in which word-final velars disappeared, apparently going through a stage in which they were reduced to a laryngeal. Hakulinen (1961:33) claims that this laryngeal is still realized intervocalically in some dialects (although not in modern standard Finnish), but most authorities mention only the most salient residue of these historical final velars, which is that they cause gemination of the onset of the following word. For example, using a single quotation mark to show the "laryngeal," *tule' pois* surfaces as *tule[pp]ois* 'come away'. True vowel-final roots do not have this effect. This development can be viewed as the loss of Place features as the modified coda condition came into the language. Eventually, the whole segment was lost, except perhaps the feature [+consonantal], which is realized as gemination.

[24] As the editors have pointed out, if this analysis is right, even surface representations may be underspecified in Finnish. See n. 21 here on Southern French.

[25] If *p* and *k* are onsets, this would of course create a new problem: Why are complex onsets allowed in this one environment only? But let us first see if the hypothesis is tenable.

[26] I thank Paul Kiparsky for help with the data in this and the following section.

[27] Both these rules also apply to *t*, even though I expect this to be an acceptable coda at all levels, as in *tk* clusters.

REFERENCES

Archangeli, D. (1984) *Underspecification in Yawelmani Phonology and Morphology,* Doctoral dissertation, MIT, Cambridge, Massachusetts.

Avery, P. and K. Rice (1988) "Underspecification Theory and the Coronal Node," *Toronto Working Papers in Linguistics* 9, 101–121.

Bloomfield, L. (1946) "Algonquian," *Viking Fund Publications in Anthropology* 6, 85–129.

Bloomfield, L. (1962) *The Menomini Language,* Yale University Press, New Haven, Connecticut.

Clements, G. N. (1985) "The Geometry of Phonological Features," *Phonology Yearbook* 2, 225–252.

Clements, G. N. (1988) "The Role of the Sonority Cycle in Core Syllabification," *Working Papers of the Cornell Phonetics Laboratory* 2, 1–68.

Clements, G. N. and S. J. Keyser (1983) *CV Phonology: A Generative Theory of the Syllable,* MIT Press, Cambridge, Massachusetts.

Collinder, B. (1957) *Survey of the Uralic Languages,* Almqvist & Wiksell, Stockholm.

Durand, J. (1988) "Les phénomènes de nasalité en français du Midi: Phonologie de dépendance et sous-spécification," *Recherches Linguistiques de Vincennes: Nouvelles Phonologies* 17, 29–54.

Hakulinen, L. (1961) *The Structure and Development of the Finnish Language,* Indiana University Publications, Uralic and Altaic Studies 3, Bloomington.

Harms, R. (1964) *Finnish Structural Sketch,* Indiana University Publications, Uralic and Altaic Series, Vol. 42, Indiana University, Bloomington.

Harris, J. (1983) *Syllable Structure and Stress in Spanish: A Non-Linear Analysis,* Linguistic Inquiry Monograph 8, MIT Press, Cambridge, Massachusetts.

Hayes, B. (1986) "Inalterability in CV Phonology," *Language* 62, 321–351.

Hewitt, M. and A. Prince (1988) "OCP, Locality and Linking: The N. Karanga verb," *Proceedings of WCCFL* 8, 176–191.

Itô, J. (1986) *Syllable Theory in Prosodic Phonology,* Doctoral dissertation, University of Massachusetts, Amherst.

Itô, J (1989) "A Prosodic Theory of Epenthesis," *Natural Language and Linguistic Theory* 7.2, 217–260.

Keyser, S. J. and P. Kiparsky (1984) "Syllable Structure in Finnish Phonology," in M. Aronoff and R. Oehrle, eds., *Language Sound Structure,* MIT Press, Cambridge, Massachusetts.

Kiparsky, P. (1985) "Some Consequences of Lexical Phonology," *Phonology Yearbook* 2, 83–136.

McCarthy, J. (1989) "Guttural Phonology," ms., University of Massachusetts, Amherst.

Paradis, C. and J.-F. Prunet (1989) "Markedness and Coronal Structure," *Proceedings of NELS 19,* 330–344.

Piggott, G. (1980) *Aspects of Odawa Morphophonemics,* Garland, New York.

Prince, A. (1984) "Phonology with Tiers," in M. Aronoff and R. Oehrle, eds., *Language Sound Structure,* MIT Press, Cambridge, Massachusetts.

Sagey, E. (1986) *The Representation of Features and Relations in Non-linear Phonology,* Doctoral dissertation, MIT, Cambridge, Massachusetts.

Sapir, J. D. (1965) *A Grammar of Diola-Fogny,* West African Language Monographs 3, Cambridge University Press, London.

Selkirk, L. (1988) "A Two-Root Theory of Length," Paper given at NELS 19. To appear in *Univesity of Massachusetts Occasional Papers* (*UMOP*) 14, E. Dunlap and J. Padgett eds.

Steriade, D. (1982) *Greek Prosodies and the Nature of Syllabification,* Doctoral dissertation, MIT, Cambridge, Massachusetts

Steriade, D. (1987) "Redundant Values," *Proceedings of CLS* 23, 339–362.

Trigo, R. L. (1988) *On the Phonological Derivation and Behavior of Nasal Glides,* Doctoral dissertation, MIT, Cambridge, Massachusetts.

Vance, T. (1987) *An Introduction to Japanese Phonology,* SUNY Press, Albany, New York.

Wintz, E. (1909) *Dictionnaire Français-Dyola et Dyola-Français,* Republished 1968, Gregg Press Ltd., Farnborough, England.

Yip, M. (1988) "Template Morphology and the Direction of Association," *Natural Language and Linguistic Theory,* 6.4, 551–578.

Yip, M. (1989) "Feature Geometry and Co-occurrence Restrictions," *Phonology* 6.2, 349–374.

PALATALIZATION AND CORONALITY

ADITI LAHIRI
VINCENT EVERS

Max Planck Institute for Psycholinguistics
6525 XD Nijmegen, The Netherlands

1. INTRODUCTION

The phenomenon of palatalization has received a great deal of attention in the literature, but there is still considerable uncertainty about its proper characterization. Part of the problem is that the assimilatory alternations that fall under this cover term do not constitute a single process, although they turn out to be related in various ways. The proposal formulated in this article is based on observations concerning the special status of the coronal consonants in palatalization processes. The phonological processes that are usually described as palatalizations often have as their output coronal consonants, in particular, palato-alveolars. What is more controversial is the characterization of the segments that act as a trigger—usually, the front vowels and the palatal glide [j].

In this article, we demonstrate that if we have the correct representation of Coronal, then the processes themselves can be characterized straightforwardly. First, we show that the interaction of certain consonants and vowels in palatalization processes argues for a unitary set of features. Second, we propose a particular feature geometry representation that groups coronal consonants, front vowels, and the palatal glide under a single articulator node Coronal. This representation also includes the separation of the traditional height features, which enables us to characterize natural classes like [high] and [low], while maintaining the classification of consonants and vowels by a single set of Place features. Third, we ar-

Phonetics and Phonology, Volume 2
The Special Status of Coronals

gue that our proposal can naturally account for different types of palatalizations as well as processes that independently require only the tongue height features.

In Section 2, we begin by identifying three common palatalization processes occurring in natural languages, and then on the basis of this overview we move on to evaluate recent feature geometry proposals. In Section 3, we develop an alternative proposal that resolves certain problems, particularly in characterizing palatalization. And in Section 4, we discuss the three palatalization phenomena in light of the proposed representation. We show that two types of palatalizations result in a primary place change, while the third involves the addition of a secondary articulation to all primary articulations. In the last type of change, the coronal consonants may pattern differently from other consonants and can undergo additional changes as well; they can become strident or even optionally undergo a place change.

2. PALATALIZATION AND THE REPRESENTATION OF CORONAL

The term palatalization suggests the involvement of the palatal place of articulation, where the forward half of the tongue is assumed to be the active articulator. The palatalizing contexts are generally believed to consist of the front vowels and the palatal glide [j], and occasionally the high back vowels (see Bhat, 1978:60–61). The process of palatalization, however, is not a unitary process. Bhat (1978) provides an exhaustive survey of the various processes that at one time or another have come under the umbrella of the term palatalization. The most frequently recurring palatalization processes are summarized below.

(1) Recurring Palatalization Processes
     a. The fronting of velars: Velar consonants are frequently fronted when followed by front vowels, especially [i], or [j]. The prototypical shift involves velar consonants becoming palato-alveolars, with a concomitant change of stops to affricates. In Slavic, for instance, [k, g, x] become [tʃ, dʒ, ʃ] when followed by front vowels and [j] (see Chomsky and Halle, 1968:421–422).
     b. Change of place within the coronal consonants: Alveolar and dental consonants become palato-alveolar or prepalatal in the context of front vowels and [j]. Again, the stops usually become affricates, while the other consonants retain their manner of articulation. In Polish, for instance, the coronal consonants [t, d, s, z, r, n, l] become prepalatal consonants before front vowels and glides (cf. Rubach, 1984:60). English alveolars also frequently become palato-alveolars when followed by the palatal glide [j].

c. Addition of secondary palatal articulation: Secondary palatal articulations can be added to any consonant. This process is seen to involve
raising the central part of the tongue while keeping the main articulator
intact (cf. Bhat, 1978:67). All places of articulation are thus subject to
this alteration. This secondary articulation is reported to occur in the
context of the high front vowel [i] or [j] (Bhat, 1978:67), often with a
prominent front off-glide articulation (cf. Rubach, 1984:166–167). For
dental or alveolar consonants, all high vowels can cause such secondary
articulation, often leading to strident sounds such as [s] and [ʃ], that is,
with or without concomitant change of place.

On the basis of the types of processes listed in (1), palatalization is widely
accepted as being assimilatory in nature (cf. Clements, 1976). If the changes
under (1a–b) are assimilatory, then there must be something in common between
the front vowels and the palatal glide [j], which are the triggers, and the palato-
alveolar consonants, which are the output of these processes. What is disputed is
the nature of this common property that characterizes the accepted coronal segments like palato-alveolars with the palatal consonants including the palatal glide
[j], and the front vowels.

The notion that front vowels, palatals (including [j]), and coronal consonants
share a common property is, of course, not a novel idea. Rather, this observation
and proposals to incorporate front vowels and glides with consonants articulated
with the tip and blade of the tongue go back to Panini. In more recent times,
Jakobson, Fant, and Halle (1963), characterizing features with both articulatory
and acoustic definitions, group these segments under the feature [−grave], which
is defined as a concentration of energy in the higher frequencies. Recall that
Chomsky and Halle (1968:304), hereafter referred to as *SPE*, made a shift from
this feature grouping to one that separates all vowels and secondary articulations
under the tongue-body features [high], [back], and [low], where the neutral position was assumed to be "raised and fronted, approximating the configuration
found in the vowel [e] in English *bed*." All vowels were by definition [−coronal]
and [−anterior]. The primary reason for this move was to be able to use tongue-
body features to characterize secondary articulations like palatalization.

Subsequently, a number of arguments were presented supporting the natural
grouping of [+coronal] consonants, front vowels, and palatal consonants including [j] based on phonological processes that treated these as a natural
class (cf. Hyman, 1973; Vago, 1976; Clements, 1976; Odden, 1978; Lahiri and
Blumstein, 1984). The feature [+coronal] was then modified to group together
dental, alveolar, and palato-alveolar consonants with palatal consonants and
front vowels. In all essential aspects [+coronal] was then identical to Jakobson
et al.'s feature [−grave].

In feature geometry accounts, however, this grouping has again become a matter of some dispute. In this approach (developed in Clements, 1985, and elaborated extensively in Sagey, 1986), a set of primary articulator features is recognized for consonants: Labial, Coronal, and Dorsal. Each of these Articulator Nodes is represented on a separate tier, allowing sequences of articulation to be expressed easily. This account also succeeds in coherently representing multiply articulated but sequentially unordered segments as single units. Other features, which may provide further refinement of these primary articulations, can be dependent on them. Thus, [anterior] and [distributed], which convey finer distinctions of the Coronal articulator, are dependent on this node. Vowel features, in this approach, are made dependents of the primary articulator features: [round] is a dependent of the Labial Node, and [high], [back], and [low] are dependents of the Dorsal Node. Such relations entail that segments distinctively characterized by a dependent feature must be specified by the node on which it is dependent. Since our concern here is mainly with the Coronal and Dorsal Nodes (which include the consonants and vowels involved in palatalization), we initially focus our attention on these articulators and their dependents. A partial sketch of the type of representation we have been discussing is given below:

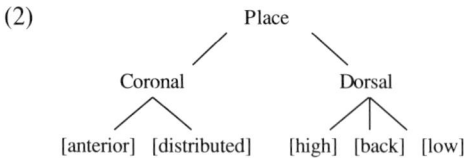

(2)   Place

              Coronal   Dorsal

       [anterior] [distributed]   [high] [back] [low]

The consonant and vowel types that fall under each node are (1) Coronal: dental, alveolar, and palato-alveolar consonants; and (2) Dorsal: palatal and velar consonants and all vowels.

This representation essentially falls back on the SPE classifications of consonants and vowels, where all vowels were by definition noncoronal, and it therefore succumbs to the same problems as before. First, the velar consonants (which must also be characterized by Dorsal) and the vowels, which are characterized by the dependent features of the Dorsal Node, do not function as a natural class in any phonological process. Second, the interaction of consonants characterized by Coronal and front vowels cannot be expressed in terms of this representation. The front vowels are [−back], and the coronal consonants are "blind" to this feature since [back] is by definition dominated by the Dorsal Node alone. A familiar assimilation process where alveolars or dentals become palato-alveolars before front vowels and [j] (see [1b]) can hardly be expressed as spreading if the segments do not share any feature. Moreover, the process in which velars front to palato-alveolars in the same context also appears to be mysterious and arbitrary if it is perceived as [−back] spreading, since the palato-alveolars are under the

Coronal Node and thus are not [−back]. The features distinguishing the pertinent segments are shown in (3).

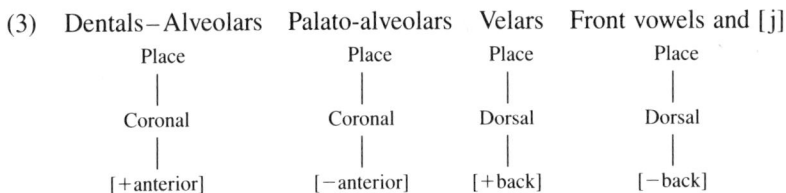

(3)   Dentals−Alveolars   Palato-alveolars   Velars   Front vowels and [j]

Place	Place	Place	Place
Coronal	Coronal	Dorsal	Dorsal
[+anterior]	[−anterior]	[+back]	[−back]

Since the dependent features imply involvement of their primary articulators, spreading of [−back] would entail spreading of the Dorsal Node to the dentals for the (1a) type of assimilation but would not result in a palato-alveolar consonant. And spreading of [−back] to a velar consonant does not change its primary articulator to a Coronal.

Indeed, other than the dependency expressed by Labial and [round], no other vowel and consonant interactions can be expressed. In response to this, Clements (1989) has proposed a unitary set of primary articulator features for consonants and vowels, linked, however, to distinct nodes labeled Consonant Place (C-Place) and Vocoid Place (V-Place). In addition, by virtue of the fact that the articulator features are duplicated on separate nodes, the traditional vowel features [back], [round], and [ATR] (advanced tongue root) turn out to be redundant. The articulator features Labial and Coronal, for instance, can be extended to characterize [round] and [back], respectively. The V-Place has two additional stricture features: [open] (the opposite of [high]) and [low].[1] A partial sketch of the structure proposed in Clements (1989) is given below:

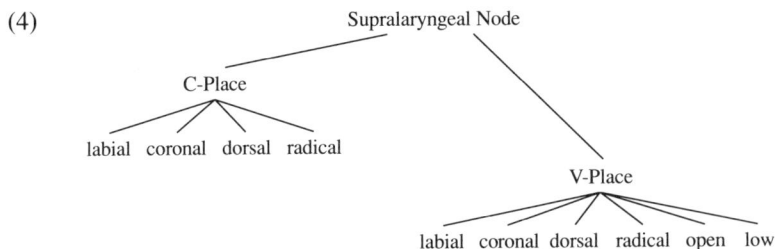

(4)   Supralaryngeal Node

        C-Place

labial   coronal   dorsal   radical
                                                V-Place

                                    labial   coronal   dorsal   radical   open   low

Clements' proposal of a unified set of features for consonants and vowels has important consequences for a theory that treats palatalization as assimilation, since palatalization processes crucially involve interaction between certain vowels and consonants. However, his proposal appears to have some disadvantages. Although Clements presents one set of articulator features that can be used in classifying both consonants and vowels, he subsequently reintroduces the distinction between the two classes of sounds by reduplicating this set and grouping them twice under distinct Place Nodes. Furthermore, his geometry incorporates the vowel–consonant distinction at least once more, namely, in the sonority features [open] and [low], which are only present under the V-Place Node and characterize only vowels. If this theory is embedded in a more complete feature geometry that also takes into account the major class features [sonorant] and [consonantal], it appears that instead of minimizing the distance between consonants and vowels, we have reinforced the distinction by representing it in three different ways. Even if one assumes that a fundamental distinction between the two major classes of sounds is necessary, this solution does not seem to be efficient and economical.

Another objection is more directly related to palatalization. Although consonants and vowels are characterized partly by the same features, contact between them is still rather indirect in this framework. This becomes particularly clear in the treatment of processes such as palatalization. Clements (1989: 32–33) proposes to account for processes such as palatalization and labialization in fundamentally the same way. First, the consonant acquires a secondary articulation by spreading the appropriate articulator feature from the V-Place tier of the following sound (usually a vowel or a glide) to that of the consonant. Subsequently, this secondary articulation becomes the primary articulation of the consonant after application of tier promotion (which moves a V-Place feature to its corresponding C-Place) and complex segment simplification (which deletes one of the C-Place articulator features). A historical process of [ku > kw > k^w] to [k͡p] or even [p] can be successfully accounted for by these processes. The change from [k^w] to [k͡p] is by tier promotion, while the change to [p] is due to complex segment simplification.

In Clements's proposal, palatalization also goes through similar stages: [k] becomes [k^j] by the addition of a V-Place [coronal] feature and then changes to [tʃ] by a second stage of tier promotion, together with complex segment simplification (and concomitant affrication). Note that in this view the processes described under (1a) and (1c) are not independent. Following Clements (1989), the complete derivation of [k] to [tʃ] via [k^j] in the context of [j] would be as in (5):

(5)

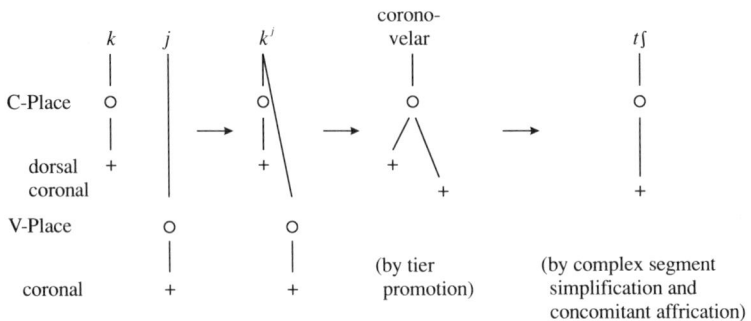

While providing a good account of the advent of a secondary articulation, this account fails to give a convincing explanation of the second part of the assimilation processes it is intended to capture. In particular, it is not clear what triggers tier promotion. If it implies simplification, is there any reason to believe a multiply articulated [k͡p] (derived by tier promotion) is any simpler than [kʷ] in the labialization process? Second, given the option of tier promotion, diachronically one might expect a [kʲ] to lead to a multiply articulated coronovelar segment as an intermediate stage during the palatalization process, just as a labialized [kʷ] may lead to a complex segment [k͡p]. This, to our knowledge, never happens.[2] Third, in this view, palatalization processes like (1a) and (1b) must necessarily go through a secondary articulation stage like (1c). But this does not seem to be the case in historical developments. Secondary palatalizations may lead to primary place changes, but there is no reason to believe (as this view suggests) that there must be this intermediate stage, or that this stage would be the most natural initial step in a diachronic process. Languages can simultaneously have both types of palatalizations (cf. Rubach, 1984:25, on Polish). In agreement with this view, Bhat (1978:68) explicitly states that it would be a mistake to consider the presence of a secondary palatal articulation as a necessary stage in every palatalization process.

In sum, then, to account for a synchronic assimilation from [k] to [tʃ] under this view, the processes of tier promotion and complex segment simplification must apply along with the spreading of the assimilation feature. This is because assimilatory features spreading from the V-Node of a vowel must link to the V-Node of the consonant before they can be promoted to a C-Place position. And as we mentioned before, the process of tier promotion is not assimilatory in character, and a velar palatalization process does not appear to be expressed as a unitary assimilatory process. We appear to be missing a generalization. In the following section, we propose an alternative solution that integrates the essential points of Clements (1989) without these problems.

3. AN ALTERNATIVE SOLUTION

Recall that the crucial reason behind Clements's proposal for separating the consonant and vocalic feature tiers was to be able to express the link between subsets of consonants and vowels that behave as a natural class, while at the same time maintaining the advantages of having the primary articulations defined by individual articulators. Further, since the secondary place features are always on the V-Node, it is possible to easily distinguish between multiply articulated complex segments and segments with secondary articulation. In Clements's (1989) terms, the representations of [k͡p] and [kʷ] are as follows:

(6) $\widehat{kp}$ k^w
    C-Place
        dorsal   +   +
        labial   +   −
    V-Place
        labial   +

The notion that vowels and consonants ought to be expressed by a unitary set of features is well taken. However, as we mentioned before, to enumerate the features in two different tiers seems to defeat the main purpose. This information is quite redundant. Clements's proposal has the same underlying tenet as the *SPE* theory of keeping the vowel features separate, except that now they have the same names as the consonant place features. An important reason for allowing two sets of Articulator Nodes is that if front and back vowels are grouped under separate nodes (along with the corresponding consonants), while the tongue-body features like [high] and [low] remain dependent on the Dorsal Node, then it is impossible to refer to natural classes of vowels by their height features alone in a tree, as proposed by Sagey (1986:14). Consider, for instance, the following schematic grouping of vowels and consonants.

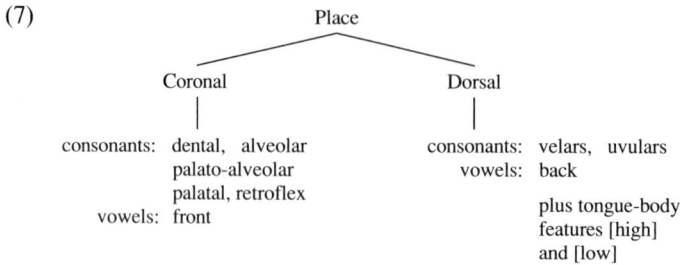

(7)   Place
                         _____
                        | |
                     Coronal   Dorsal
                        | |

     consonants: dental, alveolar   consonants: velars, uvulars
                 palato-alveolar   vowels: back
                 palatal, retroflex
        vowels: front   plus tongue-body
                                                    features [high]
                                                    and [low]

Clearly, if front and back vowels are specified under different Articulator Nodes, while the height features come under the Dorsal Node, then there is no way of expressing natural classes like the class of high vowels, which include both front and back vowels.

Thus, from all accounts, it seems that a viable feature geometry representation must have at least the following three attributes: (1) ability to express multiple articulations naturally, (2) ability to characterize vowels and consonants by a single set of features in order to capture natural classes without duplication, and (3) ability to express assimilatory (spreading) processes like palatalization, which lead to secondary articulation as well as to major place changes in a direct way. It appears to us that the basic insights of Sagey (1986), along with the recent conception of Clements (1989), can be combined in a hierarchical representation that has a unitary set of place features for consonants and vowels, but also a separate node where the so-called tongue-body features are defined. A tentative model of this conception is illustrated in (8).

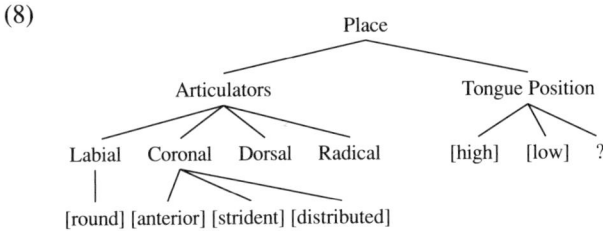

(8)

```
                              Place
                  _____/    _____
          Articulators                   Tongue Position
        ___/  /\  \___                      /  |  \
       /     /  \     \                     /   |   \
   Labial Coronal Dorsal Radical       [high] [low]  ?
     |      /\___
     |     /     \___
 [round] [anterior] [strident] [distributed]
```

We later show that this representation not only presents a satisfactory solution to the problem of relating vowel and consonant places of articulation but also accounts for different assimilation processes in a principled way. Under this conception, the Place Node dominates two nodes: the Articulator Node, which includes the major articulators, and the Tongue Position Node, which dominates the traditional tongue height features [high] and [low]. This node has been left incomplete, since further research is necessary to determine whether other features are necessary for additional height classifications. Note that [high] and [low] are features with binary values and therefore are different from the articulators that are privative (following Sagey, 1986:273, but unlike Clements, 1989). The feature [back] is dispensed with since Coronal includes all [−back] segments and Dorsal characterizes the [+back] segments. In this respect, we agree with Clements (1989:16). Based on evidence in various publications, we also assume that [round] is dependent on Labial and that [anterior] and [distributed] are dependent on Coronal (Sagey, 1986:277–278; McCarthy, 1988: 103–104). We have also included [strident] as a dependent of Coronal, under the view that this feature only distinguishes coronal consonants. The dependents mentioned here are not exhaustive; again, other features may be necessary for further segment subgroupings. Also, the Radical Node is tentative given that our understanding of the guttural consonants and their distribution and patterning is not yet clear. Our concern here is primarily with the first three class nodes.

Before we move on to discuss how such a representation accounts for different types of palatalization, we must address two issues relating to the separation of the Articulator Nodes from the tongue position. First, is there independent phonological evidence for considering the Tongue Position Node to be a separate class node? And second, how should this node be defined? With respect to the first question, a representation that separates the major articulators from the

Tongue Position Node predicts that the latter class node should be able to undergo normal nonlinear operations like spreading. Spreading of this node implies spreading not just the features [high] and [low] individually but also the node as a whole, and therefore any or all of the features dominated by it. This is analogous to the Place Node spreading as a whole in homorganic place assimilations. Evidence for this sort of spreading comes from Hyman (1988), who describes a harmony process in Esimbi that shows that height features spread as a whole.

In Hyman's analysis, the distribution of vowels in stems and prefixes in the Esimbi language is established by a synchronic transfer of underlying vowel features from the stem onto the prefix. What is of importance here is that the vowel features that spread from the stem to the prefix are just the height features, whatever their specifications may be. Note that the vowels of stems always become [+high] on the surface after having affected the prefix, as the following data on Esimbi vowel harmony reveal (Hyman, 1988:256–259). The prefix /U-/ is a vowel archiphoneme whose only underlying feature specification is [+round], and the prefix /I-/ is a vowel archiphoneme whose only underlying feature specification (in Hyman's framework) is [−back].

(9)   /U-/+/bini/   → [ubini]   'dance'
      /U-/+/kebe/   → [okibi]   'pour'
      /U-/+/rɛnɛ/   → [ɔrini]   'be poor'
      /U-/+/zomo/   → [ozumu]   'dry up'
      /U-/+/gɔnɔ/   → [ɔgunu]   'disease'

      /I-/+/jimi/   → [ijimi]   'back'
      /I-/+/gbe/   → [egbi]   'bushfowl'
      /I-/+/yɛsɛ/   → [ɛyisi]   'hole'
      /I-/+/nono/   → [enunu]   'bird'
      /I-/+/fɔmɔ/   → [ɛfumu]   'hippo'

The underlying [ɛ] in the stem /rɛnɛ/ changes the /U/ prefix to [ɔ], while the same stem vowel of /yɛsɛ/ changes the /I/ prefix to [ɛ]. Note that the prefix /I/ is changed to [ɛ] by both [ɛ] and [ɔ] in the stems /yɛsɛ/ and /fɔmɔ/. Thus, the prefix acquires only the height features of the stem, maintaining its own specifications for the round and back features. This illustrates that vowel height features can behave as a unit in phonological processes. The height features of the stem vowel, whatever they may be, are spread to the prefix. In our conception, [high] and [low] are grouped together under the Tongue Position Node separate from the Articulator Nodes, and the spreading of this class node easily accounts for the vowel alternation in the prefix. In fact, in the conclusion of his article, Hyman speculates about including height features under a separate, independent node.

The second issue is the definition of the class nodes and the dependent features, especially [high] and [low]. The primary articulators have the usual descriptions as in articulator theory (cf. McCarthy, 1988:99). Segments made by the lips are characterized as Labial; Coronal refers to the tip and blade of the tongue up to the dorsum; and Dorsal refers to the tongue body. The feature [round] characterizes labials produced with rounded or unrounded lips. Plus and minus [anterior] distinguish coronal sounds made before or after the palato-alveolar region. The feature [distributed] continues to have the somewhat unsatisfactory definition found in *SPE*, namely, constriction formed by the tongue extending for either a considerable amount or a short distance. And [strident] has an acoustic definition, namely, coronal sounds that have a considerable amount of high frequency noise (cf. Stevens, Keyser, and Kawasaki, 1986:439).

The Tongue Position Node, as we mentioned earlier, dominates the traditional tongue height features. Our definitions of these features are somewhat different from the traditional articulatory descriptions. As is well accepted, "raised tongue body" and "lowered tongue body" are rather unsatisfactory descriptions even within the same class of front and back vowels. For instance, the vowels referred to as the "high" vowels do not have the same tongue height (cf. Ladefoged, 1982:13). Moreover, since the tongue shapes differ rather dramatically, there is considerable difference between the parts of the tongue that are raised. In addition, there is often concomitant lowering of the jaw with the lowering of tongue position, a fact that is disregarded in this definition. It seems reasonable, then, to define tongue position not only with an articulatory description of "raising the tongue body" but also with respect to the acoustic formant structure, a description that is better understood. Under this conception, height is determined by the first formant frequency, [+high] being inversely correlated with F1. That is, the lower the first formant, the higher the vowel. Note that our representation permits the height features to distinguish both vowels and consonants.

In the following section, we develop the present proposal, elaborating on the combinativeness of the articulator features and the characterization of different types of palatalization, including secondary palatalized articulation.

4. PALATALIZATION AND SECONDARY ARTICULATION

We have drawn a major distinction between the primary articulators and the position of the tongue. This allows us to easily express natural classes of vowels and consonants. As we mentioned before, the front vowels are characterized by Coronal and the back vowels by Dorsal. The height distinctions are captured by the Tongue Position features. Rounded vowels are by definition multiply articulated since [round] is a dependent feature of Labial, and therefore distinctively [round] segments must also be Labial. The features for high front vowels, unrounded and rounded, and high back vowels, unrounded and rounded, would be as follows (Articulator = A, Tongue Position = TP)

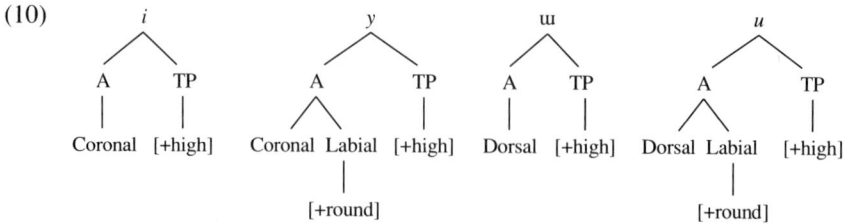

(10)

i	y	ɯ	u
A TP	A TP	A TP	A TP
Coronal [+high]	Coronal Labial [+high]	Dorsal [+high]	Dorsal Labial [+high]
	[+round]		[+round]

The representation of [i] (and simultaneously the front glide [j]), then, is Coronal and [+high], a combination of features that closely matches the description of palatal consonants given by Keating (1988:89). Based on X-ray data, Keating persuasively argues that for the articulation of prototypical palatal segments like [j], the tongue blade is used along with a simultaneous raising of the tongue body. To capture this fact in a representation such as Sagey's, Keating argues that palatals are complex, being both Coronal and [high] (and therefore Dorsal, since [high] is a dependent of Dorsal from this view). In our representation, the property of being Coronal and [high] is easily captured by having the tongue height features represented separately.

The palatalization processes summarized under (1) involve the front vowels, the palatal glide, and the dental–alveolar, palato-alveolar, and velar places of articulation. These sounds have the following featural representations:

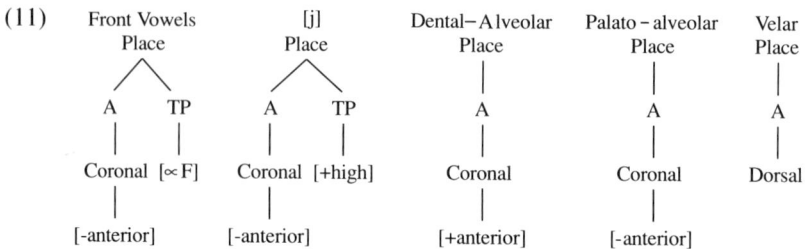

(11)

Front Vowels Place	[j] Place	Dental–Alveolar Place	Palato – alveolar Place	Velar Place
A TP	A TP	A	A	A
Coronal [∝ F]	Coronal [+high]	Coronal	Coronal	Dorsal
[-anterior]	[-anterior]	[+anterior]	[-anterior]	

The [αF] is a mnemonic for the different values of the features [high] and [low] for the various front vowels. Given this representation, the palatalization processes we have summarized in (1) are easily expressed as in (12).

(12)   a. Spreading the Coronal Node (along with the [−anterior] feature) with the concomitant deletion of the Dorsal Node for the velar fronting
   b. Spreading of [−anterior] within the Coronal class node for dental–alveolar consonants becoming palato-alveolar
   c. Spreading of [+high] to all places of articulation for the secondary palatal articulation

The first type of palatalization, where velar consonants are fronted, is best understood as a spreading of [coronal], along with its dependent features. The feature [high] is irrelevant since it is on a different node, one that does not spread. The change from [k] to [tʃ] in the context of [j] is given in (13). Due to space restrictions only the crucial features are represented.

(13)

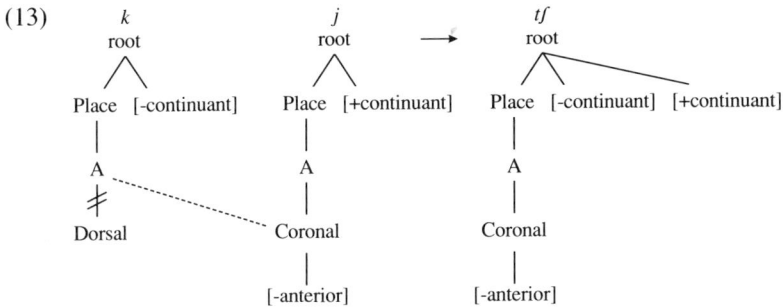

The change from stop to affricate is sometimes seen as the spreading of [+continuant] (cf. Jacobs, 1989:113–159). However, in the palatal/palato-alveolar region, only one stop and one affricate can contrast phonologically, and this affricate is usually a [−anterior] palato-alveolar affricate (Lahiri and Blumstein, 1984:143). The affrication (with stridency) in this region is completely predictable. If the palato-alveolar place of articulation is unmarked with respect to the palatal one, as seems to be generally the case, then the surface output of the assimilation should not be thought of as the result of spreading of [+continuant] but rather as the result of a redundancy rule in the language.

The second type of palatalization, where dental–alveolar consonants become palato-alveolars, is viewed as a spreading of [−anterior] within the Coronal Node. The trigger is usually a front vowel or [j] (cf. Bhat, 1978:60), both Coronal segments in our description. Again, like the previous example of velar fronting, there is a shift in the place of articulation, but this time the primary articulator remains the same. The articulation actually is a "backing," since the palato-alveolar place is further back from the dental–alveolar region. This is why an assimilation in terms of [anterior] is so much more intuitive than a spreading of [−back] in *SPE* and Sagey's featural groupings. Recall that in Sagey (1986:108–109) the assimilation from [t] to [tʃ] is accounted for by a spreading of [−back], which is linked only to the Dorsal Node. What results then is a multiply linked Coronal and Dorsal with [−back] representation. To obtain [tʃ], there is a process of "reanalysis," which Sagey claims is "a common process whereby adding the feature [−back] to a coronal results in the coronal becoming [−anterior]" (p. 109). From our viewpoint, the assimilation is easily explained since the target and the trigger are both Coronal, the only change being the spreading of [−anterior], a dependent feature of this Articulator Node.

This brings us to the third type of palatalization, the acquisition of a secondary articulation. In our proposal, multiply articulated complex segments have representations similar to those proposed by Sagey (1986) and others: a combination of two articulators. What differs crucially is the secondary palatal articulation. Like Sagey, labialization is viewed as the spreading of rounding, but palatalization is seen as raising, rather than the spreading of [−back]. This is quite similar to the proposals made in *SPE* and the traditional view that secondary palatalization results in raised articulation. A labialized segment like [kʷ], in this proposal, is not a combination of the articulator of [k] and the articulator of [u], but rather [k] plus rounding, and since [round] is dependent on Labial, a complex articulation occurs. For labialization, what spreads is neither the entire Place Node nor the entire Articulator Node, but simply [+round] and, simultaneously, Labial. The feature characterizations of the segments [kʷ], [k͡p], and [pʷ] are given in (14)

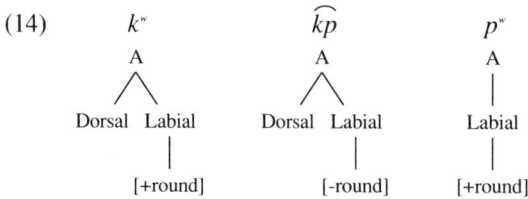

(14)   *kʷ*   *k͡p*   *pʷ*

              A   A   A
             /\   /\ |
     Dorsal Labial   Dorsal Labial   Labial
              | | |
         [+round]   [-round]   [+round]

Both [kʷ] and [k͡p] end up being complex segments in that they are multiply articulated since spreading of [round] automatically spreads Labial. In this respect, labialization crucially differs from palatalization as secondary articulation which, in our view, is the spreading of [+high], a feature not dependent on any primary articulator. The sounds [kʲ] and a coronovelar segment would have very different representations:

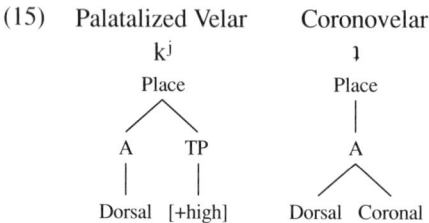

(15)   Palatalized Velar   Coronovelar
                 kʲ   ]

              Place   Place
             /‾‾‾\ |
          A   TP   A
          | | /‾‾\
      Dorsal [+high]   Dorsal Coronal

This scheme makes two predictions regarding the possible development of these articulations. For labialized consonants like [kʷ], it has been observed that they can become at a later stage [k͡p] (*Gã*, cited in Clements, 1989: 32–33). Since the Labial articulator is part of the representation of [kʷ], such a change is possible and natural, where the feature [+round] is deleted. However, secondary palatalized segments like [kʲ] never become coronovelar complex segments, which should have been possible if the representation involved the Coronal articulator, as suggested by Clements (1989).

There is also some phonetic support for our representation. Based on evidence from X-ray data, Keating (1988:81–89) argues that a fronted velar, that is, a velar with secondary palatal articulation, is primarily a Dorsal with the tongue somewhat further fronted than a normal velar, but definitely not a Coronal. A Clements (1989) or Sagey (1986) type of representation with multiple linking of Dorsal and Coronal Nodes for secondary articulation of velars would then incorrectly suggest a Coronal type of articulation. Under our view, [+high] spreading leads to secondary palatal articulation for *all* places of articulation. Thus, "fronted velars" and "raised labials and dentals," which basically all indicate "palatalized," raised, or sharp consonants, now have a uniform representation:

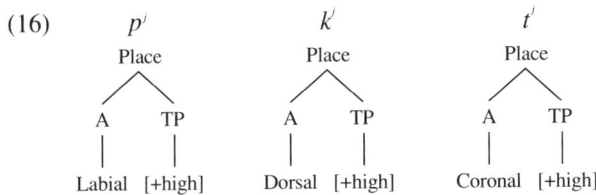

(16) p^j k^j t^j

	Place			Place			Place	
A		TP	A		TP	A		TP
Labial		[+high]	Dorsal		[+high]	Coronal		[+high]

The claim that all secondary palatalized articulations are represented as the major articulators plus [+high] has two consequences that need to be addressed. First, under the assumption that the palatalized consonants are [+high], they ought to behave as a natural class of [+high] consonants. Second, if it is [+high] that spreads, then theoretically this spreading could be triggered by other [+high] vowels and not just by Coronal high vowels and glides. For the first point, there is evidence supporting the view that palatalized consonants are [+high]. In Russian, all unaccented, nonhigh vowels are raised after palatalized consonants (except before certain affixes, Halle, 1971:70), indicating that there is [+high] spreading in this context. The initial vowel in *Pjótr* 'Peter' is raised when the accent shifts to the last syllable in the genitive form *Pjitrá*. Notice that a vowel following a nonpalatalized consonant does not raise: *tsép* 'flail' (nominative) versus *tsepá* (genitive).[3] The raising then spreads from the palatalized consonants, which by our definition are [+high]. A similar process is also attested in Gaelic (Norval Smith, personal communication). In certain paradigmatic alternations, the vowels in the genitive forms are raised when followed by a palatalized consonant: [k'ɔ:l] 'music' (nominative) versus [k'u:l'] (genitive) (Borgstrøm, 1940: 19). As for [+high] spreading from other vowels, this is not unattested, especially with the dental consonants that tend to be palatalized by high back vowels as well. Often, however, the palatalized dentals become strident, as discussed in the next section. An example of this is mentioned by Clements (1976:100). In standard Japanese, dental [t] becomes affricated before high vowels [i, ɯ];

before [i] there is a concomitant change of place to a palato-alveolar place of articulation.

However, there are some other problems we need to address. Although in the production of palatalized consonants "raising a part of the tongue" is the accepted description (Jakobson *et al.*, 1963:31–32; Bhat, 1978:67; Keating, 1988:83), the acoustic reflex is often reported to be a rise in the second formant (Jakobson *et al.*, 1963:31), a property of front or coronal segments. How can we account for this? Second, nonhigh front vowels are also reported to have secondary palatalizing effects (Sagey, 1986:209–218, 227–240). If, as we argue, secondary palatalization is spreading of [+high], this is difficult to explain. We believe that these are related problems, dealing particularly with the phonetics of this articulation, and we address this in the next section.

4.1. Secondary Palatalization, Phonetic Off-glides, and Coronality

We know from the X-ray data of palatalized velars that they are not coronal consonants (Keating, 1988:81–89). However, as we noted above, the acoustic realization of palatalized consonants compared to nonpalatalized ones is an increase in the second formant—what one expects of a high front vowel. We argue that this is a phonetic property of palatalized consonants, where, on the surface, these consonants acquire a [j]-like off-glide, even when they are phonologically single units (as opposed to stop + glide sequences). This appears to be true in languages like Polish (Rubach, 1984:166–167), Zoque (Sagey, 1986:106–112), and Gaelic (Borgstrøm, 1940:18). All phonologically palatalized (and therefore [+high]) consonants would then be articulated with a palatal off-glide. The choice of the coronal off-glide in the phonetic implementation rule (rather than any other place of articulation) can be related to the fact that the default place specification of a high glide is Coronal, and not, for instance, the labiodorsal glide [w]. When languages have only one glide, it is almost always Coronal (cf. Maddieson, 1984:92), and therefore the [+high] feature in the consonants would seek out the default glide articulation.

Sometimes it is difficult to ascertain whether the [j] off-glide is added as a phonetic rule stemming from the [+high] feature of the consonant, or if the vowel itself acquires an on-glide. In English, for instance, there is fluctuation in words like *absolute* and *allusion:* the [l], if palatalized, is followed by a [j] and then the [u]. It is difficult to establish whether the high vowel introduces the raising of the consonant, or whether the [u] is pronounced with an on-glide that produces the raising.

The second problem relates to the possibility of a nonhigh front vowel triggering secondary palatalization in the form of raising. In languages like Nupe and Kinyarwanda (Sagey, 1986:209–218, 227–240), secondary palatalization is triggered by [i] as well as [e]. As in other languages, the palatalized consonants are phonetically produced with an off-glide. In these special cases where the secondary palatalization is produced by nonhigh [e], this glide could also be present phonologically as an on-glide of the vowel. That is, the [e] would be phonologically [je]. If this is correct, then our analysis predicts that in a diachronic process, the [j] triggering the palatalization may get absorbed by the vowel, the consonant remaining a single complex unit of the major articulator plus the Tongue Position. This is often reflected in the orthography of the language, where the palatalization mark of the consonant is located on the following vowel (as in Russian). In the same vein, if palatalized consonants have a "fronting" effect (over and above the raising effect on vowels that we discussed earlier), then the assumption would be that the glide triggering the palatalization does not get absorbed in the process and theoretically could play a role in fronting neighboring vowels.

In sum, we have claimed that the processes that cause major place change rather than the addition of secondary articulation are separate. The processes summarized under (1a–b) qualify as primary place changes, the context being any front vowel or glide. The addition of a secondary articulation does not necessarily lead to a change in place. However, in many languages we find that seemingly unitary palatalization processes that can add a secondary articulation to a labial and a velar consonant can optionally have a somewhat different effect on the dental consonants. Palatalized dentals often undergo a change of place and become palato-alveolars. Under our conception, this can happen only with the high front vowel [i] or the glide [j] as the trigger, not any front vowel, that is, segments that are both [−anterior] (dominated by Coronal) and [+high]. The general process of assimilation would be the spreading of [+high]; optionally, [−anterior] would seek out an existing Coronal Node of a dental consonant and bring about a change in place as well. Here we observe the special behavior of the coronal consonants as compared to the velars and the labials, in that the former can optionally undergo a place change as well.

Another respect in which palatalized coronals, in particular the stops, can differ is that they often become strident fricatives, or at least have a strident release. Coronal consonants have relatively more energy in the higher frequencies than in the lower frequencies (Lahiri, Gewirth, and Blumstein, 1984:402). If, in addition, there is an off-glide [j] release for the [+high] palatalized coronal consonants, then there will be a greater increase in the higher frequencies, causing a concentration of energy in the high frequency range—a characteristic of strident segments. Recall, that in processes described under (1a–b) where dentals and velars can become palato-alveolars, there is a simultaneous addition of stridency, for example, [x] to [ʃ]. This change can occur in the context of any front vowel, not necessarily [+high]. As we argued earlier, this addition of [+strident] comes as a free ride, given that in the palato-alveolar region the unmarked articulation of all obstruents is with stridency (cf. Lahiri and Blumstein, 1984:142). This is somewhat different from the palatalized dentals having a strident release, or dental stops becoming strident fricatives. We have argued that [+high] consonants always have a palatal off-glide release, which for a dental causes a greater concentration of high frequency energy leading to stridency.

This pattern of alternations, where labials and velars undergo secondary palatalization, while the coronal dentals–alveolars optionally change place of articulation or have a strident release, can be found in many languages, including Dutch, as we next discuss.

4.2. The Dutch Diminutives

Facts about the Dutch diminutive construction are presented in detail in Trommelen (1984). We give here only basic examples:

(17)   a.   *-tje*
              After long vowels and diphthongs:
              zee-tje   'sea'
              After coronal nasals and liquids preceded by long vowels and schwa:
              maan-tje   'moon'
              paal -tje   'stake'
        b.   *-etje*
              After nasals and liquids preceded by short vowels:
              kam-etje   'comb'
              kan -etje   'jug'
              ring-etje   'ring'
              bal -etje   'ball'
        c.   *-je*
              After obstruents:
              snob-je   'snob'   [pʲ]
              lap -je   'rag'   [pʲ]
              hok -je   'cage'   [kʲ]
              bed -je   'bed'   [tʲ]/[tʃ]
              pot -je   'pot'   [tʲ]/[tʃ]
        d.   *-pje/-kje*
              After labial and velar nasals, respectively, in other contexts:
              raam -pje   'window'   [pʲ]
              koning-kje   'king'   [kʲ]

For a complete description of the diminutive construction within a theory of syllabification, see Trommelen's analysis. What concerns us here is the output of (17c) and (17d). On the surface, labials and velars always acquire a secondary palatal articulation, while the dentals may also undergo a change of place.[4] The

Dutch diminutive morpheme can be represented as an Obstruent Root Node (Robst) unspecified for Place Features, followed by a floating [−anterior], [+high], underspecified segment and a schwa.

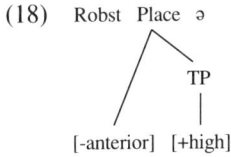

(18) Robst Place ə

             TP

    [-anterior] [+high]

This representation captures the different alternations very easily. The words under (17d) spread the Place Node of the nasal onto the unspecified Root Node, resulting in a homorganic stop: [ra:m] Robst-j-$ə$ > [ra:mp^{j}ə]. In addition, [+high] spreads onto this obstruent, which is palatalized and articulated with a [j] off-glide on the surface.

For obstruent final words, the unspecified Obstruent Root Node deletes. If the words end in labials or velars, the above observation about the spreading of [+high] holds. If, however, the word ends in a coronal consonant, there are two options. Speakers can fluctuate between a secondary "raised" palatalized dental, or a palato-alveolar/prepalatal articulation. If [+high] spreads, then the result is a palatalized coronal with a strident release; otherwise, the [−anterior] in the morpheme seeks out the coronal in the stem, resulting in a major place change. Given the nature of the morpheme, having both the properties [+high] and [−anterior], the variation in the dental articulation can be explained by our proposal of spreading [+high] for the general secondary articulations and, optionally, of spreading [−anterior] within the Coronal Node.

Similar cases of palatalization are reported in other languages like Ennemor (pointed out by Jean-François Prunet) and Japanese (Mester and Itô, 1989). In Japanese mimetics, an abstract morpheme palatalizes the rightmost dental consonant in a string, changing it to a palato-alveolar; if no dental consonant occurs, then the first consonant acquires a secondary palatal articulation. Mester and Itô (1989) claim that this morpheme consists of only [−anterior]. Since this feature normally attaches to a Coronal Node, it will first search for a coronal consonant in a string; if none occurs, it will create a Coronal Node to accommodate [−anterior]. The secondary palatalized labial and velar consonants, in their analysis, will thus be multiply articulated.

As we have argued earlier, secondary palatal articulations are *not* multiple articulations with the addition of the Coronal Node with its dependent [anterior]. Palatalized velars, for instance, do not have any coronal articulation and are clearly not [−anterior] (see [16] and related discussion). Rather, they are segments with the major articulation unaltered with the addition of [+high]. Our analysis of the Japanese facts would then be as follows. The palatalizing morpheme must have [−anterior] as a feature since it causes a change of place within the coronals (dental to palato-alveolar). This is similar to Mester and Itô. In addition, however, there must be a Tongue Position specification of [+high] that would spread to the other consonants. The morpheme would initially seek out coronal dentals to attach [−anterior], or else it would spread [+high] on the first consonant in the string, leading to secondary articulation of the labials and velars. Like the Dutch diminutives, again we see the simultaneous acquisition of secondary palatalization by velars and labials along with a change in place for dentals, which become palato-alveolars in the context of a morpheme that is both [+high] and [−anterior].

5. CONCLUSION

In this article, we have distinguished three major types of assimilatory processes that are often described as palatalizations. Our analysis of these palatalization processes supports the characterization of vowels and consonants by a unitary set of features. In particular, we argue that the front vowels and the palatal glide must be grouped together with the coronal consonants. To account for this, we propose a feature geometry representation that separates the major articulators from the traditional height features [high] and [low] grouped under a separate class node. We argue that this is not an ad hoc move, since not only can we now capture the interaction between specific vowels and consonants, but also there is independent evidence for grouping the height features together under a separate class node.

We have seen that in all the palatalization processes Coronal plays a role in one way or another. First, where velar consonants typically become palato-alveolar in the context of front vowels and glides, the change is characterized as a spreading of the Coronal Node with its dependent [−anterior]. Second, within the Coronal Node, dentals often become palato-alveolars, again in the context of front vowels and glides. We describe this process as spreading of [−anterior] within the Coronal Node. Third, we have argued that palatal secondary articulations are best understood as a spreading of [+high], where the surface phonetic form contains the unmarked palatal off-glide.

We can see the special behavior of Coronal particularly in the secondary palatal articulation. The surface phonetic off-glide that accompanies these palatalized articulations is the coronal [j], which is the default glide in most languages. In addition, when [+high] spreads to all places of articulation, the coronal consonants are often articulated with strident release and have been known to develop into strident fricatives. We have argued that this happens only with coronals, since by nature they have a predominance of high-frequency energy that is intensified by a palatal off-glide release. Moreover, if the trigger is a [−anterior] segment ([i] or [j]), then along with the spreading of [+high] there may be an additional change of place within the coronal consonants. This can happen if the [−anterior] in the trigger seeks out a coronal consonant in the input string and attaches itself to it.

ACKNOWLEDGMENTS

We thank Carlos Gussenhoven, Larry Hyman, Allard Jongman, Lisa Selkirk, Joan Sereno, and the editors, Carole Paradis and Jean-François Prunet, for comments and advice on an earlier version of this article.

NOTES

[1] Clements (1989:21) defines [open] as follows: "involves the positioning of the tongue body in a more open position than that required for the production of [i, u], with concomitant lowering of the jaw and withdrawal of the tongue root toward the rear pharyngeal wall, as in the production of mid and low vowels: [e, o, a], etc." Further, his definition of [low] "involves the lowering of the jaw, with concomitant lowering and backing of the tongue body and constriction of the pharyngeal cavity, as in low vowels: [æ, a, ɑ], etc."

[2] In most instances, coronovelar articulations are clicks, which ought not to be the outcome of palatalization.

[3] We are grateful to Allard Jongman for these examples.

[4] Berendsen (1986:69), following Neyt and Zonneveld (1980), says that the dental fricatives become palato-alveolar, while the stops end up as [c]. Unfortunately, it is unclear what [c] denotes in his description. There appears to be something of a continuum in native speakers' pronunciations of these consonants. Phonetically, they are either pronounced with a secondary palatal articulation (perhaps somewhat backed from a regular [t]) with strident release, or they are articulated as prepalatal [−anterior] sounds, with varying degrees of stridency. We have represented the two endpoints as [t^j] and [tʃ].

REFERENCES

Berendsen, E. (1986) *The Phonology of Cliticization*, Doctoral dissertation, University of Utrecht.

Bhat, D. N. S. (1978) "A General Study of Palatalization," in J. H. Greenberg, C. A. Ferguson, and E. Moravcsik, eds., *Universals of Language*, Vol. 2: *Phonology*, pp. 47–92, Stanford University Press, Stanford, California.

Borgstrøm, C. H. (1940) *The Dialects of the Outer Hebrides*, Norwegian Universities Press, Oslo.

Chomsky, N. and M. Halle (1968) *The Sound Pattern of English*, Harper & Row, London.

Clements, G. N. (1976) "Palatalization: Linking or Assimilation?" *Proceedings of CLS* 12, 96–109.

Clements, G. N. (1985) "The Geometry of Phonological Features," *Phonology Yearbook 2,* 225–252.

Clements, G. N. (1989) "A Unified Set of Features for Consonants and Vowels" (preliminary version), ms., Cornell University, Ithaca, New York.

Halle, M. (1971) *The Sound Pattern of Russian,* Mouton, The Hague.

Halle, M. and K. N. Stevens (1979) "Some Reflections on the Theoretical Bases of Phonetics," in B. Lindblom and S. Ohman, eds., *Frontiers of Speech Communication,* Academic Press, London.

Hyman, L. M. (1973) "The Feature [grave] in Phonological Theory," *Journal of Phonetics* 1, 329–337.

Hyman, L. M. (1988) "Underspecification and Vowel Height Transfer in Esimbi," *Phonology* 5, 255–273.

Jacobs, H. (1989) *Non-linear Studies in the Historical Phonology of French,* Doctoral dissertation, Nijmegen University.

Jakobson, R., G. Fant, and M. Halle (1963) *Preliminaries to Speech Analysis,* MIT Press, Cambridge, Massachusetts.

Keating, P. A. (1988) "Palatals as Complex Segments: X-ray Evidence," *UCLA Working Papers* 19, 77–91.

Ladefoged, P. (1982) *A Course in Phonetics,* Harcourt Brace Jovanovich, New York.

Lahiri, A. and S. E. Blumstein (1984) "A Re-evaluation of the Feature Coronal," *Journal of Phonetics* 12, 133–146.

Lahiri, A., L. Gewirth, and S. E. Blumstein (1984) "A Reconsideration of Acoustic Invariance for Place of Articulation in Diffuse Stop Consonants: Evidence from a Cross-language Study," *Journal of the Acoustical Society of America* 76, 391–404.

Maddieson, I. (1984) *Patterns of Sounds,* Cambridge University Press, Cambridge, England.

McCarthy, J. J. (1988) "Feature Geometry and Dependency: A Review," *Phonetica 43,* 84–108.

Mester, R. A. and J. Itô (1989) "Feature Predictability and Underspecification: Palatal Prosody in Japanese Mimetics," *Language 65,* 258–293.

Neyt, A. and W. Zonneveld (1980) *Pronominal Assimilation Phenomena,* ms., University of Utrecht/ZWO.

Odden, D. (1978) "Further Evidence for the Feature [grave]," *Linguistic Inquiry 9,* 141–144.

Rubach, J. (1984) *Cyclic and Lexical Phonology,* Foris Publications, Dordrecht.

Sagey, E. C. (1986) *The Representation of Features and Relations in Non-linear Phonology,* Doctoral dissertation, MIT, Cambridge, Massachusetts.

Stevens, K. N., S. J. Keyser, and H. Kawasaki (1986) "Toward a Phonetic and Phonological Theory of Redundant Features," in J. S. Perkell and D. H. Klatt, eds., *Invariance and Variability of Speech Processes,* Lawrence Erlbaum Associates, Hillsdale, New Jersey.

Trommelen, M. (1984) *The Syllable in Dutch,* Foris Publications, Dordrecht.

Vago, R. M. (1976) "More Evidence for the Feature [grave]," *Linguistic Inquiry 7,* 671–674.

ON THE RELATIONSHIP BETWEEN LATERALITY AND CORONALITY

KEREN RICE *
PETER AVERY †

Department of Linguistics
University of Toronto
Toronto, Ontario M5S 1A1, Canada

†*Department of Languages, Literatures and*
  Linguistics
York University
North York, Ontario M3J 1P3, Canada

1. INTRODUCTION

Recent models of feature geometry position the feature Lateral as a daughter of the Coronal Node (e.g., Levin, 1988; McCarthy, 1988:103; Pulleyblank, 1988:311), a hypothesis at odds with the classification that has considered Lateral as a manner feature rather than a place feature. If Lateral is treated as a place dependent in the feature geometry, an account of its manner properties must be presented; on the other hand, if it is a manner feature, an account of its restriction to the coronal place of articulation must be presented. In this article, we argue that the manner properties of laterals are basic and that the coronal properties of laterals are a result of universal coronal underspecification. The status of laterals as coronals follows directly from the fact that Coronal is universally the unmarked articulator node.

Current phonological theory allows at least two ways of deriving feature co-occurrence restrictions. One is to encode the restriction directly in the feature geometry. For example, as the feature [anterior] is a property of coronal segments, it is considered to be a dependent of the Coronal Node. One need not

Phonetics and Phonology, Volume 2
The Special Status of Coronals

make any statement about the nonoccurrence of this feature with labial or dorsal segments as it is simply not relevant to their specification. One need only say that [anterior] selects or projects to the Coronal Node in order to derive these restrictions. We refer to this type of co-occurrence restriction as *exclusion by structural dependency*. The second possibility is to use negative constraints to rule out certain configurations. This has been the normal approach with features that are considered to be daughters of the same node. For example, combinations of features such as [+high] and [+low] or [+nasal] and [+lateral] have generally been excluded by assuming that Universal Grammar has a constraint that rules out the co-occurrence of these features. This we refer to as *exclusion by constraint*.

While both exclusion by structural dependency and exclusion by constraint serve to rule out possible but nonoccurring representations, there is a significant difference in the way in which these representations are excluded. In the case of exclusion by structural dependency, it is assumed that two features can never co-occur because they do not occur in the same structural configuration. This is similar to what Clements (1988b) refers to as automatic underspecification and is a significant advantage of the representations posited by a theory of feature geometry. In the case of exclusion by constraint, on the other hand, it is possible during a derivation for two features that are incompatible to co-occur. However, the constraint ensures that the representation does not surface. In this way, exclusion by constraint is similar to structure preservation, which prohibits configurations absent from underlying representation from being derived lexically (Kiparsky, 1982).

In the feature geometry literature, exclusion by structural dependency is the primary motivation behind establishing geometric configurations. Segments that behave as a natural class to the exclusion of other segments are represented as dominated by the same organizing node. This strategy has been particularly successful with the place and the laryngeal features. However, the approach has been less successful in determining the position of the manner features and has led many to assume that manner features are not a natural class and are instead spread throughout the feature geometry. Based on the patterning of laterals as coronals, Levin (1988) argues that Lateral must be a Coronal dependent, a position assumed in later work in feature geometry (e.g., McCarthy, 1988:103; Pulleyblank, 1988:311). Noncoronal laterals are ruled out by this structural configuration, with the coronal–lateral relationship encoded directly in the representation of laterals.

In this article, we examine the position of the feature Lateral, focusing on the relationship between it and the Coronal Node. We examine a number of properties of laterals and conclude that, despite its coronal properties, Lateral forms a constituent with the other sonorant features, in particular Nasal. In order to account for its coronal properties, we explore the use of a constraint that disallows the co-occurrence of Lateral with specified place features. We show that a specific version of exclusion by constraint is problematic and suggest that a more general constraint excluding complex structure at both the Place and Manner Nodes must be proposed. This constraint, plus a condition on spreading, properly predicts the coronal place of articulation of laterals.

In the first section of the article, we set out our assumptions concerning phonological rules and representations. We then turn to arguments that Lateral is a sonorant feature. Having established this, we examine the coronal properties of laterals and show how they are derived.

2. ASSUMPTIONS

2.1. Feature Geometry

Following Clements (1985), Archangeli and Pulleyblank (1986), Sagey (1986), McCarthy (1988), and others, we assume that segments are not unordered feature bundles but have hierarchical structure. This structure is universal in nature, with invariant dependencies across languages. The model that we adopt is shown in (1). Features that are not relevant to this article are suppressed; default features are enclosed in parentheses.

(1)

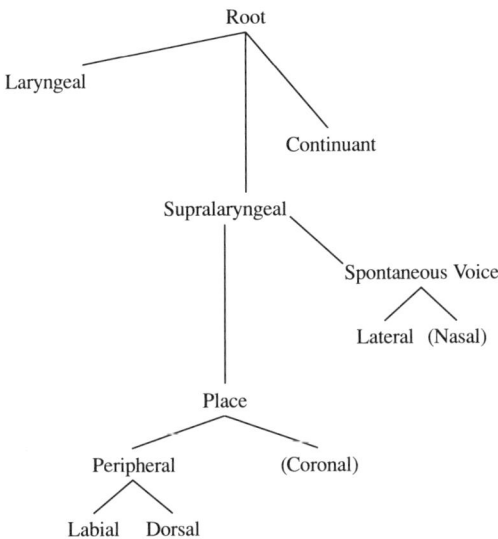

Several aspects of this representation require comment. First, we argue for the existence of an organizing node called Spontaneous Voice (SV). Generally, sonorants have a SV Node and obstruents do not. (See Rice and Avery, 1989, for discussion of the term "Spontaneous Voice" for this node; see also Piggott, 1989, for a similar proposal.)

Second, we distinguish two major node types, organizing nodes and content nodes. Organizing nodes (roughly equivalent to Clements's, 1985, class nodes) serve to define major organizational units such as Supralaryngeal, Place, and Spontaneous Voice. The content nodes, often called features, are actual articulatory instructions. We propose that the organizing and content nodes have very different properties. The required organizing nodes of a segment are specified individually for each segment, while content nodes can be shared between segments. For instance, the geminate sequence /bb/ has the structure in (2).

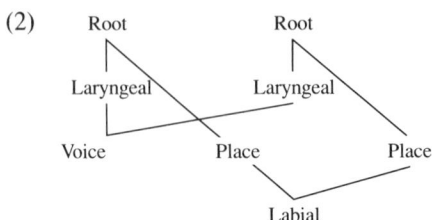

(2)

Root   Root

Laryngeal   Laryngeal

Voice   Place   Place

Labial

The hypothesis represented in this view is that distinctive organizing structure is inherent in segments and that content features give an articulatory dimension to the segmental representation. Because distinctive organizing structure is inherent in each segment, it cannot be dispensed with in the representation of any individual segment. Thus, processes such as fusion affect content structure only, leaving organizing structure alone. The content nodes, on other other hand, give an articulatory reality to a segment and can be shared between segments.

In addition to theoretical considerations, several empirical considerations lead to this hypothesis. Part of the motivation comes from the observation that empty Place Nodes do not fuse (Avery and Rice, 1989). In addition, processes are found that transmit organizing structure from one node to another but do not transmit actual content (Rice and Avery, 1989).

Finally, the absence of plus and minus values on the nodes should be noted. Their absence follows from our assumption that all features are monovalent in nature, with presence versus absence giving the appearance of binarity. This assumption is a natural extension of the move made in Sagey (1986) to monovalent articulator nodes and leads potentially, we believe, to a more highly constrained theory. See Anderson and Ewen (1987), van der Hulst (1989), and Rice (1990) for work that argues for monovalency.

2.2. Underspecification

What we call underspecification differs in some respects from the usual use of this term (e.g., Archangeli, 1984, 1988; Steriade, 1987). Given binary features, two types of underspecification can be distinguished: redundant feature underspecification and redundant value underspecification. With single-valued features, only redundant feature underspecification is relevant. We assume that redundant content nodes are absent from underlying representation. The redundant content nodes are those that are unmarked, as determined by a universal theory of markedness. The least marked of the content nodes at any particular organizing node is normally absent from underlying representation. Universal markedness theory can be overridden by contrasts within an inventory that force the least marked of the content nodes to be present. (See Avery and Rice, 1989, for development of this theory.) The particular Place and SV Nodes that are considered to be the least marked are important to this article. Avery and Rice (1989) argue, following work by Kean (1975) and Maddieson (1984), that the Coronal content node is the least marked of the Place dependents, and that as such it is generally absent from underlying representation. (See also other contributions to this volume for similar arguments.) It is present only if two segments are distinguished by a feature that is a Coronal dependent. A typical coronal stop thus has the phonological representation in (3), where irrelevant structure is omitted. The feature Coronal is added by a default rule in phonetic implementation.

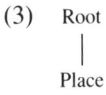

(3)   Root
        |
        Place

In this article, we suggest that the least marked of the SV dependents is Nasal and that Lateral is specified underlyingly. The feature Nasal is added to the representation of the nasal consonant by a default rule in phonetic implementation, its insertion being triggered by the presence of the contentless organizing SV Node. This is consistent with observations found in the literature concerning the least marked of the sonorant consonants (e.g., Kean, 1975). The proposed representations for /n/ and /l/ are given in (4).

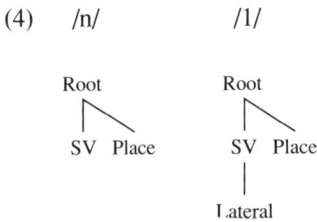

(4)   /n/   /l/

        Root   Root
        ⟋⟍   ⟋⟍
       SV Place   SV Place
                        |
                      Lateral

The role of default rules in our framework is less elaborate than that found in other work on underspecification theory (e.g., Archangeli and Pulleyblank, 1986; Kiparsky, 1982). While in most frameworks default rules function to fill in both redundant features and redundant values, we claim that they function only to fill in redundant features. We view these rules as largely restricted to the phonetic implementation component of the grammar. Thus, if a feature or node is underspecified in the phonology of a language, then that feature cannot play a role in the phonology of the language. Default rules merely supply articulatory instructions; for example, such rules specify whether a /t/ is dental or alveolar in a particular language.

2.3. Rules

We assume that the phonology is restricted to at most four operations: spreading, delinking, copying, and OCP (obligatory contour principle)-based fusion.

Spreading is a language-particular operation that may include trigger and target conditions as well as a directionality parameter. The theory of spreading that we adopt is summarized in (5).

(5)   a. Spreading can occur only if the spreader is spreading to the same node that dominates it, that is, a structural target must be present.
      b. A feature or node can spread only to an empty position.

Rule (5a) disallows node generation through spreading, and (5b) rules out cases of spreading triggering delinking. The workings of this spreading theory are illustrated in (6), where γ is an organizing node and α and β are content nodes.

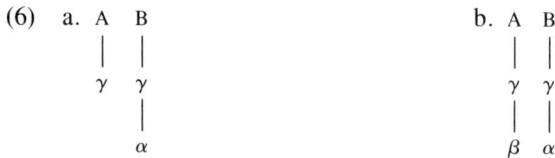

(6)   a. A   B   b. A   B
         | | | |
         γ γ γ γ
             | | |
             α β α

In (6a), spreading of α to γ can occur since γ is present in the representation of A, has no dependents, and is the structural node that dominates α. In (6b), α cannot spread to γ because γ has the dependent β. Only if an independent rule delinking β existed could α spread to γ. See Mascaró (1987) and Piggott (1989) for similar views and Avery and Rice (1989) for further details.

Given the assumption that each segment has its own organizing structure, the process of copying is necessary in order to transmit organizing structure from one segment to another. Copying takes an organizing node of one segment and copies it to another segment under conditions of locality. It is generally motivated by the need to meet sonority restrictions. The general operation of copying is illustrated in (7), where γ is an organizing node and α is a content node.

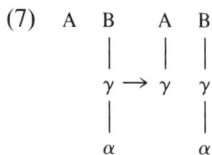

(7)   A   B   A   B
         | | |
         γ $\rightarrow$ γ γ
         | |
         α α

Delinking is a neutralization process that delinks content nodes in neutralizing positions such as morpheme-final or syllable-final. Fusion takes identical, locally adjacent content nodes and fuses them. See Avery and Rice (1989) and Rice and Avery (1989) for discussion of the differences between fusion, copying, and spreading.

3. THE SV HYPOTHESIS

We now turn to arguments for the position of Lateral in the feature geometry. We propose that Lateral is a dependent of a node that organizes the sonorant features Nasal and Lateral (and R-features, a general term referring to manner features, other than Continuant, that are present in the representation of /r/, if indeed there are any.) This node we term Spontaneous Voice. The arguments that we present are similar to those often given for an organizing node. For example, frequent place assimilation across languages has been taken as strong evidence for Place as an organizing node (see Clements, 1985; McCarthy, 1988). We argue that a node dominating the sonorant features is necessary based on assimilations found within the sonorant consonants, desonorantization, and assimilations to the sonority (but not the place) of an adjacent segment.

3.1. Spreading: SV as a Target

In this section we examine sonorant–sonorant assimilations. Given our assumptions about spreading (see [5]), if a sonorant assimilates to the manner of an adjacent sonorant, the consonants must both contain an identical node that functions as the holder of the spreading feature. In this section we examine a number of sonorant–sonorant assimilation processes that suggest the need for a common node dominating the sonorant segments.

3.1.1. ENGLISH ASSIMILATION

Sonorant–sonorant assimilations are found in English level-1 phonology, with the prefix /in-/. This prefix assimilates to a following consonant in terms of place of articulation, as in (8a). More important, it assimilates totally to a following sonorant consonant, as in (8b), with subsequent, independently necessary degemination (see Borowsky, 1986; Schein and Steriade, 1986, for discussion of degemination in English).

(8) a. *i[m]balance*   *i[n]dentured*   *i[ŋ]grown*
         i[m]possible   *i[n]tangible*   *i[ŋ]credible*
      b. *i[r]rational*   *i[l]legible*   *i[n]numerable*   *i[m]measurable*

Borowsky (1986) argues that the /n/ of the prefix /in-/ is specified merely as [sonorant], with [nasal] supplied by default. We agree with the spirit of this analysis, but for us the nasal is simply the organizing node SV (see [4]).[1]

The rule of spreading in English for (8b) can be formulated as in (9). In this rule, we show Lateral and R-features as dependents of the organizing SV Node, while the nasal is simply the SV Node. The conditions for spreading are met (there is an empty structural target), and the SV Node dependent spreads leftward to the empty SV Node.

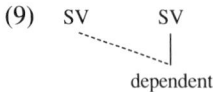

(9)   SV   SV

                    |

          dependent

When the nasal is followed by a nonsonorant consonant, the structural description of the rule in (9) is not met since there is no SV Node from which to spread. Place assimilation occurs and the default rule realizing a bare SV Node as nasal applies, yielding a nasal of the same place of articulation as the following consonant.

3.1.2. KLAMATH *n-l* ASSIMILATION

In Klamath, as in English level 1, /n-l/ becomes /l-l/, as illustrated in (10). See Barker (1964) for discussion. (The single quotation mark following a segment indicates glottalization.)

(10)   *honlina* → *hollina*   'flies along the bank'
         w'inl'ga → *w'illga*   'lies down on the stomach'
                                                    (from Barker, 1964:79)

In our terms, the Klamath rule is like that of English, with the Lateral dependent of the SV Node on the right-hand side spreading to the empty SV Node on the left-hand side. The rule is shown in (11).

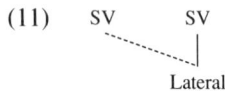

(11)   SV   SV

                    |

          Lateral

3.1.3. PONAPEAN ASSIMILATION

Ponapean is another language that exhibits assimilation within the sonorants. We illustrate the Ponapean assimilations with the *n-l* alternation.[2] In rapid speech, Ponapean exhibits the same assimilation found in Klamath and English, /n/ assimilates to /l/. This is illustrated in the words in (12). Data are from Rehg and Sohl (1981:57).

(12)   *nan-leng* → *nalleng*   'heaven'
         pan lingan → *pallingan*   'will be beautiful'

This assimilation can be accounted for in the same way as the Klamath and English assimilations, with the daughter of the right-hand node spreading to the left-hand node.

3.1.4. TOBA BATAK ASSIMILATION

Toba Batak is another language with numerous sonorant–sonorant assimilations. These are shown in (13). (Data are from Hayes, 1986:479.)

(13) $nn \rightarrow nn$ $rn \rightarrow rn$ $ln \rightarrow ln$
      $nr \rightarrow rr$ $rr \rightarrow rr$ $lr \rightarrow lr$
      $nl \rightarrow ll$ $rl \rightarrow ll$ $ll \rightarrow ll$

We assume the representations in (14) for the Toba Batak sonorants.

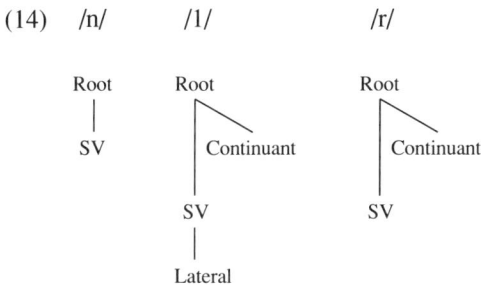

(14)   /n/   /l/   /r/

```
       Root       Root             Root
        |         /  \             /  \
        SV      SV  Continuant   SV  Continuant
                 |                |
                SV               SV
                 |
              Lateral
```

The nasal /n/ is represented as a bare SV Node; /l/ is a SV Node with a Lateral dependent and Continuant as a daughter of the Root Node; and /r/ is a bare SV Node with Continuant as daughter of the Root Node. With /n/, a default rule in phonetic implementation fills in Nasal, while with /r/, the specification of Nasal is blocked due to the presence of Continuant.

The *n-l* sequences are analyzed in the same way as the *n-l* sequences in Klamath, English level 1, and Ponapean, with spreading of Lateral (and Continuant) onto the left-hand unspecified SV Node. In the *n-r* case, Continuant spreads from the /r/ onto the /n/ and the entire sequence is realized as [r-r] as the nasal default rule will not insert Nasal onto a continuant. Assimilation in *l-n* is blocked since the nasal has no features to spread. In *r-l*, Lateral spreads from the /l/ to the /r/, yielding [l-l]. Assimilation in *l-r* is blocked for the same reason that there is no assimilation in *l-n;* the left-hand SV Node has specified features (Lateral) and therefore spreading cannot apply.

So far, we have argued for the SV Node based on spreading, and in all of the cases discussed we have hypothesized that the SV Node organizes sonorant features and serves as a target for spreading. In the next two sections we provide further evidence for this hypothesis by demonstrating that the SV Node displays typical node-like behavior, that is, it delinks and copies.

3.2. Delinking–Desonorantization

Delinking provides a second type of argument for node status. As discussed by McCarthy (1988:92), debuccalization can be viewed as the delinking of the Place Node. If the SV Node is independent of the Root Node, one might expect to find a parallel process to debuccalization involving the SV Node, namely, desonorantization. Processes in Yagaria and Kuman present some evidence for desonorantization.

3.2.1. YAGARIA

In the Move dialect of Yagaria, a language of the East New Guinea Highlands, there are alternations between sonorants and obstruents. Yagaria has the consonant inventory shown in (15). (See Renck, 1967, 1975, for Yagaria data.)

(15)   Obstruents   p   t   k   ʔ
                    b   d   g
                    f   s   h
        Sonorants   m   n
                    v   l   y

The lateral consonant in Yagaria is phonetically a velar consonant (Renck, 1967, 1975) but patterns phonologically as a coronal (Levin, 1988).

The sonorant–obstruent alternations found in Yagaria involve *l-t, v-p,* and *m-b,* with the sonorant form occurring after a vowel and the obstruent form after a glottal stop, the only possible syllable-final consonant in Yagaria. The glottal stop is subsequently lost.[3] This is illustrated in (16).

(16)   a. *l-t* alternation
            bade 'boy' + *lata* 'dual' → *badelata* 'two boys'
            aʔ 'female' + *lata* 'dual' → *atata* 'two women'
        b. *v-p* alternation
            agoʔ do va   'I am already eating'
              do + *va* (emphatic)
            legiʔ aʔ elidu pa 'we have truly not taken it'
              eliduʔ + *va* (emphatic)

As discussed by Levin (1988), this process can be viewed as strengthening, where a sonorant becomes an obstruent of the same place of articulation.[4] We formulate this rule as in (17).

(17)   Root]$_{\sigma\sigma}$ [Root
                  $\neq$
                  SV

The SV Node delinks when it follows another consonant (a glottal stop). The delinking of the SV Node produces obstruents, with the right-hand element being realized as a coronal by default if it has no specified place of articulation.

3.2.2. KUMAN

Kuman, a Papuan language, also provides some evidence for SV delinking. In Kuman, a lateral loses its sonorancy and becomes a [t] when it is followed by /n/, as illustrated in (18). (Data are from Levin, 1988, based on Lynch, 1983.)

(18)   *yobul + na → yobutna*   'my bone'
        yal + nga → yatnga   'you plant' (Aorist)

We can think of this case as involving delinking of the left-hand SV Node in the presence of a following SV Node. Once SV is delinked, the consonant is realized as the default coronal, [t].

3.3. Copying–Transmission of the SV Node

We take copying to be a diagnostic for a node. While it is beyond the scope of this paper to defend our analysis of copying, we observe that copying is generally motivated by the need to conform to sonority restrictions. In the cases discussed here, copying ensures that rhymal segments are not less sonorous than following onsets. (See the work on syllable contact by Hooper, 1976; Murray and Vennemann, 1983; Kaye, Lowenstamm, and Vergnaud, 1990; Clements, 1988a.) In this section we examine two cases that can be analyzed as copying of the SV Node with subsequent spreading of SV dependents.

3.3.1. KOREAN

An example of copying of the SV Node is found in Korean, a language with extensive assimilation. Stops assimilate in nasality to a following segment (19a–d), and /t/'s assimilate to a following lateral (19e). (Data are from Cho, 1988:45, and Iverson and Kim, 1987:186.)

(19)   a. *kukmul → kuŋmul*   'soup'
        b. *kakmok → kaŋmok*   'wood'
        c. *napnita → namnita*   'to sprout'
        d. *katʰni → kanni*   'to be the same'
        e. *tikitliil → tikilliil*   'the letters *t* and *l*'

In (19a) the final consonant of the first syllable, /k/, becomes [ŋ] in order to conform to sonority restrictions that hold between rhymes and following onsets. Examples (19b–d) are similar. In (19e), the /t/ becomes [l] before the following lateral. When a stop of another place of articulation precedes the lateral, a nasal–nasal sequence results, as in (20).

(20)   *kɯk-lak* → *kɯŋnak*   'paradise'
      tsap-lok → *tsamnok*   'a miscellany'

Assuming that the nasals are characterized as having a bare SV Node and the lateral as a SV Node dominating Lateral, the Korean process can be analyzed as copying of a SV Node and spreading of SV dependents, if any. This assimilatory process is illustrated in (21) for a /k-m/ sequence, where [ŋm] results.

(21)   *k*   *m*   *ŋ*   *m*

The SV Node copies from /m/ to /k/ to satisfy trans-syllabic sonority restrictions. As there are no SV dependents, the SV Node is specified as Nasal by default.

The illustration in (22) shows the derivation of a /t-l/ sequence, where [ll] results.

(22)   *t*   *l*   *l*   *l*

The SV Node is copied from the /l/ to the /t/. The Lateral dependent of SV can spread from right to left, resulting in [ll].

The derivation involving the /p-l/ sequence, where [mn] results, is somewhat more complex. First, the SV Node is copied from the /l/ to the /p/. Spreading of Lateral is blocked because Lateral cannot co-occur with a specified Place Node; see the discussion in Section 4.2 for details. Finally, sonorant–sonorant sequences must be identical in SV features in Korean (e.g., see Cho, 1967). Since Lateral cannot spread, the only way of achieving this is for this feature to delink. The Place Node of the /l/ is suppressed in this derivation.

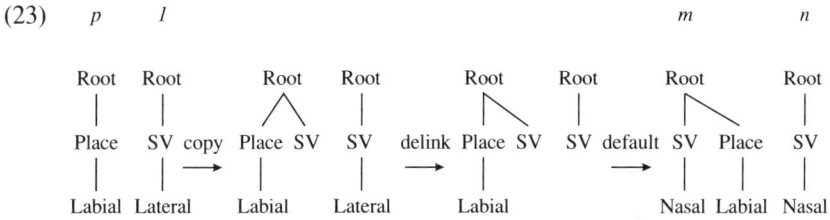

(23)   *p*   *l*   *m*   *n*

Root Root		Root Root		Root Root		Root	Root

Place SV copy Place SV   SV   delink Place SV   SV default SV Place   SV

Labial Lateral   Labial   Lateral   Labial   Nasal Labial Nasal

3.3.2. SANSKRIT

Sanskrit illustrates a process quite similar to that found in Korean. In Sanskrit, stops can assimilate to the nasality of a following segment, and /t/'s can assimilate to a following lateral. These processes are illustrated in (24). (Data are from Whitney, 1889, Section 161.)[5]

(24)   *tat namas → tan namas*
        vak me → vaŋ me
        baṭ mahan → baṇ mahan
        triṣṭup nunam → triṣṭum nunam
        vak + maya- → vaŋmaya
        mṛt + maya → mṛnmaya
        tat labhate → tal labhate
        út luptam → úl luptam

If nasals are characterized as having a SV Node dominating Nasal and laterals as having a SV Node dominating Lateral, then Sanskrit, like Korean, shows the copying of a SV Node on the right-hand side to an adjacent segment on the left-hand side with no SV Node, followed by the spreading of SV dependents from right to left.[6] As in Korean, copying results in forms that conform to cross-syllable sonority restrictions.

3.4. Summary

We have argued that sonorants are best characterized as having a SV Node dominating sonorant features. We have attempted to show that this node displays typical node-like behavior: It serves as a target of spreading (Klamath, English, Ponapean, Toba Batak), it delinks (Yagaria, Kuman), and it copies (Korean, Sanskrit). We now turn to an important question that is as yet unanswered by our analysis, the question of why laterals are coronals.

4. THE CORONAL PROPERTIES

While we have argued that Lateral is not a Coronal dependent, but rather a dependent of the SV Node, it is undeniable that laterals show coronal properties in the phonology. Based on these properties, Levin (1988) argues that non-coronal laterals are excluded by structural dependency because Lateral is a Coronal dependent, a claim assumed by McCarthy (1988) and Pulleyblank (1988). In this section we explore an alternative solution to the coronal problem.

4.1. Phonological Restrictions on the Place of Laterals

The first question that we address concerns how laterals get to be coronal. In Avery and Rice (1989), we argue that the Coronal Node is generally not present underlyingly but is added by a default rule in the phonetic implementation component of the grammar. Given this, we suggest that the coronality of laterals can be derived by treating them like other coronals, that is, they are generally unspecified for place, with the coronality following from phonetic implementation.[7]

While we can derive the coronality of laterals from universal markedness theory, laterals remain distinct from other manners of articulation in another way: They are underlyingly restricted to the coronal place of articulation and do not co-occur with the other articulator nodes. The question of why laterals are restricted phonologically to the coronal place of articulation is the second question that we address. Exclusion by structural dependency is ruled out since we have argued that Lateral is a SV dependent rather than a Coronal dependent. A reasonable alternative hypothesis is that this distribution results from a universal constraint against Lateral occurring with a specified place in the phonology. Thus, the configuration in (25a) is permissible, but those in (25b–c) are not.

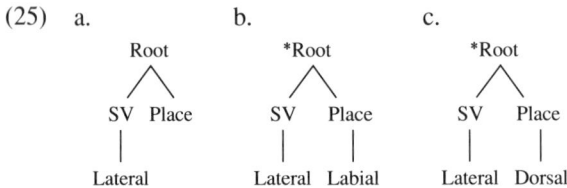

(25)   a.   b.   c.

        Root   *Root   *Root
        /\   /\   /\
      SV Place   SV   Place   SV   Place
       | | | | |
     Lateral   Lateral Labial   Lateral Dorsal

Such constraints block the derivation of a segmental representation that contains both Lateral and specification for place.

While this type of constraint is a descriptively adequate device, we must question why it would exist universally. Constraints against the co-occurrence of features such as [+high] and [+low] or [+spread glottis] and [+constricted glottis] are often claimed to have an articulatory basis, that is, the co-occurrence is impossible phonetically. The exclusion of Lateral and the specified peripheral places,

Labial and Dorsal, does not seem to be a result of such articulatory incompatibility; as Catford (1977:132) points out, airflow at the sides of an articulation is possible at places of articulation other than coronal. In fact, Catford claims that labial laterals are articulatorily possible. It would thus be desirable to find an alternative way of excluding Lateral from co-occurring with Labial and Dorsal places of articulation. We suggest a more general means of excluding the non-coronal laterals underlyingly, exclusion by a constraint on the structural complexity of a segment.

When consonant inventories are examined, the difference in range of places available for obstruents and nasals, on the one hand, and for liquids, on the other, is striking. Obstruents occur in the full range of places of articulation, nasals occur either in the full range or in a slightly more restricted range of places of articulation than the obstruents, and liquids are limited to the unmarked coronal place of articulation.[8] When the structural properties of obstruents, nasals, and laterals are compared, we find that obstruents in general are lacking in SV structure, nasals contain a SV Node and possibly a specified Place Node, and laterals contain a SV Node with a dependent and no specified Place Node. Laterals are structurally more complex with respect to SV structure than nasals, which have little or no SV structure. It appears that there is a tension between the Place structure and the SV structure of a segment. We refer to the amount of specified structure allowed underlyingly as structural complexity. We suggest that only a certain level of structural complexity is tolerated in the underlying representation of a segment. Specification of SV implies no specification of Place and specification of Place implies no specification of SV. Obstruents can occur in the full range of places of articulation because they lack any specification at the SV Node. Nasals can occur in the full range of places of articulation because they contain only the organizational node SV beyond their place structure. That nasal inventories are often smaller than stop inventories might be expected since nasals have a SV Node while obstruents do not. Laterals, on the other hand, with specified SV structure, cannot tolerate any specification of Place structure beyond the organizing node Place. This observation is summarized in (26).

(26)   STRUCTURAL COMPLEXITY CONSTRAINT (SCC)
       Specified SV structure implies lack of specified Place structure, and
           specified Place structure implies lack of specified SV structure.

The SCC allows the representation in (25a), where only SV structure is specified, but disallows the representations in (25b–c), where both Place structure and SV structure are specified underlyingly. We assume that the SCC holds throughout the phonology, where representations are underspecified.

The notion of structural complexity is undoubtedly related to sonority. Clements (1988a), in an illuminating discussion of sonority, examines the major class features (obstruent, nasal, liquid, glide, and vowel) in terms of structural complexity. He measures sonority by counting the number of plus values of the features [syllabic], [vocoid], [approximant], and [sonorant] present. Within the consonants, the obstruents are the least complex, and the liquids the most complex. In a theory without binary features, complexity cannot be measured in terms of the number of plus values present. However, it can be measured in terms of structure present at a particular node. For instance, /l/ is more sonorant than /n/ because /l/ has more SV structure. An examination of the complex relationship between the SV Node and the Place Node may provide fresh insight into the nature of sonority among the consonant segments.

We cannot explore the details of this suggestion or the full range of consequences—for example, can structural complexity be used to account for the relative infrequency of glottalized and aspirated (voiceless) sonorants as opposed to glottalized and aspirated obstruents? The SCC allows us to derive the restricted place distribution of laterals without forcing the unacceptable exclusion by structural dependency. It also explains why noncoronal laterals cannot be phonologically derived: Assuming that the SCC holds throughout the phonology until phonetic implementation, when default rules apply, the derivation of a noncoronal lateral would violate the SCC.

The SCC has certain advantages over exclusion by structural dependency. Some evidence for this can be found in the derivation of noncoronal laterals. Consider the following data from Catalan. (Data based on Mascaró, 1976:46.)

(27) a. Unassimilated alveolar *e[l]*   'the'
      b. Labial   *e[lʷ] pa*   'the bread'
      c. Labiodental   *e[lʷ] foc*   'the fire'
      d. Dental   *e[l̪] dia*   'the day'
      e. Alveolar   *e[l] sol*   'the sun'
      f. Postalveolar   *e[l̠] ric*   'the rich'
      g. Laminopalatal   *e[l̯] [ʒ]ermá*   'the brother'
      h. Palatal   *e[l̯] [ʎ]ibre*   'the book'
      i. Velar   *e[ɫ] gos*   'the dog'

In Catalan, the lateral assimilates not just to the coronal but also to the labial and velar. Assimilation of the lateral to the labial is not noted in the sources, but J. Mascaró (personal communication, 1989) suggests that there is labialization before labials. Assimilation to noncoronals is problematic if the coronal–lateral co-occurrence restriction is accounted for by structural dependency: The lateral is already coronal, so assimilation to the labial and velar is unexpected.[9] Under the SCC, the assimilation of the lateral to labials and velars is not unexpected. Any assimilation is blocked so long as the SCC holds. However, the SCC does not hold in phonetic implementation when default values are filled in, as all structure must be specified at this point. In a language that allows assimilation late in a derivation, as Catalan does (see Kiparsky, 1985), that noncoronal laterals exist phonetically is not surprising since at this point Place dependents can spread to the lateral without violating the SCC. Noncoronal laterals are ruled out phonologically by the SCC, but at the point that the SCC is no longer relevant, there is no reason not to expect them.[10]

Further empirical evidence for the SCC over structural dependency exists. The hypothesis that the Lateral is a Coronal dependent predicts that whenever Place dependents spread, Lateral will also spread. However, in Dutch, /n/ assimilates in place of articulation to a following consonant, but it does not assimilate to the laterality of a following lateral, as seen in the forms in (28).

(28) a. Assimilation to place of articulation of following consonant
  i[n] elf uur   'in eleven hours' (Trommelen, 1984:167)
  i[m]-brengen   'to bring in'
  i[ŋ]-kopen   'to purchase'
  i[ñ] jullie huis 'at your house'
  i[ɱ] vieren   'in four parts'
 b. No assimilation to the laterality of following lateral
  i[n]-laten   'let in, admit'
  i[n]-leggen   'lay in, put in'

If Lateral is a Coronal dependent, the failure of Lateral to spread in the forms in (28b) is unexplained; however, if it is a SV dependent, Dutch can be characterized as showing spreading only to the Place Node.

Transparency facts involving laterals also present an argument against the structural dependency approach to the lateral–coronal relationship. In languages such as Mau and Guere (see Paradis and Prunet, 1989, 1990), laterals are transparent to a vowel harmony process, just as are other coronal consonants. If Lateral is a dependent of the SV Node, this transparency can be accounted for. If, on the other hand, Lateral is a Coronal dependent, one would expect the harmony to be blocked.[11]

4.2. Laterals in Phonetic Implementation

We have a constraint that blocks noncoronal laterals underlyingly. We now turn to another aspect of this issue: If noncoronal laterals can be derived from lateral–noncoronal obstruent sequences phonetically by the spreading of Place features, why can't noncoronal laterals be derived from nasal–lateral sequences by the spreading of Lateral to the preceding consonant? For instance, in Klamath, *n-l* becomes [ll], but *m-l* remains [ml]. Similar facts are found in Ponapean, Toba Batak, and Korean. The observation that we make is that Lateral can spread only when Place is identical to that of the preceding consonant, as in *n-l*. Lateral does not spread when the places of articulation of the two consonants are distinct.

There are other cases in which spreading of a feature is limited to cases where Place is identical. In Sudanese Arabic, for example, a stop becomes a continuant before a continuant, but only when the consonants have the same place of articulation, as in (23). (Data are from Kenstowicz, 1989, in turn from Hamid, 1984. See these sources for additional data.)

(29) a. *kitaab*   'book'
          kitaaf faṭḥi   'Fathi's book'
          kitaap samiir   'Samiir's book'
          kitaap šariif   'Shariif's book'
          kitaap xaalid   'Xaalid's book'
          kitaap ḥasan   'Hasan's book'
      b. *bit*   'girl'
          bit fariid   'Fariid's girl'
          bis saamya   'Saamya's girl'
          ʔal-biš šaafat   'the girl saw'
          bid ɣariiba   'strange girl'

In addition, continuancy can spread only when two segments are identical in terms of SV structure. This can be seen in Ponapean, where continuancy spreads from an onset to a rhyme when the consonants have the same SV structure, as in (30), from Rehg and Sohl (1981:57).

(30)   *nan-rek → narrek*   'season of plenty'

In this form, the adjacent consonants /n/ and /r/ both have a bare SV Node, as in the representations in (14). Here continuancy can spread. In a form where the first consonant has a SV Node and the second does not, continuancy is not allowed to spread, as in (31).

(31)   *sin-sinom → sinsinom*   'sink in' (reduplicated form)
              *sirsinom

If continuancy spread in (31), the ungrammatical form *[sirsinom] might be expected since /r/ is a continuant sonorant.

The generalization can be drawn that dependents of the SV Node can spread only when Place is identical, and continuancy can spread only when both Place and SV structure are shared. To offer a preliminary explanation for this observation, we turn to a proposal made by Selkirk (forthcoming). Selkirk suggests, based on Mester (1986), that feature structure can be viewed as encoding domination and sisterhood relations that obtain between features. When a feature H immediately dominates a feature F, H and F are in a dependency relationship, where H is the head and F the dependent. This is illustrated in (32), from Selkirk (forthcoming), in turn based on Mester (1986).

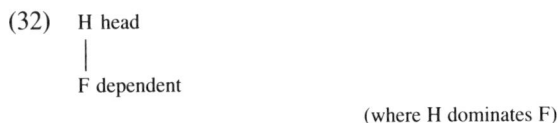

(32)   H head
       |
       F dependent
                                        (where H dominates F)

For instance, the Place Node is a head and the articulator nodes are dependents; SV is a head with Lateral as a dependent.

Selkirk extends the notion of head-dependent relationships beyond these organizing node–content node relationships, arguing that the Place Node is a dependent of Continuant. We accept this proposal and further propose that SV also enters into the head-dependent relationships with the Place Node and continuancy.

(33)   SV is a head for Place. Continuancy is a head for SV and for Place.

We have thus far been agnostic as to the status of continuancy as representing organizing- or content-type structure. We suggest that Continuant is a content node that is dominated by an organizing node, one that we call Air Flow (AF). Given this view of continuancy, the organizing structure of a segment has Place as a dependent of all organizing structure and SV as a dependent of AF. The organizing structure of a segment thus has internal headedness relationships, as in (34).

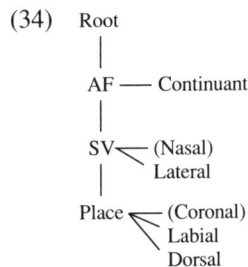

(34)   Root
       |
       AF —— Continuant
       |
       SV⟨— (Nasal)
       | Lateral
       Place ⟨— (Coronal)
              Labial
              Dorsal

In this structure SV and Place are both dependents of AF, and Place is a dependent of the SV Node.

Selkirk proposes that head-dependent relations constrain representations: Linked dependents must share a head. We state the head-dependent constraint differently, in essentially the opposite way from Selkirk.

(35)   HEAD-DEPENDENT CONSTRAINT (HDC)
       For daughters of heads to be linked, dependents must have identical structure.

The HDC allows continuancy to spread only if there is identity at both the SV Node and the Place Node, and it allows SV dependents to spread only if there is identity at Place. In the case of nasal–lateral sequences, HDC allows the SV Node, a head, to be a target for spreading only under identity of Place, the dependent. It thus allows spreading of Lateral, a daughter of the SV Node, in *n-l* since the structure of Place is the same. In *m-l*, on the other hand, Lateral cannot spread since the dependent, Place, is not identical. This is illustrated in (36), where the AF Node is omitted.

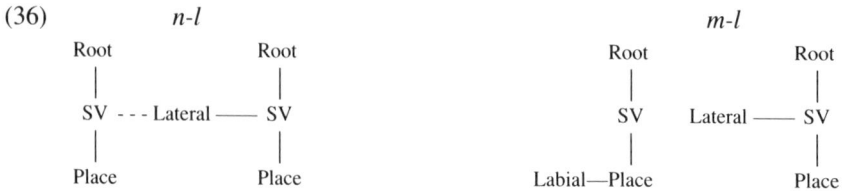

(36)   *n-l*   *m-l*

```
    Root            Root                        Root             Root
     |               |                           |                |
    SV - - - Lateral ─── SV                      SV   Lateral ─── SV
     |               |                           |                |
   Place           Place                  Labial—Place          Place
```

In Sudanese Arabic, continuancy can spread in *p-f* since Place (Labial) is shared. It cannot spread in *p-s,* where Place is distinct. This is shown in (37).

(37)   *p-f*   *p-s*

```
    Root            Root                        Root             Root
     |               |                           |                |
    AF - - - Continuant ─── AF                   AF   Continuant ─── AF
     |               |                           |                |
   Place ─── Labial ─── Place            Labial—Place           Place
```

Finally, the spreading of continuancy in the Ponapean *n-s* case is blocked since these segments do not both have SV Nodes.

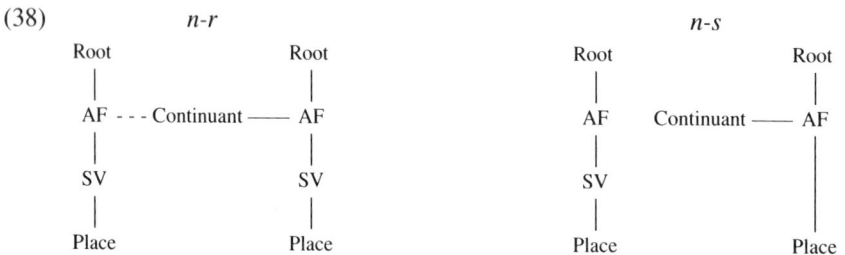

(38)   *n-r*   *n-s*

```
    Root            Root                        Root             Root
     |               |                           |                |
    AF - - - Continuant ─── AF                   AF   Continuant ─── AF
     |               |                           |                |
    SV              SV                           SV               |
     |               |                           |                |
   Place           Place                       Place            Place
```

While the HDC works to constrain spreading, it says nothing about copying. It is our contention that copying produces new organizing structure and is constrained by sonority conditions rather than by the HDC.

The HDC may serve as a constraint on the statement of rules, allowing spreading to be stated only on the highest node affected. For instance, in languages such as Ponapean, Sudanese Arabic, and Korean, where continuancy can spread, it may be enough simply to state this; it follows automatically that SV and Place dependents spread. Constraints such as identity of place could be eliminated from rules, as they would follow from a more general constraint on representations. We leave the exploration of these consequences for further work.

5. CONCLUSION

We have argued for a revision of the feature geometry, namely, the addition of a node that organizes the sonorant features Nasal and Lateral. This analysis is based on the observation that these features group together in spreading, delinking, and copying. While laterals have coronal properties phonologically, we suggest that this is not a result of Lateral being a dependent of Coronal but instead follows from a structural constraint, the structural complexity constraint. Given the SCC, laterals can only be coronal because Coronal is the unmarked articulation. The SCC is supplemented by the head-dependent constraint, which prohibits spreading to SV unless the segments involved are identical in place of articulation. The implications of these proposals require further study, but both the SCC and the HDC seem to be otherwise motivated and thus provide a direction for further research.

ACKNOWLEDGMENTS

We thank the editors, Carole Paradis and Jean-François Prunet, Moira Yip, Glyne Piggott, Elan Dresher, and Tom Wilson for helpful comments. We accept sole responsibility for any errors.

NOTES

[1] This is true only of English level 1. See Rice and Avery (1989).

[2] Ponapean shows a wider range of assimilations within sonorants than we discuss. The assimilations are consistent with the theory proposed here, but a detailed analysis would take us beyond the scope of this article. See Rice and Avery (in preparation) for discussion.

[3] There is a clear connection between the loss of the glottal stop and desonorantization. Both the sequence [ʔ-l] and the single segment [t] occur in Yagaria; [ʔ-t] is not found. This suggests a connection between loss of the glottal stop and desonorantization since the obstruent occurs only when the glottal stop is absent. We have not attempted to capture this connection in our description of Yagaria.

[4] We do not attempt to deal with the problem of why /y/ alternates with /g/ rather than /k/, and why /m/ alternates with /b/ rather than with /p/.

[5] There is a second form in Sanskrit, where assimilation is simply to voicing and not to nasality or laterality. See Rice and Avery (1989) for details.

[6] Under the proposal of Rice and Avery (1989), Nasal is present underlyingly in Sanskrit. The presence or absence of Nasal in the representation of nasal consonants has no effect on the analysis offered here.

[7] A caveat is necessary. As discussed in Section 1, Avery and Rice (1989) propose that while Coronal is generally absent in the underlying representation of languages, if there are segments that contrast only with respect to a Coronal dependent, Coronal must be present underlyingly. In just such a case, Lateral can occur with a dependent of Place.

[8] We ignore the representation of laterals in languages that have coronal contrasts for stops and laterals.

[9] See Levin's (1988) discussion on Biscayan Basque. She argues that in Basque the lateral assimilates to a following coronal, but not to other places of articulation, as expected if Lateral is a Coronal dependent. She implies that a system such as Catalan is not possible. We have not examined the phonetics of the Basque data and thus do not know if these data are a real counterexample to our proposal.

[10] English appears to offer similar facts. The actual articulation of the laterals in the following words is dependent on the place of articulation of the word-final consonant.

(i)   *well, whelp, welt, welch, whelk*

The lateral clearly assimilates to the place of articulation of a following nonlabial. Even with the labial, the articulation of the lateral seems to be quite far forward. The SCC predicts that such assimilations might be found, whereas the structural dependency and constraint hypotheses do not.

[11] Shaw (1988a,b) argues on grounds of transparency to a consonant harmony process that Lateral cannot be a Coronal dependent in Tahltan, an Athapaskan language. In Athapaskan languages in general, unlike the languages discussed in this article, the laterals function as continuants within the system rather than as sonorants (see, e.g., Krauss and Leer, 1981). For these languages, Lateral (or whatever the relevant feature of laterals turns out to be) is not to be regarded as a SV dependent.

REFERENCES

Anderson, J. and C. Ewen (1987) *Principles of Dependency Phonology*, Cambridge University Press, Cambridge, England.

Archangeli, D. (1984) *Underspecification in Yawelmani Phonology and Morphology*, Doctoral dissertation, MIT, Cambridge, Massachusetts.

Archangeli, D. (1988) "Aspects of Underspecification Theory," *Phonology* 5.2, 183–207.

Archangeli, D. and D. Pulleyblank (1986) *The Content and Structure of Phonological Representations*, ms., University of Arizona, Tucson, and University of Southern California, Los Angeles.

Avery, P. and K. Rice. (1989) "Segment Structure and Coronal Underspecification," *Phonology* 6.2, 179–200.

Barker, M. (1964) *Klamath Grammar,* University of California Press, Berkeley.

Borowsky, T. (1986) *Topics in English Phonology,* Doctoral dissertation, University of Massachusetts, Amherst.

Catford, J. C. (1977) *Fundamental Problems in Phonetics,* Indiana University Press, Bloomington.

Cho, S.-B. (1967) *A Phonological Study of Korean,* Almqvist & Wiksell, Stockholm.

Cho, Y.-M. (1988) "Korean Assimilation," *Proceedings of WCCFL* 7, 41–52.

Clements, G. N. (1985) "The Geometry of Phonological Features," *Phonology Yearbook* 2, 223–250.

Clements, G. N. (1988a) "The Role of the Sonority Cycle in Core Syllabification," *Working Papers of the Cornell Phonetics Laboratory,* No. 2, 1–68.

Clements, G. N. (1988b) "Towards a Substantive Theory of Feature Specification," *Proceedings of NELS* 18.1, 79–93.

Hamid, Abdul-Halim (1984) *A Descriptive Analysis of Sudanese Colloquial Arabic,* Doctoral dissertation, University of Illinois, Urbana.

Hayes, B. (1986) "Assimilation as Spreading in Toba Batak," *Linguistic Inquiry* 17, 467–500.

Hooper, J. B. (1976) *An Introduction to Natural Generative Phonology,* Academic Press, New York.

Iverson, G. and K.-H. Kim (1987) "Underspecification and Hierarchical Feature Representation in Korean Consonantal Phonology," *Proceedings of CLS* 23, 182–198.

Kaye, J. D., J. Lowenstamm, and J.-R. Vergnaud (1990) "Constituent Structure and Government in Phonology," *Phonology* 7.2.

Kean, M. L. (1975) *The Theory of Markedness in Generative Grammar,* Doctoral dissertation, MIT, Cambridge, Massachusetts.

Kenstowicz, M. (1989) "Comments on 'The Structure of (Complex) Consonants' by Harry van der Hulst and Norval Smith," Paper presented at the MIT Conference on Feature and Underspecification Theories, MIT, Cambridge, Massachusetts.

Kiparsky, P. (1982) "Lexical Morphology and Phonology," in I.-S. Yang, ed., *Linguistics in the Morning Calm,* pp. 3–91. Hanshin, Seoul, Korea.

Kiparsky, P. (1985) "Some Consequences of Lexical Phonology," *Phonology Yearbook* 2, 85–138.

Krauss, M. and J. Leer (1981) *Athabaskan, Eyak, and Tlingit Sonorants,* Alaska Native Language Center Research Papers, No. 5, Alaska Native Language Center, Fairbanks.

Levin, J. (1988) "A Place for Lateral in the Feature Geometry," ms., University of Texas, Austin.

Lynch, J. (1983) "On the Kuman 'Liquids'," *Languages and Linguistics in Melanesia* 14(1–2), 98–112.

Maddieson, I. (1984) *Patterns of Sounds,* Cambridge Studies in Speech Science, and Communication, Cambridge University Press, Cambridge, England.

Mascaró, J. (1976) *Catalan Phonology and the Phonological Cycle,* Doctoral dissertation, MIT, Cambridge, Massachusetts.

Mascaró, J. (1987) "A Reduction and Spreading Theory of Voicing and other Sound Effects," ms., Universitat Autonoma de Barcelona, Barcelona, Spain.

McCarthy, J. (1988) "Feature Geometry and Dependency," *Phonetica* 43, 84–108.

Mester, R.-A. (1986) *Studies in Tier Structure,* Doctoral dissertation, University of Massachusetts, Amherst.

Murray, R. and T. Vennemann (1983) "Sound Change and Syllable Structure in Germanic Phonology," *Language* 59, 514–528.

Paradis, C. and J.-F. Prunet (1989) "On Coronal Transparency," *Phonology* 6.2, 317–348.

Paradis, C. and J.-F. Prunet (1990) "On Explaining Some OCP Violations," *Linguistic Inquiry* 21.3, 456–466.

Piggott, G. (1989) "Variability in Feature Dependency," ms., McGill University, Montreal.

Pulleyblank, D. (1988). "Underspecification, the Feature Hierarchy, and Tiv Vowels," *Phonology* 5.2, 299–326.

Rehg, K. L. and D. G. Sohl (1981) *Ponapean Reference Grammar,* University Press of Hawaii, Honolulu.

Renck, G. L. (1967) "A Tentative Statement of the Phonemes of Yagaria," *Pacific Linguistics* A-12, 19–48.

Renck, G. L. (1975) "A Grammar of Yagaria," *Pacific Linguistics* B-40.

Rice, K. (1990) "Blocking Effects in a Theory of Privative Features," ms., University of Toronto.

Rice, K. and P. Avery (1989) "On the Interaction between Sonorancy and Voicing," *Toronto Working Papers in Linguistics* 10, 65–82.

Rice, K. and P. Avery (in preparation) *Ponapean Assimilations,* University of Toronto.

Sagey, E. (1986) *The Representations of Features and Relations in Nonlinear Phonology,* Doctoral dissertation, MIT, Cambridge, Massachusetts.

Schein, B. and D. Steriade (1986) "On Geminates," *Linguistic Inquiry* 17, 691–744.

Selkirk, E. O. (forthcoming) "A Two-Root Theory of Length," *University of Massachusetts Occasional Papers in Linguistics.*

Shaw, P. (1988a) "Feature Geometry and Coronality," Paper presented at the annual meeting of the Canadian Linguistic Association, University of Windsor.

Shaw, P. (1988b) "On the Phonological Representation of Laterals and Affricates," Paper presented at the annual meeting of the Linguistic Society of America, New Orleans, Louisiana.

Steriade, D. (1987) "Redundant Values," *Proceedings of CLS* 23, 339–362.

Trommelen, M. (1984) *The Syllable in Dutch,* Foris Publications, Dordrecht.

van der Hulst, H. (1989) "Atoms of Segmental Structure: Components, Gestures, and Dependency," *Phonology* 6.2, 253–284.

Whitney, W. D. (1889) *Sanskrit Grammar,* Harvard University Press, Cambridge, Massachusetts.

CONSONANT HARMONY SYSTEMS: THE SPECIAL STATUS OF CORONAL HARMONY

PATRICIA A. SHAW

Department of Linguistics
University of British Columbia
Vancouver, British Columbia V6T 1W5, Canada

1. INTRODUCTION

Whereas a long-standing body of research has contributed substantially to our understanding of vowel harmony systems, significantly less is known about consonant harmony systems. Consonant harmony is here defined as phonological assimilation or dissimilation between consonants that are not necessarily adjacent in the surface phonological string and where, crucially, other intervening vocalic or consonant segments do not interact with the harmony in any way. Such cases entailing "action-at-a-distance" present a rich body of data relevant to testing a number of current hypotheses regarding constraints on phonological representation and rule-governed behavior. From the present research on consonant harmony systems, three fundamental questions emerge which one must ask of a theory of phonology that aims toward explanatory adequacy.

The first question concerns the seeming rarity of consonant harmony compared to vowel harmony. Is this a fortuitous and arbitrary fact, or does this follow from a principled conception of phonological organization and interaction?

The second question derives from a striking asymmetry in the kinds of consonant harmony found cross-linguistically. Specifically, considering possible harmony patterns across each of the four major places of articulation, why is it that coronal harmony is so much more frequently attested than any of the others? Labial harmony is at best rare, while dorsal and pharyngeal harmony are, according

125

Phonetics and Phonology, Volume 2
The Special Status of Coronals

to the present survey, nonexistent. This observed generalization thus reiterates the fundamental question addressed by this volume: Why, in harmony processes as well as in the broad range of other phonological phenomena investigated in this book, do coronals once again stand out as having "special status"?

The third and final question pertains to another curious behavioral asymmetry that characterizes these coronal harmony processes. Specifically, why do coronal harmony systems typically involve only a subset of the coronal segments in a language and systematically ignore other coronal segments?

It is argued here that the observed cross-linguistic properties underlying the above questions follow as logical consequences of three interacting hypotheses about phonological representation and interaction. First, the internal structure of phonological segments postulated in the hierarchically organized model of feature geometry embodies restrictive claims regarding what features and groups of features may function as constituents in phonological processes. Two particular claims receive strong empirical support here. One claim is that the feature [lateral] is not dominated by the Coronal articulator but rather must hang higher in the tree. The unmarked coronal articulation of laterals may then be linked to the unmarked status of coronals in general. A second claim is that the place features of both vowels and consonants are represented by a single, uniform set of articulator nodes. From this follows the answer to the second major question raised above. That is, the observed frequency of coronal harmony (and, as a corollary, the absence or rarity of consonant harmonies involving the other places of articulation) is explained by the fact that the coronal features ([anterior], [strident], [distributed]) function exclusively to define distinctive consonant articulation. Because these features never function to define vowel properties, coronal consonant harmony can propagate uninterrupted by intervening vowel specification. In contrast, because each of the other articulators may define *both* vowel and consonant articulation, consonant harmony cannot occur between these places of articulation to the exclusion of intervening vowels.

The second major hypothesis contributing to an explanation of the properties of consonant harmony systems derives from underspecification theory. The claim that certain aspects of phonological structure are not overtly specified in lexical representation imposes a severe constraint on what features of the melodic form are a priori available to participate in harmonic interaction. In answer to the third question above of why only a subset of the coronal inventory of a language characteristically participates in a harmony process, it is here argued that this is a direct consequence of the fact that those coronals that do not require distinctive specification in terms of a subcoronal feature will be unspecified for a Coronal articulator node. This research on harmony processes thus provides further support for the conclusion reached on independent grounds by several other research initiatives in the present volume: The articulator node for coronals is, under systematic and predictable conditions, underspecified in underlying representation.

The third major hypothesis is that these two subtheories of phonological representation (hierarchical feature organization and underspecification) interact with postulated locality conditions on rule application. Accepting the restrictive hypothesis that harmonic interaction between segments that are not strictly adjacent in the phonological string can only occur if both trigger and target are adjacent on the relevant autosegmental tier, it is here argued that the relative rarity of consonant harmony compared with vowel harmony derives from inherent restrictions on tier scansion possibilities. That is, drawing on Archangeli and Pulleyblank's (1987a) characterization of a maximal–minimal scansion parameter, it is shown that pure consonant harmony is necessarily restricted to minimal scansion. A further conclusion, based on the present analysis of the rich coronal harmony system of Tahltan, is that Archangeli and Pulleyblank's definition of minimal scansion requires reinterpretation.

Thus, the basic thrust of this research is to demonstrate the considerable explanatory power that results from the combined interaction of these three sets of hypotheses—hierarchical feature organization, underspecification, and locality conditions—in constraining the possible properties of consonant harmony in ways that receive strong empirical support from attested systems.

The remainder of the paper is organized as follows. Section 2 presents a survey of attested cases of consonant harmony, this substantiating the existence of certain striking typological asymmetries. Section 3 explicates two specific tenets of the assumed theoretical framework: the feature geometry model and the formal characterization of locality conditions. Section 4 illustrates how these hypotheses define a restrictive typology of possible harmonies, with specific reference to cases of vowel harmony, vowel–consonant harmony, and laryngeal harmony. Section 5 examines place-of-articulation harmony between consonants, focusing on the question of why coronal harmony is so predominant. Section 6 reviews the relatively familiar case of coronal harmony in Chumash, providing a context for the discussion of critical issues regarding underspecification and segment transparency. Section 7 presents a detailed analysis of coronal harmony in Tahltan, where the behavior of the five independent series of coronals provides significant insights into the appropriate representation of coronal articulations within the feature geometry model and into the function of locality constraints. Section 8 provides a summary of the conclusions reached and discusses their implications for future research.

2. CROSS-LINGUISTIC SURVEY OF CONSONANT HARMONY

The following survey of documented cases of consonant harmony aims to provide a broadly representative sample. In addition to the major articulatory subclassification that structures the present taxonomy, some other relevant, defining characteristics merit clarification. On the assumption that dissimilation is governed by identical constraints on tier scansion, feature specification, etc., "harmony" is here taken to embrace both assimilatory and dissimilatory processes. To qualify as consonant harmony, the process must entail action-at-a-distance, that is, across intervening classes of segments that do not participate. Therefore, for example, the pharyngealization triggered by Chilcotin "flat" consonants (e.g., Cook, 1987) does not qualify since it propagates on a strictly string-adjacent basis, thus affecting intervening vowels as well.

Further, under the assumption that different kinds of harmonies may be subject to different constraints, the following compendium differentiates three kinds of harmonies. Following Cole (1987), a distinction is made between morphological harmony (MH), where the harmony instantiates or signifies a particular morpheme (e.g., the glottalization that spreads to all resonants within the word domain to mark diminutive in the Salish languages referenced below), and phonological harmony (PH), where the harmony is a well-defined phonological process of the language (e.g., Tahltan coronal harmony). This distinction is very relevant, for Cole (1987) argues that the morphemic tier hypothesis allows certain MH processes to apply throughout a domain without being blocked by phonological specification. Given Cole's conclusion that MH is not necessarily subject to the same constraints on phonological specification and scansion as is PH, the present article has aimed instead to define the more restrictive and predictive set of constraints that pertain to PH processes. A third harmony type, morpheme structure constraints (MSCs), is also differentiated in the taxonomy, although the assumption made here, on the basis of the Tahltan data discussed below and the argumentation in Davis (this volume), is that harmonic MSCs are subject to the same constraints as PH rules. Indeed, many PH rules also function as MSCs; the properties of these two subclasses constitute the focus of the present analysis.

(1)   Consonant Harmony Typology

     a. Laryngeal Harmony
        PH: Grassman's Law in Indo-European (e.g, Steriade, 1982)
        PH: Grassman's Law in Salish (Thompson and Thompson, 1985)
        PH: Rendaku/Lyman's Law in Japanese (Itô and Mester, 1986)
        PH: Dahl's Law in Kikuyu (Davy and Nurse, 1982; D. Pulleyblank, 1986)
        MH: Salish diminutive glottalization (e.g., Reichard, 1938; Mattina, 1973; Hukari, 1981; Cole, 1987)
        MH: Nisgha ʔ-spread (Shaw, Bagemihl, and Walsh, 1989)

     b. Place Harmony
     Coronal harmony
        PH: Chumash sibilant harmony (e.g., Beeler, 1970; Applegate, 1972; Harrington, 1974)
        PH: Sanskrit *n*-retroflexion (e.g., Schein and Steriade, 1986)
        PH: Wiyot coronal harmony (Teeter, 1964)

PH: Quechua sibilant harmony (Mannheim, 1988)
PH: Harari dental palatalization (Leslau, 1958; Halefom, 1988)
PH: Kinyarwanda sibilant fricative harmony (Kimenyi, 1979)
PH: Navaho sibilant harmony (Sapir and Hoijer, 1967; Kari, 1976)
PH: Tahltan coronal harmony (Shaw, 1989)
PH: Latin *l-r* dissimilation
MSC: English (e.g., Davis, this volume)
Labial harmony
    MSC: Arabic (Greenberg, 1950; McCarthy, 1988)
    MSC: Chinese (Yip, 1988)
    MH: Chaha labialization (Leslau, 1966; McCarthy, 1983)
    PH: not attested
Dorsal harmony
    PH: not attested
    MSC: not attested
Pharyngeal harmony
    PH: not attested
    MSC: not attested

Although this survey is by no means exhaustive, the documented asymmetry in the types of consonant harmony that exist cross-linguistically is striking. Only two common classes occur: laryngeal harmony and coronal harmony. Why? The present thesis is that this observed asymmetry is not fortuitous or arbitrary but rather follows from a principled and constrained conception of phonological representation and interaction.

3. THEORETICAL FRAMEWORK

Two of the theoretical components that prove to have considerable explanatory power in addressing the questions here advanced are (1) a hierarchical model of feature organization and (2) postulated constraints on locality conditions governing phonological interaction. The basic tenets of each of these are clarified below.

3.1. Feature Organization

It is here claimed that there is a crucial interdependence of current postulates regarding phonological representation and a typology of possible harmony processes. Consider, therefore, the formal structure of the proposed hierarchy of feature organization. Although further research will contribute to a more precise characterization of certain components of the feature hierarchy, the following model combines several independently substantiated claims regarding the content and locus of particular nodes and features (see Clements, 1985; Sagey, 1986; Archangeli and Pulleyblank, 1986; Piggott, 1987; McCarthy, 1988, 1989; Shaw, 1989): [1]

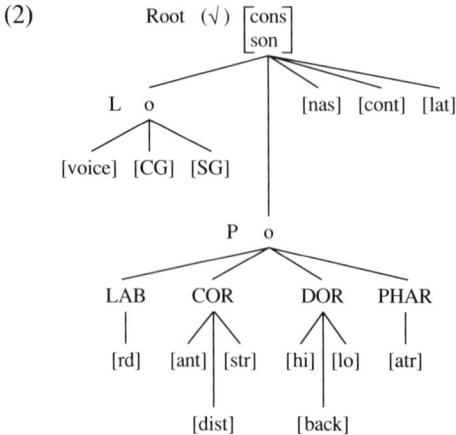

(2)   Root (√) [cons]
                        [son]

        L   o   [nas] [cont] [lat]

    [voice] [CG] [SG]

                         P   o

        LAB   COR   DOR   PHAR

         | /\   /\ |
        [rd] [ant] [str] [hi] [lo] [atr]

              [dist]   [back]

Some controversial claims regarding the appropriate organization of specific features and node dominance relations merit comment. First, the locus of the feature [lateral] as a dependent of the Root Node rather than the Coronal articulator node is argued for in Section 6 below.

A second substantive area of controversy involves the postulated representation of the articulator nodes. The model here maintains the traditional position of Sagey (1986) of three major articulators—Labial, Coronal, and Dorsal—supplemented by recent proposals (McCarthy, 1988; Clements, 1989) that there is a fourth articulator node, Pharyngeal. [2] Note that these Articulator Nodes are here assumed to be privative (following Halle, 1986; Sagey, 1986), with only the plus values being specifiable. Thus, if an articulator is not actively involved in the production of a sound, it will not be specified at any level of representation. This embodies the claim (contrary, for example, to Christdas, 1988) that specifications such as [−coronal] or [−labial] do not characterize possible natural classes of sounds, and that phonological processes can only make reference to classes definable in terms of the positive specification of these nodes. A second significant empirical claim encoded in this proposed organization is what may be called the "integrated articulators" hypothesis, that is, the hypothesis that both consonant and vowel articulations are defined by the same Articulator Nodes and features. This position contrasts, for example, with various interpretations of what I call a "segregated articulators" hypothesis. For example, Steriade (1987a) proposes an independent Velar Node for consonant articulation in addition to a Dorsal Node for vowel articulation, although the other articulators are shared by both consonants and vowels. Even more representative of the segregated articulators position is Clements (1989), who proposes that all four primary articulators are independently available for consonants and vowels under separate superordinate

Consonant-Place and Vowel-Place Nodes. It is here argued that not only is the integrated articulators hypothesis preferable on a priori grounds, as it is inherently more restrictive, but also the explanatory power that it contributes to an understanding of the restrictive typology of consonant harmony systems must be taken as significant empirical support.[3]

3.2. Locality Conditions and Adjacency

The theory of autosegmental phonology allows for an insightful characterization of locality constraints such that adjacency is defined relative to the specific tier of the autosegmentalized representation that is relevant to the process under consideration. This allows, therefore, that two segments /A/ and /D/ that are not themselves adjacent in the phonological string /ABCD/ may nonetheless have subcomponents of melodic structure, such as [F], that are adjacent on their respective autosegmental tier:

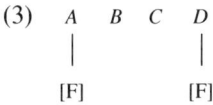

(3)   A   B   C   D
      | |
     [F]   [F]

The autosegmental tier hypothesis thus underlies a very restrictive formalization of locality conditions on segmental or subsegmental interaction as being constrained by a requirement of strict adjacency (cf. Archangeli and Pulleyblank, 1987a; Steriade, 1987a):

(4)   STRICT ADJACENCY
      The target of a phonological operation must be adjacent to the trigger on the relevant autosegmental tier.

Archangeli and Pulleyblank (1987a) claim further that the notion of "relevant" tier is restricted to two possibilities, which they define in terms of a minimal–maximal scansion parameter:

(5)   SCANSION PARAMETER (Archangeli and Pulleyblank, 1987a: 21, 25)
      Maximal Scansion: A rule whose target is node or feature α scans the highest level of syllabic structure providing access to α.
      Minimal Scansion: A rule whose target is node or feature α scans the tier containing α.

Consider the implications of these hypotheses for a theory of possible harmony processes. Under the assumption that all phonological rules are constrained to apply under conditions of strict adjacency, the seeming contradiction that harmony processes apply at a distance, that is, to nonadjacent segments, is explained by the autosegmental tier hypothesis. Thus, the claim is that if two nonadjacent segments are participating in a harmony process, then they must have distinctive melodic specification that is adjacent on the autosegmental tier that is crucially relevant to defining the trigger–target conditions of the harmony.

Given the well-defined predictive content of this theoretical framework, consonant harmony processes can reveal very significant aspects of the specified (and underspecified) content of phonological representation.

4. HARMONY SYSTEMS AND THE SCANSION PARAMETER

How these combined hypotheses apply to define a restrictive typology of possible harmony systems can now be illustrated. Cases of vowel harmony, vowel–consonant harmony, and laryngeal harmony are each considered, prior to the cases of consonant-place harmony.

4.1. Vowel Harmony

The familiar cases of vowel harmony effects, which ignore intervening consonants (including dorsals), are described as cases of maximal scansion where the vowel nuclei (heads) of contiguous syllables are strictly adjacent on their tier. Consider, for example, the operation of back harmony in Turkish where, following Archangeli and Pulleyblank's (1987a) analysis, an underlying form such as /ayak+ten/ 'foot (ablative)' harmonizes to [ayaktan]:

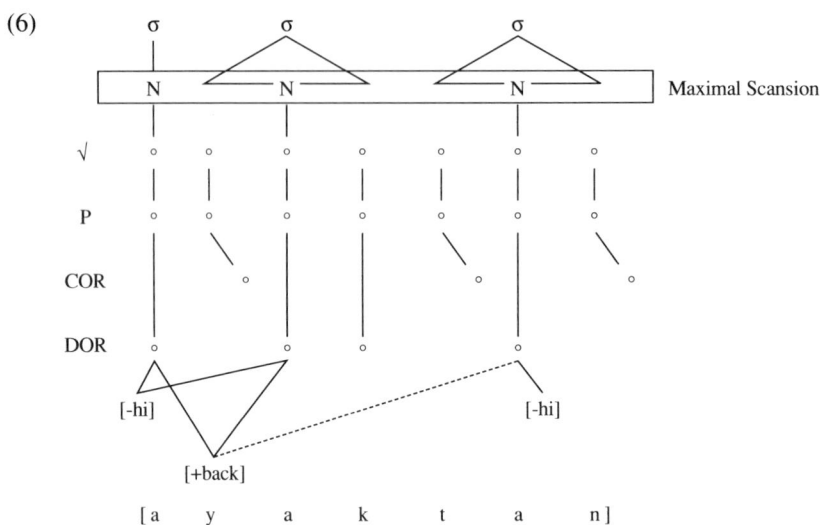

In a case such as this, the trigger /a/ and the target vowel in the suffix /-ten/ cannot meet the strict adjacency criterion at the lowest level of relevant structure, that is, the Dorsal tier, since consonants with Dorsal specification can intervene on this tier, yet they do not function to block the harmony.[4] Consequently, adjacency must be defined at the prosodic level by maximal scansion across the syllabic nuclei (N).

4.2. Vowel–Consonant Harmony

In contrast, cases of vowel–consonant harmony where the harmonic effect may skip over intervening "irrelevant" consonants can be accounted for in terms of minimal scansion. Consider, for example, the following Turkish data (from Clements and Sezer, 1982:234) where the velar consonants /k g/ are seen in (7a) to assimilate to the [−back] value of a tautosyllabic vowel, becoming palatal [ḵ g̱]. The important fact in these data is that nonvelar consonants, such as /r n/, may intervene without blocking or being affected by the harmonic spread.[5]

(7)　a.　*sirḵ*　　'circus'　　　　　　　*denḵ*　'equal'
　　　　　ḵürḵ　　'fur'
　　b.　*fark*　　'difference'　　　　　*kirk*　'forty'
　　　　　zamk　　'glue'　　　　　　　　*burk*　'sprain'
　　c.　*haḵi:kat*　'truth'　　　　　　　*diḵkat*　'attention'

The forms in (7b) illustrate the regular velar realization in the nonharmonic context of central and back vowels, and the data in (7c) show the domain of spread to be limited to tautosyllabic segments. The fact that this harmony in Turkish targets tautosyllabic velars across other (nonvelar) consonants can be explained by hypothesizing that the harmonic spread of [−back] is scanning the Dorsal tier, that is, the tier that immediately dominates the trigger feature [−back] and that uniquely identifies the appropriate targets. Because /r/ and /n/ have no Dorsal specification, they are transparent to the spread, as shown below (features noncritical to the point at hand are not specified here):

(8)

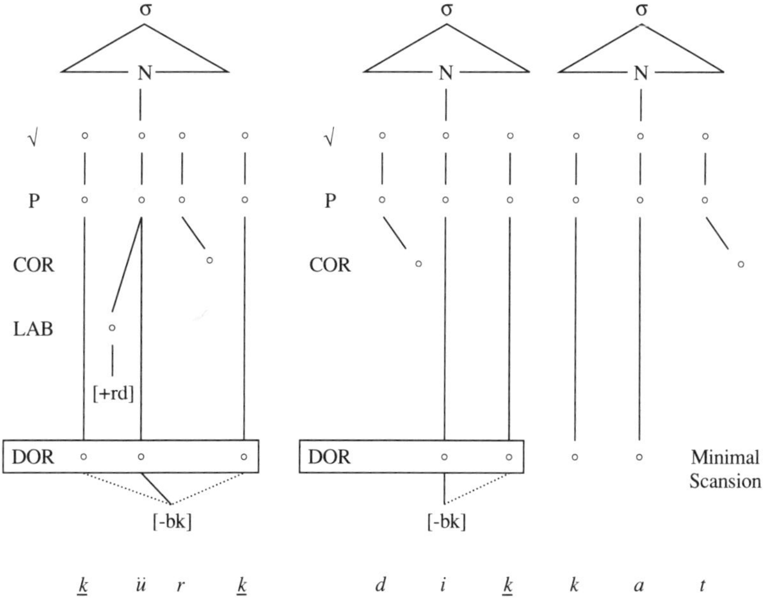

Note that strict adjacency is necessarily defined in terms of minimal scansion in this case, for in [kürk] the trigger /ü/ and the final consonant /k/ are not adjacent at any other level of structure. Parenthetically, this example serves to establish another important observation: The fact that the harmony process here is restricted to tautosyllabic velars shows that the specification of the domain of rule application (here, the σ-domain) must be independent of the specification of the level of rule scansion for locality (here, minimal scansion along the Dorsal tier).

4.3. Laryngeal Harmony

Given this discussion of locality conditions and the role of the proposed distinction in maximal–minimal scansion in defining adjacency, we can now turn to an examination of how well these hypotheses characterize the attested classes of consonant harmony. As already noted from the cross-linguistic survey in (1) above, laryngeals comprise one of the two major subclasses of sounds that commonly participate in consonant harmony. From the perspective of current feature geometry theory and underspecification theory, it is highly significant that there is a relatively substantial set of consonant harmony processes involving the features [voice], [constricted glottis], and [spread glottis], since on the basis of independent phonological processes, such as debuccalization (Clements, 1985; McCarthy, 1988) and translaryngeal vowel harmony (Steriade, 1987a), these laryngeal features are well recognized as a class of features that have the potential to behave independently of other melodic features. This observed autonomy is well accounted for by the postulation of the independent Laryngeal Node in the feature hierarchy model in (2) above. Given this broad base of evidence that laryngeal features are defined on their own tier, it is not surprising that natural languages exhibit such a broad range of laryngeal harmonies; rather, this is in fact predicted by the model. Moreover, the particular properties of possible laryngeal harmonies are severely constrained in ways that directly match attested systems. First, the identification of appropriate triggers and targets for spreading or delinking must be confined to strictly adjacent, specified segments on this tier. Second, under the assumption of underspecification theory that only those segments that are phonologically distinctive or contrastive for laryngeal articulation will in fact bear overt Laryngeal feature specification, it follows that those consonants that are distinctively specified for [voice], [spread glottis], or [constricted glottis] can interact only with each other. Furthermore, this interaction can occur not only across vowels but also across sonorant consonants, since both these latter classes of sounds are, in the unmarked case, entirely predictable with respect to laryngeal articulation and therefore have no distinctive Laryngeal feature specification.

By way of exemplification, consider briefly the Japanese restriction, commonly referred to as Lyman's Law (see Itô and Mester, 1986), which prohibits the rule of Rendaku [+voice] specification from voicing the initial obstruent of the second member of a compound if that lexical stem already contains a voiced obstruent elsewhere in the string. Thus, compare the forms in (9a), which undergo Rendaku, with the forms in (9b), where the expected application of Rendaku is blocked by the presence of a distinctively voiced segment further on in the string (data from Itô and Mester, 1986:55):

(9)   a.   Forms showing Rendaku   b.   Forms showing Lyman's Law

      nuri-futa   'lacquered lid'   *nuri-fuda*   'lacquered
      [nuributa]   *[nuribuda]   sign'

      oharai-kuši   'purification   oharai-kuji   'purification
      [oharaiguši]   comb'   *[oharaiguji]   ticket'

      taikutsu-haraši   'boredom-   *taikutsu-šinogi*   'boredom-
      [taikutsubaraši]   dispel'   *[taikutsujinogi]   endure'

As Itô and Mester argue, the nonlocal behavior of Lyman's Law constitutes strong motivation for two of the hypothesized aspects of phonological representation. First, voicing must be represented on an independent autosegmental tier, given that the introduction of the Rendaku [+voice] specification is sensitive to the presence of any other [+voice] specification already present on that tier. Second, the fact that Rendaku is blocked only by voiced obstruents, but not by voiced resonants (cf. /iro-kami/ → [irogami] 'colored paper', /asa-kiri/ → [asagiri] 'morning mist'), is a direct consequence of the claim of underspecification theory that it is only the distinctive [+voice] specification on obstruents that is present in lexical phonological representation, since the [+voice] value of sonorants (and the [−voice] value of obstruents) is predictable and therefore filled in only later in the derivation by redundancy rules. The essential aspects of this analysis are illustrated in the partial representation of the form [taikutsu-šinogi] 'boredom-endure' given below, showing the effect of Lyman's Law in prohibiting two adjacent specifications of [+voice] within the domain of the second member of the compound:

(10)

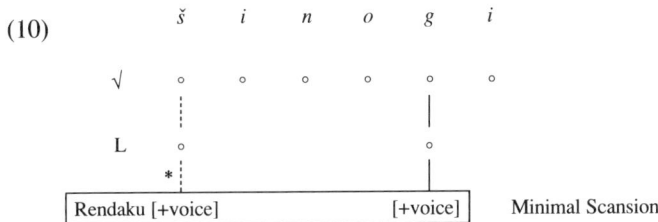

4.4. Toward an Explanatory Theory of Consonant Harmony

Let us consider the further implications of the hypotheses discussed thus far. Archangeli and Pulleyblank (1987a) present the two scansion possibilities, maximal and minimal, as a binary parameter, the setting of which must presumably be specified for each individual rule. The empirical strength of this hypothesis is its restriction against any arbitrarily selected intermediate level of representation ever being involved. Still, the available and seemingly arbitrary choice of maximal–minimal raises several deeper questions. For example, are both settings of this parametric option freely available to any kind of phonological rule? Are there broad classes of phonological rules characterizable by each scansion value? Is a change in the specified setting of the parameter (i.e., from maximal to minimal scansion, or vice versa) a possible type of diachronic language change?

The assumptions made in the present analysis of consonant harmony systems lead to a significant generalization: All consonant harmony necessarily involves minimal scansion. Note, however, that this restriction is not a stipulated constraint; rather, it is a logical consequence of the combined hypotheses adopted in this model. That is, although maximal scansion can define as adjacent vowels that are nonadjacent in the phonological string, but that are the prosodic heads of adjacent syllables, maximal scansion cannot possibly embrace non-string-adjacent consonants, for consonants are simply not represented by any unique prosodic constituency node(s) above the melodic level in any current model of subsyllabic prosodic constituency.

We have arrived then at a very narrowly constrained definition of the range of possible consonant harmony systems that can occur in natural language. First, consonant harmony is necessarily restricted to minimal scansion. Second, it can involve only features (or higher levels of structure) that are, under the constraints of a well-defined theory of underspecification, distinctively specified. The prediction, then, is straightforward: All and only those features that are uniquely or distinctively specified for consonants will define an autosegmental tier not utilized by vowels and can therefore participate in consonant harmony.

What features fall within the set that can be uniquely or distinctively specified only for consonants? The example from Lyman's Law in Japanese illustrates nicely the point that the Laryngeal features commonly undergo consonant harmony because a feature such as [+voice], although an obvious and pervasive feature of vowel articulation at the surface level, is not a specified or functional vowel feature in deeper phonological representation. A second set of possible candidates are the features [nasal], [continuant], and [lateral], postulated to hang directly from the Root Node. The feature [lateral], for example, may be defined only on consonants, as it is not a possible distinctive articulation for vowels; yet I know of no long-distance lateral harmony systems. The case of [continuant] is more like that of [voice], in that the [+continuant] value is an indisputable phonetic property of vowels, though an entirely redundant one. Given, then, that continuancy is distinctive only for consonants and given the relative frequency of [continuant] assimilation rules between string-adjacent segments, one might also expect long-range spirantization or occlusivization as possible consonant harmony processes. Again, I am not aware of any such cases. Consider, finally, [nasal]. This feature may function distinctively on consonants and/or vowels. Yet, despite the commonality of nasal harmony, I am not aware of any nasal harmony processes that target only consonants. As each of these three features is (1) available for distinctive consonant representation and (2) a terminal constituent of the tree model capable of defining its own autosegmental tier, each should in principle define a possible consonant harmony type. The apparent absence of such systems may be an accidental gap, in that the body of assumptions adopted thus far predicts their occurrence. Alternatively, it may be a systematic gap attributable to some independent principle(s) related, for example, to the possible monovalent status of [nasal] and [lateral], or to the level of scansion for processes involving these features necessarily being at the Root Node level and therefore not being able to skip across vowels. These issues await further research.

The only other possible candidates for consonant harmony are the Place articulator nodes and their dependent features. Their harmonic behavior receives close study in the following section.

5. CONSONANT HARMONY ACROSS PLACE OF ARTICULATION

As discussed in Section 3.1 above, the present analysis adopts the integrated articulators hypothesis, which claims that the behavior of consonants and vowels requires unified specification in terms of the four articulator nodes and their dependent features. Thus, the distinctive place specifications for vowels, as well as for velar consonants, are defined under the Dorsal Node. Similarly, if a vowel is distinctively [round], it will have Labial Node specification, as of course will labial and labialized consonants. Finally, the Pharyngeal Node is interpreted as involved in the distinctive specification of vowel systems where the feature [advanced tongue root] is functional, as well as of consonant systems with uvular and/or pharyngeal articulation.

An important consequence of this conception of feature organization is that the Labial, Dorsal, and Pharyngeal Node tiers are all in principle available to *both* consonant and vowel articulator specification. In contrast, however, none of the distinctive features under the Coronal Node, namely, [distributed], [anterior], and [strident], are ever relevant to the specification of vowels. That is, the Coronal Node tier is the *only* articulator node tier that is exclusively relevant to the distinctive specification of consonants. This conclusion has profound significance for a theory of possible consonant harmony processes as it offers a principled explanation for the first two questions raised in the introductory section of this article.

The first question was, Why is consonant place harmony rarer than vowel harmony? The answer is because vowel feature specifications under Labial, Dorsal, and Pharyngeal disrupt the requisite adjacency of consonant segments at the level of minimal scansion, whereas vowel harmony has recourse to the parametric setting of maximal scansion whereby it can meet the strict adjacency requirement without interference from consonant feature specification. Consequently, the relative "rareness" of consonant harmony does not require special stipulation or accommodation with markedness theory or learnability theory; rather, it is a direct and straightforward consequence of several interacting tenets of a single, integrated, coherent theory of phonological representation and rule-governed behavior.

The second question was, Why does consonant harmony that involves place of articulation most typically involve Coronal segments? Again, the answer is a direct reflection of the postulated form of representations and constraints on their interaction. That is, under the model assumed here, vowels cannot possibly disrupt adjacency of coronal consonants because the feature specifications found under the Coronal Node are simply incompatible with the articulation of vowels. Consequently, minimal scansion along the Coronal tier will readily identify only coronal consonants without encountering any interference from other intervening segments. The observed "special status" of coronals in the consonant harmony typology is, then, directly attributable to the uniquely consonantal status of its dependent features.

5.1. Labial Harmony

A corollary of this second question demands an explanation for the much less frequently attested, but possible, cases of labial harmony. Consider the implications of the present model with respect to consonant–consonant and consonant–vowel interaction between labial segments. In the absence of a clear case of labial consonant harmony as an active phonological process, consider instead the morpheme structure condition of Arabic, postulated by McCarthy (1988), which prohibits more than one labial consonant per root morpheme, even if the labial consonants are separated by a nonlabial segment:

(11)   Arabic MSC: [labial] can appear, at most, once in a root morpheme.

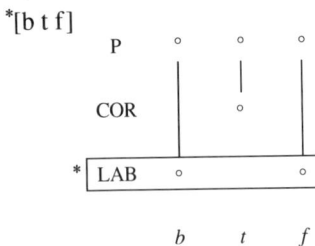

It is evident, from the autosegmental properties of the feature hierarchy model developed, that this constraint again reduces to a characterization of strict adjacency, and consequently to a violation of the obligatory contour principle (McCarthy, 1986).

Similarly, consider the implications of the claim that distinctively round vowels and labial consonants are both specified under the Labial Node. Given the apparent freedom of choice that a vowel harmony process has in the parametric option of maximal–minimal scansion, one would expect to find cases where the scansion parameter for a [+round] vowel harmony is set as minimal, rather than as maximal. In such cases, the present theory predicts that the labial consonants would function to block the [+round] harmonic spread. Precisely this situation occurs in Warlpiri (Nash, 1979), Igbo (Hyman, 1975), and Tulu (Campbell, 1974; Sagey, 1986).

Among the further predictions of the set of assumptions developed here is the following. Consider a language where the the values of [+back] and [+round] in the vowel system are not both distinctive; for example, in the system /i e a o u/, the vowels /u o/ may be distinctively specified as [+back, (−low)] with their [+round] value predictable by redundancy rule, or they may be underlyingly [+round] with their [+back] value being predictable. The prediction is that if such a language were to exhibit a labial harmony process, where the harmony exclusively affected consonants and not vowels (i.e., vowels are not targets, triggers, or blockers), then it must be the case that [+back], and not [+round], is the functional distinctive feature in the vowel system. This would then allow the consonant harmony process to scan and spread across the Labial tier without encountering any vowel specifications.

5.2. Dorsal and Pharyngeal Consonant Harmony

These proposals also offer a principled account of the nonexistence of dorsal and pharyngeal consonant harmony systems, in that both the Dorsal and Pharyngeal Nodes are also integrally involved in the specification of vowel articulation. In the case of Dorsal harmony, the prediction is absolute. That is, extensive cross-linguistic investigation seems to substantiate the claim that all vowel systems require some distinctive specification under the Dorsal Node. Thus, for example, it is logically possible that a two-vowel system would simply contrast rounded versus unrounded vowels, where the former were marked labial and the latter were unmarked: Such a system would thereby entail no distinctive vowel specification under the Dorsal Node. However, despite this logical possibility, it appears that no natural language vowel system functions in such a way, that is, without specification of some Dorsal feature. It follows therefore that a phonological harmony process exclusively restricted to consonants along the Dorsal tier is precluded.

In the case of pharyngeal harmony, it is premature to articulate clear predictions because our current understanding of the behavior and the appropriate representation of phonological properties in this articulatory range is much less well understood (but see McCarthy, 1989). Nonetheless, the cases of which I am currently aware involving pharyngeal harmony between consonants (e.g., Chilcotin in Cook, 1987; Arabic emphasis) also all affect any eligible vowels encountered in the harmonic domain.

To summarize, it has been argued that because the Labial, Dorsal, and Pharyngeal articulator nodes are in principle available to both consonant and vowel distinctive feature specification, the potential long-range spreading of a consonant feature value will automatically be blocked by any vowel feature specification along the same tier. The absence (or, in the case of Labial, rarity) of consonant harmony of these types follows, therefore, as a direct logical consequence. In contrast, the Coronal articulator node defines exclusively consonantal articulation in terms of the features [distributed], [anterior], and [strident]. Because vowels are never specified for these features, the harmonic spread of these consonant feature values will never encounter vowel specification and will therefore proceed unimpeded. Consider briefly the alternative conception of representing vowels and consonants by separate Articulator Nodes, that is, the segregated articulators hypothesis discussed earlier in Section 3.1. This hypothesis predicts falsely that because consonants are on a completely independent tier from vowels, any kind of consonant harmony should be able to occur. This fails to account, therefore, for the basic generalization that the places of articulation that define the attested kinds of consonant harmony are in complementary distribution with the places of articulation that define vowels.

In the following two sections, we turn to a consideration of what general properties characterize coronal harmony systems, and, in particular, to the third question asked at the beginning, namely, Why do these coronal harmony systems typically involve only a subset of the coronal segments in the language and systematically ignore other coronal segments?

6. CHUMASH CORONAL HARMONY

Consider first the case of "sibilant" harmony in Chumash, which is well documented in Beeler (1970, 1976), Applegate (1972, 1976), and Harrington (1974), and is familiar from recent theoretical discussion (e.g., Poser, 1982; Steriade, 1987b). The forms in (12) establish that, within the domain of a word, all coronal sibilants agree in anteriority with the rightmost sibilant.

(12)   Chumash [anterior] Harmony
    a. *k-sunon-us*   'I obey him'
       k-šunon-š   'I am obedient'
    b. *ušla*   'with the hand'
       usla-siq   'to press firmly by hand'
    c. *uqsti*   'of throwing'
       š-uxšti-meš   'throw over to'

   d. /s-iš-tiši-yep-us/   'they two show him'
      [s-is-tisi-yep-us]   (3-dual-show-3obj)

The process is analyzed by both Poser (1982) and Steriade (1987b) as a feature-changing rule because of the contrast in data such as (12b) versus (12c). That is, in (12b) the unaffixed root has an underlying [−anterior] /š/, but this changes to the [+anterior] [s] if followed by a suffix with /s/. In contrast, in (12c), the root clearly has [+anterior] /s/ underlyingly but this changes to [−anterior] [š] before a suffix with /š/. Further, the forms in (12c, d) illustrate the unbounded effect of the harmony: It propagates right-to-left throughout the word.

   Consider now the data in (13), which show that not all coronal segments in the language participate in the harmony process (note that the relevant neutral segments are underlined; [c] symbolizes the alveolar affricate [tˢ]).

(13)   Chumash Transparent Segments
       a. š-api-čo-it̲   'I have good luck'
          s-api-co-us̲   'he has good luck'
       b. k-šun̲on̲-š̲   'I am obedient'
          k-sun̲on̲-us   'I obey him'
       c. ha-s-x̲in̲tila   'his Indian name'
          ha-š-h̲in̲tila-waš 'his former Indian name'

The segments /t n l/ are systematically transparent in three ways. First, they do not trigger [+anterior] harmony despite their being [+anterior]. See, for example, the seemingly disharmonic root /ušla/ in (12b) where the [−anterior] /š/ does not agree with the rightmost [+anterior] coronal /l/ in anteriority; similarly, in the cyclically derived contexts of (13a) and (13c), /t n l/ exert no triggering influence. Second, none of these segments ever undergoes the harmony. Third and most crucially, they never function to block the harmony: It freely applies across them. The challenge, therefore, is to provide a principled account of the selective application of the harmony to only a subset of the coronal consonants in the Chumash inventory.

   There are two particular components of the analysis proposed by Poser (1982) and essentially adopted by Steriade (1987b) that are noteworthy in the present context. First, their analysis of the harmony process entails that *both* the plus and minus values of the feature [anterior] spread, this triggering in turn the delinking of whatever the former value of [anterior] was on the target. Thus, they treat the Chumash harmony as an unbounded, directional, feature-changing rule, these properties being represented in the following formalization (following Poser, 1982; Steriade, 1987b):

(14)   COR   ∘   ∘

              ǂ- - - - - - - -|

           [α ant]   [β ant]

The application of this rule is illustrated by the derivations from (12b) and (12c):

(15)   /u š l a - s i q/   /s - u x s t i - m e š/

COR   ○   ○   COR   ○   ○   ○

   [-ant]   [+ant]   [+ant]   [+ant]   [-ant]

The second interesting component of this analysis pertains to the issue of locality conditions. Specifically, how is it that the other coronal segments /t l n/ do not trigger, block, or undergo the harmony? To account for this, Steriade (1987b) proposes what I call the "transparency hypothesis":

(16) TRANSPARENCY HYPOTHESIS
       If a segment intervening between the target and the trigger of a harmony process propagating the feature F is transparent to the process, then that segment is *unspecified* for F when the rule applies.

Consider what this hypothesis entails in the context of (17), the full phonemic inventory of Chumash (from Beeler, 1970) (parenthesized segments represent segments of marginal or questionable status):

(17) p   t   c   č   k   q
      pʰ   tʰ   cʰ   čʰ   kʰ   qʰ
      p'   t'   c'   č'   k'   q'   ʔ
                s   š   x   h
                sʰ   šʰ   (xʰ)
                s'   (š') x'

      m   n
      m'   n'
      w   l   y
      w'   l'   y'

Basically, there are three series of coronal segments present in this inventory. Given the transparency hypothesis of (16), the series comprising /t n l/ must be unspecified for the harmonic feature [anterior]. The remaining two series, that is, the /c/ and /č/ columns, must both be specified: the /c/ series as [+anterior] and the /č/ series as [−anterior], because both (according to the Poser/Steriade analysis) can trigger harmony.[6]

But, what is unformalized and remains unclear in this analysis is the precise nature of the locality conditions that must be assumed in order for the strict adjacency requirement to be met. More explicitly, Archangeli and Pulleyblank (1987a: 25) specify that minimal scansion is determined "by having rules scan the tier in the feature hierarchy that immediately dominates the feature affected by the rule."

Consider, for example, how this stated condition on minimal scansion would be applied in the application of the harmony rule to the first form in (13b):

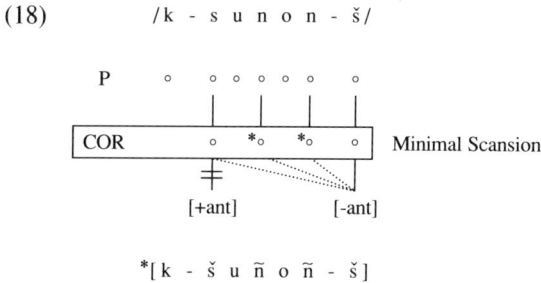

(18)　　　　　　/k - s u n o n - š/

```
P        o     o o o o o      o
               |   |   |   |
 ┌──────────────────────────────┐
 │ COR       o  *o   *o    o     │   Minimal Scansion
 └──────────────────────────────┘
            ‡ ⁚⁚⁚⁚⁚⁚⁚⁚⁚⁚⁚⁚⁚⁚⁚⁚⁚
         [+ant]          [-ant]
```

*[k - š u ñ o ñ - š]

Here it is seen that applying the transparency hypothesis of (16), such that /t n l/ are not specified for the feature [anterior], is insufficient, for they would still be expected to be eligible targets for the harmony process if, as claimed by Archangeli and Pulleyblank (1987a), the rule scans the immediately dominating tier (i.e., Coronal) to define adjacency. Since /t n l/ clearly do not function as targets, we can consider revising the analysis in one of two possible ways.

The first is to hypothesize that the transparent segments /t n l/ are not only not marked for the feature [anterior] but are also not marked with a specified Coronal Node (cf. Avery and Rice, 1989). This would clearly have the effect of making the trigger and target segments strictly adjacent on the Coronal tier, that is, the tier that "immediately dominates" the spreading feature. Support for this hypothesis would be in the form of independent phonological evidence in Chumash that coronals (except for the /c/ and /č/ series) are completely unspecified for place of articulation.

In the absence of such independent evidence, however, an alternative hypothesis is worthy of consideration. This is to reinterpret the definition of minimal scansion so that it is not necessarily defined with respect to the "immediately dominating" tier but may be defined on the tier of the spreading constituent itself. In the Chumash case, adjacency would then be defined with reference to segments overtly specified on the [anterior] tier. Since only the sibilants are contrastively specified on this tier, only they would be identified by the scansion process. All other coronal segments would be transparent.

It is clear that either of these hypotheses will result in an observationally adequate account of the transparency of the /t n l/ coronals in Chumash. However, in the absence of compelling language-internal evidence in favor of one or the other, it is illuminating to consider the power of each of these hypotheses in handling a more complex coronal harmony case, that of Tahltan. In the following section, it is argued that an optimal analysis of the Tahltan facts relies on both these hypotheses.

7. TAHLTAN CORONAL HARMONY

As shown in (19), the rich inventory of consonant phonemes in Tahltan, an Athapaskan language spoken (by probably fewer than forty speakers now) in northern British Columbia, contains five contrastive series of coronals: [7]

(19) b   d   dl   dð   dz   dž   g   gʷ   G
          t   tɬ   tθ   ts   tš   k   kʷ   q
          t'   tɬ'   tθ'   ts'   tš'   k'   kʷ'   q'   ʔ
               ɬ   θ   s   š   x   xʷ   χ   h
               l   ð   z   ž   γ   γʷ   ʁ
      m   n   y   w
          n'

These series are referred to here, respectively, as the *d* series, *dl* series, etc. Of particular interest is a coronal harmony process that involves three of the five series, specifically the *dð, dz,* and *dž* series. The basic characteristics of this process are illustrated by the alternations in (20), where the first-person singular subject marker /s/ (underlined for ease of reference) surfaces as [θ] if followed anywhere in the string to the right by a dental affricate or fricative, that is, by any member of the *dð* series (20a); as [š] if followed by any member of the *dž* series (20b); and as [s] elsewhere (20c):

(20)   Tahltan Coronal Harmony: /s̲/ {1-sing subj}
       a. *θεθð̲εɬ*   'I'm hot'
           dεθ̲kʷʊθ   'I cough'
           εθ̲du:θ   'I whipped him'
           mεθεθ̲εθ   'I'm wearing (on feet)'
           naθtθ̲'εt   'I fell off (horse)'
       b. *hudištš̲a*   'I love them'
           εšdž̲ɪni   'I'm singing'
           ɬεnεštš̲u:š   'I'm folding it'
           nεš̲yεɬ   'I'm growing'
       c. *εsk̲'a:*   'I'm gutting fish'
           nadεdε:sba̲:tɬ   'I hung myself'
           εsdan̲   'I'm drinking'
           sεsxε̲ɬ   'I'm going to kill it'
           nεstε̲ɬ   'I'm sleepy'

To show that the target of the harmony is not exclusively /s/ but may be any member of any of the participating *dð, dz,* and *dž* series, consider the additional data below, where the initial underlying /θ/ of the first-person dual subject prefix /θi(d)/ surfaces as [s] or [š] in appropriate harmonic contexts (again, the target segment is underlined): [8]

(21) a. *dɛθigɪtɬ*   'we threw it'
         naθiba:tɬ   'we hung it'
         θi:tθædi   'we ate it'
      b. *dɛsidzɛl*   'we shouted'
         xasi:dɛts   'we plucked it'
         dɛsit'ʌs   'we are walking'
         nisit'a:ts   'we got up'
      c. *išitšotɬ*   'we blew it up'
         tɛɛdɛnɛšidžu:t   'we chased it away'
         ušidžɛ   'we are called'

These data establish the basic parameters of the coronal harmony process in Tahltan as the following. First, the harmony is directional, spreading from right to left. Second, the triggers and targets of the process are both composed of any member of the *dð*, *dz*, and *dž* series. Third, only the place of articulation spreads, not the manner (e.g., [−continuant] from the affricates) or the voice specification of the triggering segment.

The data in (22) below provide additional evidence of two other significant facts. The base representation of the target segment is given in phonemic slashes on the left; the locus of the target is again identified as the underlined portion of the surface representations.

(22) a. /s/   *ɛdɛdɛθdu:θ*   'I whipped myself'
         /s/   *taθtθaɬ*   'I'm dying'
         /s/   *xaʔɛθt'aθ*   'I'm cutting the hair off'
         /θ/   *dɛsit'ʌs*   'we are walking'
         /θ/   *nisit'a:ts*   'we got up'
         /θ/   *mɛʔɛšit'otš*   'we are breast-feeding'
      b. /s/   *noʔɛdɛ:šɬɛdži*   'I melted it over and over'
         /s/   *yaštɬ'ɛtš*   'I splashed it'

As seen in (22a), members of the *d* series of coronal obstruents /d t t'/ never function to block the harmony from applying across them; nor do they function as targets of the harmony, for they are never changed; nor do they trigger a harmony of their own. Similarly, as evidenced in (22b) as well as in some of the forms of (20) and (21), the lateral *dl* series is also fully transparent.

Thus, the coronal harmony process in Tahltan possesses several interesting properties requiring principled explanation. Note in particular that, in contrast to the Chumash case discussed in Section 5, Tahltan has (1) two separate series of transparent coronal segments, not just one, and (2) the segments that participate in the harmony cannot be analyzed in terms of a straightforward binary opposition of a single contrastive feature because *three* distinct coronal series are involved, not simply two as in Chumash.

As argued in detail in Shaw (1989), the optimal formalization of the Tahltan harmony spreads the rightmost Coronal Node leftward, with concomitant delinking of the previous Coronal specification of the target:

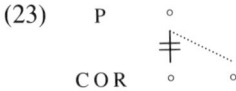

(23)   P   ∘

                 ╪ ⋯⋯⋯⋯

        COR ∘   ∘

Thus, the trigger of the rule is a specified Coronal Node, and the target of the rule is an immediately adjacent, specified Coronal Node.

Consider first the claim that it is indeed the superordinate Coronal Node that spreads, rather than any of its dependent features. The inescapable fact here is that there are three separate series of coronals (the *dð*, *dz*, and *dž* series) that participate in the harmony, and that require distinctive specification from each other. The present analysis proposes that these series are underlyingly distinguished by the distinctive feature specification of [+distributed] for the *dð* series, [+strident] for the *dz* series, and [−anterior] for the *dž* series.[9] Although there are various other proposals in the literature differing in nomenclature and content for what the universal set of terminal features under the Coronal Node should be (e.g., [±apical], [±dental], [±grooved]), it is clear that no single binary feature under the Coronal Node could function either to characterize this tripartite phonemic contrast or to effect the full participation of all three coronal series in the harmony process. Thus, assuming a maximally binary-valued feature theory, spreading cannot be solely of any one feature below the Coronal Node. The essential unity and generality of the process can only be captured by spreading the lowest common node that uniquely dominates the class of features involved, that is, the Coronal Node.

The transparent behavior of both the *d* and the *dl* series of coronals has yet to be explained. It is argued in Shaw (1989) that there is strong independent motivation, both language-internal and cross-linguistic, that the major structural differences (ignoring, as not directly relevant, distinctive laryngeal and nasal specification) between the five coronal series of stops–affricates in the Tahltan phonemic inventory should be represented as follows:

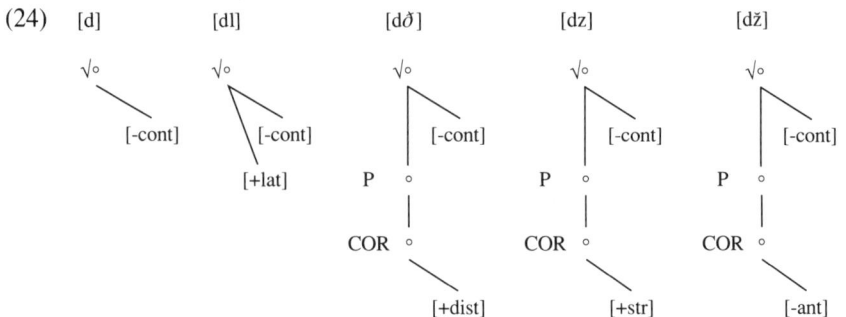

(24)   [d]   [dl]   [dð]   [dz]   [dž]

         √∘   √∘   √∘   √∘   √∘

             [-cont]   [-cont]   [-cont]   [-cont]   [-cont]

                          [+lat]   P   ∘   P   ∘   P   ∘

                                    | | |

                                 COR ∘   COR ∘   COR ∘

                                    [+dist]   [+str]   [-ant]

Given space limitations, not all aspects of this analysis can be recapitulated here. Consider briefly, however, some of the major claims integral to these representations.

First, it is hypothesized, following the theory of radical underspecification (e.g., Archangeli, 1988), that only one value (i.e., [+F] or [−F]) is lexically specified for any given feature in a particular context. The most relevant particular instantiation of this principle involves the feature [continuant], with the claim here being that for consonants the only lexically available feature value is [−continuant]. This hypothesis has significant consequences for the representation of fricatives and affricates. That is, if the only functional feature value is [−continuant], then it follows that fricatives are all underlyingly unspecified for continuancy. It further follows that the postulated representation of affricates (e.g., Sagey, 1986; Hualde, 1988) as having internal branching structure with both [−continuant] and [+continuant] specification cannot be adopted as the correct underlying representation, since [+continuant] is simply not a lexically available specification. Instead, it is proposed that affricates and stops are both exclusively [−continuant] in underlying representation, and that they are differentiated from one another primarily in terms of the feature specification that identifies the distinctive nature of the affricate release.[10] These premises underlie, therefore, the representations in (24) where the *dl* series is distinctively [+lateral], the *dð* series is distinctively [+distributed], the *dz* series is distinctively [+strident], and the *dž* series is distinctively [−anterior] (and redundantly [+strident]). This leaves the *d* series of stops represented exclusively by the specification [−continuant], with its unmarked place of articulation being predictable by a later redundancy rule to the following effect:

(25)　[0Place] → Coronal

In the light of the growing body of evidence in favor of the unmarked status of the coronal place of articulation cross-linguistically, this may well be a candidate for a universal redundancy rule.

Further compelling language-internal motivation for these proposed representations is found in the seemingly unusual behavior of a completely independent and widespread Athapaskan phenomenon known in the traditional literature as the D-effect (Howren, 1971). One of the morphemes illustrating this effect has already been introduced in the data of (21), where it is seen that the final *d* of the first-person dual pronoun /θid/ sometimes surfaces as a [d] and other times seems to be deleted, and still other times its underlying presence is deduced only through mutation of the following consonant. These various manifestations comprise the D-effect; its particular realizations in Tahltan are summarized informally as follows:[11]

(26)　$d + ł → dl$　　$d + x → g$
　　　　$d + θ → dð$　　$d + ʔ → t'$

$d + s \rightarrow dz$ $d + C \rightarrow C$ (C = any other consonant)
$d + š \rightarrow dž$

Several Athapaskan scholars (e.g., Wright, 1984, and Speas, 1984, for Navaho; Rice, 1987, for Slave; Hargus, 1985, for Sekani) have recognized that the resources of autosegmental phonology provide an insightful way of representing the most fundamental aspect of the D-effect, namely, by positing (or deriving) a floating segment that crucially contributes the feature [−continuant] to a following fricative or glottal stop. However, these previous analyses are each based on significantly different assumptions regarding underspecification, representation, rule formalism, etc. Consequently, each requires various additional assumptions or mechanisms to correct or repair the resultant configurations (e.g., Rice, 1987; Paradis, 1988).[12] In the present analysis, given the proposed underlying representations in (24), the spread of a floating [−continuant] to whatever segment follows results in exactly the appropriate structural representations without necessary recourse to repair strategies of any kind. Three derivations are presented below to illustrate this:

(27) $d + ? \rightarrow t'$ $d + š \rightarrow dž$ $d + x \rightarrow g$

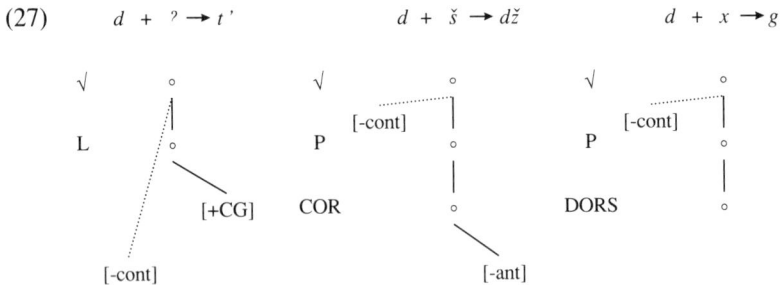

Thus, the proposed representation of the D-effect trigger as simply [−continuant], in combination with the postulated underspecification of Tahltan obstruents, results in an optimally simple and elegant analysis of what otherwise requires complex and idiosyncratic stipulation to effect the correct output. Although this floating *d* and the full-fledged phoneme /d/ differ in that the latter is anchored to a skeletal–prosodic position of its own, they are identical in their feature content, that is, both are distinctively defined only by the feature [−continuant].

The hypothesis that the series of coronal stops /t d n/ in Tahltan is simply represented as [−continuant] (plus, of course, distinctive laryngeal–nasal specification) has another correct empirical consequence: The absence of a specified Coronal Node automatically accounts for their observed transparent behavior (cf. [22a]) with respect to the coronal harmony process in (23). That is, since the trigger of the harmony is a specified Coronal Node and the target is an immediately adjacent, specified Coronal Node, then the transparent behavior of the stops /t d n/ follows directly from their not having a Coronal Node to make them either a trigger or blocker. This transparency is illustrated in the derivation below, where the lack of any articulator specification on the /d/ that intervenes between the trigger /θ/ and the target /s/ allows the coronal harmony to spread right past it.

(28)   /ɛ d ɛ d ɛ s d u: θ /   ⟶   [ɛ d ɛ d ɛ θ d u: θ]

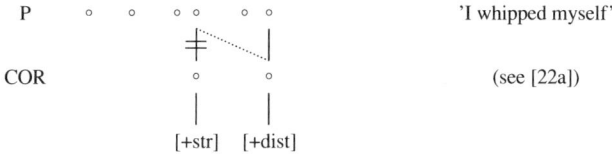

P   ○   ○   ○ ○   ○ ○   'I whipped myself'

COR   ○   ○   (see [22a])

                [+str]   [+dist]

The major residual question is the attested transparency of the lateral *dl* series to the coronal harmony process (see [21] and [22b]). There has been significant controversy in the literature as to where [+lateral] should hang in the tree geometry: Whereas some authors, such as Sagey (1986:281), argue that [lateral] should be attached relatively higher in the tree, others, including Steriade (1986) and, most notably, Levin (1988), contend that it should be under the Coronal Node. While agreeing that laterals are indeed basically coronal, I argue in Shaw (1989) that it does not necessarily follow that the feature [lateral] is therefore dominated by the Coronal Node. Rather, if [+lateral] is represented at a higher level of the feature hierarchy, the unmarked status of its coronal articulation can be predicted by a redundancy rule to the following effect:

(29)   [+lateral] → Coronal

Indeed, the transparent behavior of the lateral series in Tahltan with respect to the coronal harmony process requires that [+lateral] *not* be under the Coronal Node, for if it were, it would block the coronal harmony process from applying across it. That is, as illustrated in the unsuccessful derivations for [yaštɬ'ɛtš] 'I splashed it' below, one would first of all (see [30a]) expect the spread of the rightmost Coronal Node to target and change the lateral /tɬ'/, which does not happen. Further, even if one were to stipulate some sort of condition on the harmony rule such that [+lateral] segments were not appropriate targets, this would still leave the problem of how the rightmost Coronal Node is to successfully spread leftward *past* the intervening Coronal Node with its specified [+lateral], without violating the prohibition against crossing of association lines, as in (30b).

(30)   a.   /y a s   tɬ' ɛ tš /   b.   /y a s   tɬ' ɛ tš /

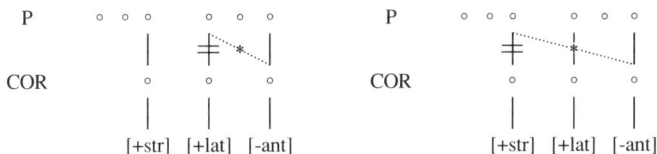

P   ○ ○ ○   ○ ○ ○   P   ○ ○ ○   ○ ○ ○

COR   ○   ○   ○   COR   ○   ○   ○

      [+str] [+lat] [-ant]   [+str] [+lat] [-ant]

It is only under the hypothesis that the feature [lateral] hangs higher up the tree, as proposed in the representations in (24), that their transparent behavior to the coronal harmony can be accounted for. Thus, as illustrated in the derivation below, the rightmost Coronal Node can spread uninterrupted past the intervening /tɬ'/ to the next specified coronal segment:

(31)   /y a s   tɬ' ɛ tš /

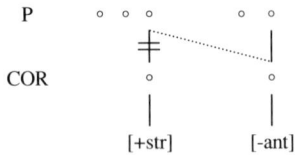

We are now in a position to return to the question, triggered by the Chumash harmony analysis in Section 5, of what specific conditions define adjacency at the level of minimal scansion. Recall that Archangeli and Pulleyblank (1987a: 25) specify that minimal scansion is determined "by having rules scan the tier in the feature hierarchy that immediately dominates the feature affected by the rule." The details of the Chumash analysis, as adopted from Poser (1982) and Steriade (1987b), were not sufficiently determinate to resolve how the observed transparency of /t n l/ segments should be handled so that the constraints on strict adjacency at the level of minimal scansion were also met. Two possible revisions were proposed. First, to preserve Archangeli and Pulleyblank's contention that minimal scansion is of the immediately dominating tier, one could postulate that not only are the transparent segments /t n l/ not specified for the harmonic feature [±anterior], but they are also not specified for Coronal. Referring back to the derivation in (18), it is evident that since Coronal is the tier that immediately dominates the affected feature [anterior], minimal scansion would now define the trigger and target as strictly adjacent at this level. This solution is represented in (32a) below. The second alternative is to revise the interpretation of minimal scansion so that it need not refer to the next tier up but rather should refer to the lowest tier that crucially defines both trigger and target. In the Chumash case, strict adjacency would then be defined with reference to any segments specified on the [anterior] tier, as illustrated in (32b).

(32)   a.   /k - s u n o n - š/   b.   /k - s u n o n - š/

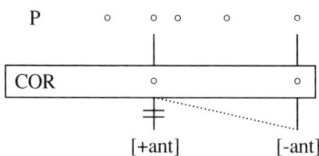
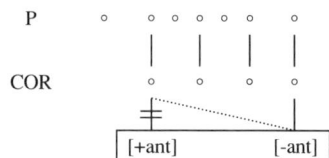

Although either hypothesis is capable of accommodating the Chumash facts, this is not the case with Tahltan. Because in Tahltan it is the Coronal Node itself that spreads, the next higher level is that of the Place Node. However, the harmony process consistently spreads across vowels, and even though one vowel might be totally underspecified within a vowel system, all other vowels are necessarily linked to their dorsal specification through a Place Node. Moreover, the harmony also consistently spreads across all other noncoronal consonants, which also patently have Place Node specification. Consequently, as shown in (33a), minimal scansion at the level of the "immediately dominating" tier would not correctly identify trigger and target as strictly adjacent. If, however, minimal scansion is interpreted as applying to the lowest tier that identifies the crucial properties defining both trigger and target, then the appropriate level for Tahltan is the Coronal tier. As illustrated in (33b), strict adjacency of the relevant segments is successfully defined at this level.

(33) a.   / y a s   tɬ' ɛ tš /   b.   / y a s   tɬ' ɛ tš /

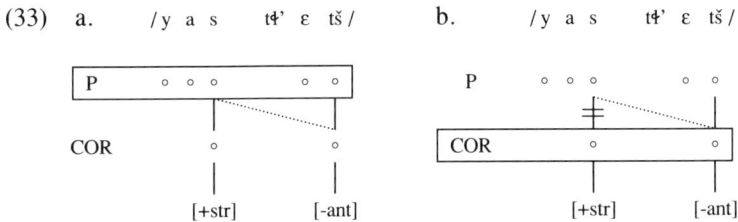

Finally, we must ask what broader generalizations apply to characterize possible coronal harmony systems. In the analysis of Tahltan, it has been argued that two independent series of coronal obstruents, the *d* series of stops /t d n/ and the *dl* series of laterals, are both unspecified for the Coronal articulator node in underlying representation. Their ultimate realization as coronals is effected by two separate redundancy rules, both of which receive significant cross-linguistic reaffirmation: The first, in (34a), expresses the unmarked status of coronal articulation for laterals; the second, in (34b), expresses the unmarked status of coronal articulation, relative to all other places of articulation, for obstruent systems in general.

(34) a. [+lateral] → Coronal   [=(29)]
      b. [0Place] → Coronal   [=(25)]

A strong hypothesis emerges from this: Let us postulate that the two redunancy rules of (34) are in fact part of Universal Grammar, and that the Coronal articulator node will therefore only be present in the underlying repertoire of a phonemic system if the inventory contains segments that require distinctive specification by features that are daughters of the Coronal Node. Recall the third question asked at the beginning of this paper: Why do coronal harmony systems typically involve only a subset of the coronal segments in a language and systematically ignore other coronal segments? The hypothesis offered here makes very precise and restrictive predictions regarding coronal harmony systems that do not apply to the full inventory of coronals within the language. Specifically, if a harmony selectively applies to a subset of coronals, then it will be to only those coronals that, independently of the harmony process and based solely on the phonemic contrastiveness of the underlying inventory, require distinctive feature specification under the Coronal articulator node.

8. CONCLUSIONS

The present research has examined several asymmetric properties of consonant harmony systems with the aim of providing a coherent explanation for these characteristics within a constrained theoretical framework. Coronals have emerged repeatedly as playing a unique role, compared with other places of articulation. The major contention of the argumentation developed here is that the observed characteristics of consonant harmony systems in general, and coronal harmony in particular, follow as logical consequences of three interacting hypotheses regarding phonological representation and interaction: the hierarchical model of feature organization, underspecification theory, and postulated constraints on locality conditions for rule application.

With respect to feature organization, a major claim is that the place specification of both vowels and consonants is represented by a single, uniform set of articulators. This position, here called the integrated articulators hypothesis, provides a systematic explanation for the striking asymmetry in what kinds of consonant place harmonies occur. That is, the overwhelming prevalence of coronal harmony (and the corollary absence, or rarity, of consonant harmonies across the other places of articulation) follows from the fact that the coronal terminal features ([anterior], [strident], [distributed]) function exclusively to define distinctive consonant articulation. In contrast, each of the other major articulators is available, in principle, for both vowel and consonant specification. The alternative conception of representing vowels and consonants by separate Articulator Nodes, here called the segregated articulators hypothesis, predicts falsely that because consonants are on a completely independent tier from vowels, any kind of consonant harmony should be able to occur. This fails to account, therefore, for the basic generalization that the places of articulation that define the attested kinds of consonant harmony are in complementary distribution with the places of articulation that define vowels.

A second claim, based on the transparent behavior of laterals to coronal harmony in Tahltan, is that the locus of the feature [lateral] in the tree hierarchy is not subordinate to the Coronal Node but is instead a dependent of the Root Node. Its unmarked coronal articulation is then linked, through the postulated universal redundancy rules in (34), to the unmarked status of coronals universally. Thus, the behavior of laterals is related directly to the additional and independent claim that the Articulator Node for coronals is underspecified in underlying representation, unless the segment in question requires distinctive specification in terms of a subcoronal feature. Thus, this research on harmony processes provides further support for this same conclusion, reached on independent grounds, by several other studies in the present volume.

A final contribution, motivated by the properties of the rich coronal harmony system of Tahltan, relates to the precise formalization of postulated conditions on tier scansion in order to define adjacency. With reinterpretation of the definition of minimal scansion so that it applies not necessarily to the "immediately dominating" tier but rather to the lowest tier that identifies the crucial trigger–target properties, Archangeli and Pulleyblank's (1987a) characterization of a maximal–minimal scansion parameter functions significantly in restricting a typology of possible harmony systems.

ACKNOWLEDGMENTS

This article was originally presented to the Canadian Linguistic Association at the University of Windsor, May 1988, and subsequently at the University of Arizona, Tucson, December 1988. I thank D. Archangeli, B. Bagemihl, T. Borowski, E. Czaykowska-Higgins, M. D. Kinkade, C. Paradis, J-F. Prunet, C. Ulrich, and L. Walsh for their comments. I also gratefully acknowledge the support of the British Columbia Provincial Museum, Linguistics Division, and of SSHRCC Grant 451-85-0925.

NOTES

[1] In (2), and in all subsequent examples, cons = consonant, son = sonorant, L = Laryngeal, nas = nasal, cont = continuant, lat = lateral, cg = constricted glottis, P = Place, sg = spread glottis, LAB = Labial Node, COR = Coronal Node, DOR = Dorsal Node, PHAR = Pharyngeal Node, rd = round, ant = anterior, str = strident, hi = high, lo = low, atr = advanced tongue root, dist = distributed, sing = singular, subj = subject, and obj = object.

[2] The relationship of the feature [low] to the postulated Pharyngeal Node requires further investigation (e.g., Shaw *et al.*, 1989), as does the relationship of the feature [back] to the Coronal Node. The present analysis treats front vowels as not distinctively specified as Coronal. This claim is based on the transparent behavior of all vowels, including front vowels, to coronal harmony between consonants. If front vowels were distinctively coronal, then they would be expected to block, or otherwise interact with, coronal harmony processes, whereas none of the languages investigated in detail here show any such effects. At the same time, however, I must acknowledge that the independent body of evidence presented by Clements (1989), E. Pulleyblank (1989), and Lahiri and Evers (this

volume) is also compelling in establishing strong links between front vowels and coronal properties in processes such as palatalization. At present, these two separate types of evidence seem to lead to contradictory conclusions. There are further inconsistencies here, though, that demand explanation: For example, what is traditionally viewed as [−back] specification is what is seemingly tied to the Coronal Node, whereas what is traditionally considered [+back] is still tied in its behavioral manifestations to the Dorsal articulator. If this is truly a single feature, how can its two values be split under two independent nodes? Perhaps a deeper understanding of this apparent discrepancy will lead to a more relativized hypothesis. For example, if the markedness specification for the frontness–backness of vowels is not universal (i.e., in some languages [−back]/coronal is the marked value, whereas in other languages it is [+back]/dorsal), then perhaps those languages that have coronal harmony will present independent evidence that [−back]/coronal is not underlyingly marked for vowels, whereas for those languages with coronal palatalization effects it is. This hypothesis would predict, then, that coronal harmony (where all vowels are transparent) and coronal palatalization triggered by front vowels should not be found (at least at the same lexical level of feature [under]specification) in the same language.

[3] Further empirical support for the "integrated" representation of both consonants and vowels under the same Dorsal and Pharyngeal Nodes comes from the consonant–vowel harmonic interactions considered in Shaw et al. (1989).

[4] A model based on the weaker segregated articulators hypothesis, which states that consonants and vowels are defined on separate tiers (e.g., Clements, 1989), would predict that even at the level of minimal scansion dorsal consonants would not block vowel harmony, unless specified with secondary articulation features on the vowel tier.

[5] The lateral /l/ also assimilates to a palatal variant, though as Clements and Sezer (1982:236ff.) point out, its harmonic behavior is considerably more complex than that of the velars. However, it is well documented cross-linguistically that /l/ often has dorsal properties (see Kenstowicz and Kisseberth, 1979:74, on Serbo-Croatian).

[6] A point of clarification can be interjected here. Considerable controversy persists regarding the status of two competing subtheories of underspecification: contrastive specification, represented by this analysis of [±anterior] in Chumash, and radical underspecification, which restricts lexical feature specification to a single value. Although I argue below that the optimal analysis of Tahltan requires radical underspecification, I have not attempted, due to space limitations, to address a possible reanalysis of the Chumash /c : č/ opposition in radical terms. Regardless of the ultimate resolution of this aspect of the analysis, however, the important point served by the Chumash case is that the segments /t n l/ must be totally unspecified on the relevant harmonic tier in order to account for their transparency.

[7] The Tahltan data presented here are from my own fieldnotes, collected in Telegraph Creek, British Columbia, between 1981 and 1983. More detailed documentation of the coronal harmony process and more explicit argumentation for certain aspects of the present analysis are presented in Shaw (1989). A description of the harmony as a condition governing canonical root structure, based on the closely related Iskut dialect, is found in Nater (1989). See also Hardwick (1984).

[8] The parentheses around the d in this representation signify a floating segment that has various surface realizations according to the D-effect (Howren, 1971), to be discussed shortly.

[9] Although [+strident] is not a distinctive specification on the *dž* series (being predictable, given [−anterior]), a grammar incorporating the redundancy rule ordering constraint (RROC) of Archangeli and Pulleyblank (1986) would presumably effect its specification on this series once [+strident] is phonologically activated in the course of the derivation.

[10] Subsequent to the original presentation of this article at the Linguistic Society of America (December 1988), Steriade (1989a,b) has reported on independent research leading to a very similar conclusion regarding the [−continuant] status of affricates.

[11] Although it is beyond the scope of this article to motivate the laryngeal system of Tahltan in detail, the present analysis assumes that the stop–affricate series orthographically represented as /d g (etc.)/ is underlyingly plain, that is, unmarked for voice.

[12] Although Rice (1987) postulates that the D-effect trigger is lexically specified as [−continuant], she also posits that [+continuant] is the specified distinctive value for the regular obstruent inventory. Thus, both values are functional. This results in considerable complexity in having to account for the "loss" of the underlying [+continuant] value of segments like /x/ in D-effect derivations such as /d + x/ → [g]. In the analysis proposed in the present article (cf. [27] above), this problem is obviated by the claim that [+continuant] is not lexically specified in the first place.

REFERENCES

Applegate, R. B. (1972) *Ineseño Chumash Grammar,* Doctoral dissertation, University of California, Berkeley.

Applegate, R. B. (1976) "Reduplication in Chumash," in M. Langdon and S. Silver, eds., *Hokan Studies: Papers from the First Conference on Hokan Languages,* pp. 271–283. Mouton, The Hague.

Archangeli, D. (1988) "Aspects of Underspecification Theory," *Phonology* 5.2, 183–207.

Archangeli, D. and D. Pulleyblank (1986) "The Content and Structure of Phonological Representations," ms., University of Arizona, Tucson, and University of Southern California, Los Angeles.

Archangeli, D. and D. Pulleyblank (1987a) "Maximal and Minimal Rules: Effects of Tier Scansion," *Proceedings of NELS* 17, 16–35.

Archangeli, D. and D. Pulleyblank (1987b) "Yoruba Vowel Harmony," ms., University of Arizona, Tucson, and University of Southern California, Los Angeles.

Avery, P. and K. Rice (1989) "Segment Structure and Coronal Underspecification," *Phonology* 6.2, 179–200.

Beeler, M. S. (1970) "Sibilant Harmony in Chumash," *IJAL* 36.1, 14–17.

Beeler, M. S. (1976) "Barbareño Chumash Grammar: A Farrago," in M. Langdon and S. Silver, eds., *Hokan Studies: Papers from the 1st Conference on Hokan Languages,* pp. 251–270. Mouton, The Hague.

Campbell, L. (1974) "Phonological Features: Problems and Proposals," *Language* 50, 52–65.

Christdas, P. (1988) *The Phonology and Morphology of Tamil,* Doctoral dissertation, Cornell University, Ithaca, New York.

Clements, G. N. (1985) "The Geometry of Phonological Features," *Phonology Yearbook* 2, 225–252.

Clements, G. N. (1989) "A Unified Set of Features for Consonants and Vowels," ms., Cornell University, Ithaca, New York.

Clements, G. N. and E. Sezer (1982) "Vowel and Consonant Disharmony in Turkish," in H. van der Hulst and N. Smith, eds., *The Structure of Phonological Representations*, pp. 213–255. Foris Publications, Dordrecht.

Cole, J. S. (1987) *Planar Phonology and Morphology*, Doctoral dissertation, MIT, Cambridge, Massachusetts.

Cook, E. D. (1987) "An Autosegmental Analysis of Chilcotin Flattening," in A. Bosch *et al.*, eds., *Papers from the CLS Parasession on Autosegmental and Metrical Phonology*, pp. 51–65.

Davy, J. I. M. and D. Nurse (1982) "Synchronic Versions of Dahl's Law: The Multiple Applications of a Phonological Dissimilation Rule," *Journal of African Languages and Linguistics* 4, 157–195.

Greenberg, J. (1950) "The Patterning of Root Morphemes in Semitic," *Word* 6.2, 162–181.

Halefom, G. (1988) "Palatalization in Harari," Paper presented at the Canadian Linguistic Association, University of Windsor.

Halle, M. (1986) "On Speech Sounds and their Immanent Structure," ms., MIT, Cambridge, Massachusetts.

Hardwick, M. (1984) "Tahltan Phonology and Morphology," ms., University of Toronto.

Hargus, S. (1985) *The Lexical Phonology of Sekani*, Doctoral dissertation, UCLA.

Harrington, J. P. (1974) "Sibilants in Ventureno," *IJAL* 40.1, 1–9.

Howren, R. (1971) "A Formalization of the Athapaskan D-Effect," *IJAL* 37, 96–113.

Hualde, J. I. (1988) "Affricates are not Contour Segments," *Proceedings of WCCFL* 7, 143–157.

Hukari, T. (1981) "Glottalization in Cowichan," in *Working Papers of the Linguistics Circle of the University of Victoria* 1(2), 233–250.

Hyman, L. (1975) *Phonology: Theory and Analysis*, Holt, Rinehart and Winston, New York.

Itô, J. and A. Mester (1986) "The Phonology of Voicing in Japanese," *Linguistic Inquiry* 17.1, 49–73.

Kari, J. H. (1976) *Navaho Verb Prefix Phonology*, Garland, New York.

Kenstowicz, M. and C. Kisseberth (1979) *Generative Phonology*, Academic Press, London.

Kimenyi, A. (1979) *Studies in Kinyarwanda and Bantu Phonology*, Linguistic Research Inc., Edmonton.

Leslau, W. (1958) *The Verb in Harari (South Ethiopic)*, University of California Publications in Semitic Philology, Vol. 21, University of California Press, Berkeley and Los Angeles.

Leslau, W. (1966) "The Impersonal in Chaha," in *To Honor Roman Jakobson*, Janua Linguarum, Series Major 32, pp. 1150–1162. Mouton, The Hague.

Levin, J. (1988) "A Place for Lateral in the Feature Geometry," ms., University of Texas at Austin.

Mannheim, B. (1988) "On the Sibilants of Colonial Southern Peruvian Quechua," *IJAL* 54.2, 168–208.

Mattina, A. (1973) *Colville Grammatical Structure*, Doctoral dissertation, University of Hawaii, Honolulu. Published in *University of Hawaii Working Papers in Linguistics*.

McCarthy, J. J. (1983) "Consonantal Morphology in the Chaha Verb," *Proceedings of WCCFL* 2, 176–188.

McCarthy, J. J. (1986) "OCP Effects: Gemination and Antigemination," *Linguistic Inquiry* 17, 207–263.

McCarthy, J. J. (1988) "Feature Geometry and Dependency: A Review," *Phonetica* 43/45, 84–108.

McCarthy, J. J. (1989) "On Gutturals," ms., University of Massachusetts, Amherst.

Nash, D. (1979) "Warlpiri Vowel Assimilations," in K. Safir et al., eds., *MIT Working Papers in Linguistics 1*, Linguistics Dept., MIT, Cambridge, Massachusetts.

Nater, H. F. (1989) "Some Comments on the Phonology of Tahltan," *IJAL* 55.1, 24–42.

Paradis, C. (1988) "On Constraints and Repair Strategies," *Linguistic Review* 6.1, 71–97.

Piggott, G. L. (1987) "On the Autonomy of the Feature Nasal," in A. Bosch et al., eds., *Papers from the CLS Parasession on Autosegmental and Metrical Phonology*, pp. 223–238. Chicago Linguistic Society, Chicago, Illinois.

Poser, W. J. (1982) "Phonological Representations and Action-at-a-Distance," in H. van der Hulst and N. Smith, eds., *The Structure of Phonological Representations, Part II*. Foris Publications, Dordrecht.

Pulleyblank, D. (1986) "Rule Application in a Noncylic Stratum," *Linguistic Inquiry* 17, 573–580.

Pulleyblank, E. (1989) "The Role of Coronal in Articulator-Based Features," Paper presented at the Chicago Linguistics Society, Chicago, Illinois.

Reichard, G. A. (1938) "Coeur d'Alène," *Handbook of American Indian Languages* 3, 517–707.

Rice, K. (1987) "The Function of Structure Preservation: Derived Environments," *Proceedings of NELS* 17, 501–520.

Sagey, E. C. (1986) *The Representation of Features and Relations in Nonlinear Phonology*, Doctoral dissertation, MIT, Cambridge, Massachusetts.

Sapir, E. and H. Hoijer (1967) *The Phonology and Morphology of the Navaho Language*, University of California Publications in Linguistics, Vol. 50, University of California Press, Berkeley and Los Angeles.

Schein, B. and D. Steriade (1986) "On Geminates," *Linguistic Inquiry* 17.4, 691–744.

Shaw, P. A. (1989) "On the Phonological Representation of Laterals and Affricates," ms., University of British Columbia.

Shaw, P. A., B. Bagemihl, and L. Walsh (1989) "Report on SSHRCC Project on Syllable Structure in Northwest Coast Languages," ms., University of British Columbia.

Speas, M. (1984) "Navajo Prefixes and Word Structure Typology," *MIT Working Papers in Linguistics* 7, 86–109.

Steriade, D. (1982) *Greek Prosodies and the Nature of Syllabification*, Doctoral dissertation, MIT, Cambridge, Massachusetts.

Steriade, D. (1986) "A Note on Coronal," ms., MIT, Cambridge, Massachusetts.

Steriade, D. (1987a) "Locality Conditions and Feature Geometry," *Proceedings of NELS* 17, 595–617.

Steriade, D. (1987b) "Redundant Values," in A. Bosch et al., eds., *Papers from the CLS Parasession on Autosegmental and Metrical Phonology*, pp. 339–362. Chicago Linguistic Society, Chicago, Illinois.

Steriade, D. (1989a) Paper presented at the Conference on Parameters in Phonology, LSA Summer Institute, University of Arizona, Tucson.

Steriade, D. (1989b) "Affricates and the Analysis of Place Features," Paper presented at the Conference on Feature and Underspecification Theories, MIT, Cambridge, Massachusetts.

Teeter, K. V. (1964) *The Wiyot Language*, University of California Publications in Linguistics, Vol. 37, University of California Press, Berkeley and Los Angeles.

Thompson, L. C. and M. T. Thompson (1985) "A Grassman's Law for Salish," in V. Z. Acson and R. L. Leed, eds., *For Gordon H. Fairbanks*, Oceanic Linguistics Special Publication 20, Honolulu, Hawaii.

Wright, M. (1984) "The CV Skeleton and Mapping in Navajo Verb Phonology," *Proceedings of NELS 14*.

Yip, M. (1988) "The OCP and Phonological Rules: A Loss of Identity," *Linguistic Inquiry* 19.1, 65–100.

ON THE UNIVERSALITY OF
THE CORONAL ARTICULATOR

YOUNG-MEE YU CHO

Department of Asian Languages
Stanford University
Stanford, California 94305

1. INTRODUCTION

The question has not yet been asked in the literature whether all of the properties of a feature geometry are universally given or whether some properties are determined on a language-particular basis.[1] It is true that the logic of restrictiveness favors the universalist position, according to which a feature geometry is provided once and for all in Universal Grammar and is never subject to language-specific stipulation. When the universalist position cannot be maintained for whatever reason, it is clearly more desirable to require any language-particular aspects of geometry to be minimized so that cross-linguistic variation can be accounted for in a principled manner.

In this article, I question the universality of the subplace nodes such as the Labial, the Coronal, and the Dorsal Nodes, which are assumed to be distinct class nodes under the Place Node in more recent versions of feature geometry (Sagey, 1986; McCarthy, 1988; Levin, 1987). While there is ample evidence in some languages that each of these subplace articulator nodes functions as a real phonological entity, in other languages not only is such evidence lacking but the postulation of the articulator nodes makes incorrect predictions in defining certain natural classes of segments. Furthermore, in some languages simpler analyses of various phonological processes obtain if one assumes no class nodes under

159

the Place Node but instead binary features such as [±coronal]. One of the most crucial differences between the theory with the Coronal articulator and the theory without concerns the use of the feature [coronal].

The universalist position, however, does not seem warranted when we consider the organization of the Place Node for two languages, Sanskrit and Korean. When we are confronted with two cases that seem to argue for two different structures, a universal structure internal to the Place Node cannot be easily determined.

This article is organized as follows. In Section 2, I compare the two theories that deal with the internal organization of the Place Node. In Section 3, I discuss coronal assimilation and /n/-retroflexion in Sanskrit with the conclusion that the Coronal articulator node should be present. In Section 4, Korean assimilation is presented to show that a representation with no articulator nodes makes better sense in accounting for the data. In the conclusions of Section 5 it is suggested that given the compelling arguments for both of the representations, the choice of the relevant structure for the Place Node (i.e., Coronal/[±coronal]) should be parameterized rather than universally determined.

2. TWO THEORIES FOR THE PLACE NODE

As has been argued extensively, one of the most important motivations for a hierarchical structure for segment-internal structure is the assumption that distinctive features are organized into sets constituting natural classes. In such a structure each feature or node of the feature tree constitutes a possible locus for phonological rules and various well-formedness conditions. McCarthy (1988) contains a brief comparison of the two theories concerning the internal organization of the Place Node, what he calls place of articulation theory (PT) and articulator theory (AT), which are represented in (1).[2]

(1)   a. Place of Articulation Theory   b. Articulator Theory

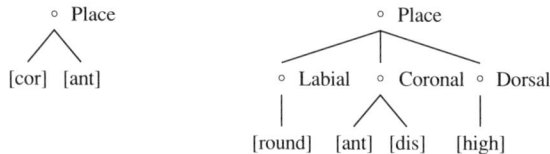

McCarthy compares these two theories and concludes that AT is a better theory in several respects. First, it provides a coherent account for complex segments since complex segments are represented with two different articulators linked to a single Place Node (Sagey, 1986). Second, it is consistent with the evidence of phonological processes that independently manipulate labials, coronals, and dorsals. Third, it is supported by the fact that obligatory contour principle (OCP) effects like root-morpheme co-occurrence restrictions are based on the articulator rather than on the place of articulation.[3]

Given that there are formidable arguments for AT, it seems only natural to give up PT once and for all and adopt AT as part of the universal feature geometry. However, I argue here that such a move cannot be accomplished as easily as we might hope when we consider a set of different languages.[4]

The two theories make different predictions regarding the natural grouping of segments. In a hierarchical representation every node of the tree represents a set of features designated by the theory as a natural class: Every node, terminal and nonterminal, represents a distinct class. PT predicts that each terminal feature such as [coronal] and [anterior] represents a distinct class and that both values of these features play a role in phonological representations and rules.[5] On the other hand, AT proposes that such class nodes as Labial, Coronal, and Dorsal function as monovalent "privative" features, so that the presence of a Coronal Node, for instance, indicates what would have been interpreted in a binary system as [+coronal] and the negative value is not present in any part of the grammar.

PT expresses places of articulation primarily in terms of values of the features [coronal] and [anterior] (Chomsky and Halle, 1968; Clements, 1985; Archangeli and Pulleyblank, forthcoming). Segments that are coronal are produced with the blade or the tip of the tongue; segments that are anterior are produced with a primary constriction in or forward of the palato-alveolar region.[6] Given these two features, one can characterize the four places of articulation as follows.

(2)

	Labials	Dentals	Palatals	Velars
Ant	+	+	−	−
Cor	−	+	+	−

Labials are characterized as [+anterior, −coronal], dentals and alveolars are characterized as [+anterior, +coronal], palatals are characterized as [−anterior, +coronal], and velars are characterized as [−anterior, −coronal]. A primary argument against the feature makeup shown in (2) has been based on the fact that the feature [anterior] does not refer to a single articulator and plays only a definitional role (McCarthy, 1988). However, as noted by Keating (1988), [anterior] is not the only feature with this problem, and it is not even clear whether every place feature should correspond to a single articulator; the features [lateral] and [distributed] are widely used to distinguish a place of articulation but it is disputable whether they in fact refer to a single articulator. Another objection against [anterior] has been based on the putative fact that it never characterizes a natural class of segments referred to by phonological processes, as noted by Kenstowicz and Kisseberth (1979). Contrary to these objections, I argue that all the possible

natural classes of segments are indeed attested as shown below, even though
some groupings are more common than the others. The scheme in (3) shows a
logically possible classification of segments within PT according to each value of
the two distinctive features in question.

(3)   a. [+ant]: labials and dentals
         e.g., Philadelphia English /æ/ tensing (Ferguson, 1975; Labov, 1981;
         Kiparsky, 1988)
         Klamath syllabification (Levin, 1985)
      b. [−ant]: palatals and velars (often as the feature [+high])
      c. [+cor]: dentals, palatals, and retroflex
         e.g., Baule vowel fronting (Vago, 1976)
         Fe?fe? vowel backing, Igbo vowel reduplication (Hyman, 1973)
      d. [−cor] ([+grave]): labials and velars
         e.g. Korean vowel rounding (Lee, 1971)
         Hungarian lenition (Collinder, 1965)
         Old English lenition (Lass and Anderson, 1975)

In Chomsky and Halle (1968) the feature [anterior] is defined to distinguish
sounds produced with a constriction in front of the alveopalatal region from those
produced with a constriction at the back of it. There is evidence that this feature
in fact defines a natural class. In Philadelphia English (Ferguson, 1975; Labov,
1981; Kiparsky, 1988), /æ/ is tensed before tautosyllabic front nasals /m/ and /n/
and front voiceless fricatives /f/, /θ/, and /s/ (e.g., in *jam, pan, staff, path,* and
glass but not in *bang, catch, cap, cash, rash,* and *badge*). Thus, labials and
alveolars but not alveopalatals and velars trigger the rule, a class that can be
specified as [+anterior]. Labov also notes that this Philadelphia set is the minimal set that conditions the tensing of low vowels in English in general.[7]

Another case for the feature [anterior] involves Klamath syllabification, as reported in Levin (1985). According to Levin, sonority ranking is responsible for
characterizing tautosyllabic clusters, and in Klamath labial and dental consonants
(/p/, /t/) should be regarded as more sonorous than palatal, velar, and uvular consonants (/c/, /k/, /q/) and therefore are found closer to a syllable nucleus. This
fact has been incorporated into the grammar in terms of the so-called minimal
sonority distance that assigns the [+anterior] consonants to be more sonorous
than the [−anterior] consonants.

Now let us look at the use of the feature [coronal] in the two theories. AT
(McCarthy, 1988; Sagey, 1986; Mester, 1986; Steriade, 1987b) distinguishes
segments in terms of the active articulators making the constricting gesture
rather than in terms of articulation. Gestures by the lips are characterized by
[labial]; gestures by the blade or tip of the tongue are characterized by [coronal];
gestures by the tongue body are characterized by [dorsal]. The Place Node is
divided into these three Articulator Nodes, which in turn dominate sets of termi-

nal features. Proponents of this theory assume that the Articulator Nodes constitute monovalent features. The presence of a unary node automatically implies the absence of the other Articulator Nodes for noncomplex segments. Postulation of the monovalent Articulator Nodes groups segments into natural classes in a manner quite different from that in PT. PT makes use of both values of the features involved, [+anterior] in addition to [−anterior], [+coronal] as well as [−coronal]; the use of the binary value for each feature results in four natural classes, as shown in (3). On the other hand, in AT the complement of a natural class is not a natural class, that is, the classes of segments that are captured by such features as [−labial], [−coronal], and [−dorsal] in PT no longer constitute a natural class.

A classification of segments in AT is illustrated in (4).

(4) Natural Classes in AT
     Labial: labials
     Coronal: dentals, alveolars, palatals, retroflexes, laterals
     Dorsal: velars

In this account, labial, coronal, and dorsal consonants each form a natural class by themselves, but noncoronals such as labials and velars are not a natural class since there is no apparent feature (e.g., [−coronal]) that groups them together. They are a set just as arbitrary as a set of coronals and labials. I have cited in (3), however, cases where labials and velars are grouped together to the exclusion of coronals, on the one hand, and cases where labials and alveolars are grouped together, on the other. There is, in fact, quite an extensive literature that motivates the feature [−coronal] (or [+grave] with the same attributes) (Jakobson, Fant, and Halle, 1963; Hyman, 1973; Lass, 1976; Vago, 1976; Odden, 1978).

Hyman (1973:329) cites a common historical process of a fricative "at one end of the oral cavity turning into a fricative at the other end of the oral cavity" (/x/ > /f/ in Germanic and /f/ > /h/ in Hausa). This suggests a common feature shared by peripheral consonants.[8]

Another example is the lenition of intervocalic voiced stops in Old English (Lass and Anderson, 1975; Lass, 1976); here labials and velars are grouped as a leniting class, with dentals excluded. The Old English data are shown in (5a), and (5b) states the rule that crucially refers to the [−coronal] segments. The same grouping of consonants by the feature [−coronal] is found in Hungarian and Tavgi initial lenition and in Mordvin and Cheremis intervocalic lenition (Collinder, 1965).

(5) a. Old English Lenition
         būgan → [būɣan] 'bow'
         plēgan → [plējan] 'play' (ɣ → *j* by palatalization)

    gavol < *gabala* (Old High German)
    hydan 'hide' *hyðan
    glīdan 'glide' *glīðan

  b. Intervocalic Continuancy Adjustment

$$\begin{bmatrix} +\text{obs} \\ -\text{cor} \\ \alpha\text{voice} \end{bmatrix} \rightarrow [\alpha\text{cont}]/V\underline{\hspace{2em}}V$$

(Lass and Anderson, 1975:183)

In addition, Hyman (1973:333) cites the rule of vowel reduplication in Fe?fe?
where there is a change of [+grave] to [−grave] in the vowel where the required
stem consonant is also [−grave]. In our terms, it is translated as coronals patterning with front vowels, on the one hand, and labials and velars with back vowels,
on the other.[9]

Also in Korean, there is another phenomenon that justifies the use of [−coro-
nal] as a feature that designates a natural class. As shown in (6), Lee (1971) reports a fifteenth-century rounding in which /ɨ/ (the back unrounded vowel) becomes [u] before /m/, /p/, /ph/, /k/, and /kh/ but not before dentals and palatals.[10]

(6) $ɨ \rightarrow u$ / $\underline{\hspace{2em}}$ *m, p, ph, k, ph*
    ətip- > *ətup*   'dark'
    təik > *təuk*   'more'
    cɨzɨm > *cuzum*   'at the time' (the first [u] due to vowel harmony)

Of course, some arguments for the feature [grave] found in the literature are
the arguments for the feature [−grave], (i.e., [+coronal]) and can be easily
translated into AT. For instance, in Baule the glide /w/ is fronted when preceded
by an alveolar or palatal consonant and followed by /i/ (Vago, 1976). Likewise,
Sanskrit /n/-retroflexion (which I later discuss in detail) treats coronal consonants
(dentals, retroflexes, and palatals) as a blocker of the rule. These cases can be
equally well handled in AT where coronals are grouped as a natural class to the
exclusion of noncoronals. The crucial difference between the two theories lies in
the fact that one, but not the other, allows us to capture noncoronals as a natural class.

One possible way out for AT is to assume radical underspecification and to
propose that what classifies labials and velars as a natural class, as opposed to
dentals, is the presence or the absence of the Place Node.[11] It is true that some
cases reported in the literature can be accounted for by assuming that labials and
velars pattern as if the Place Node has content whereas coronals are transparent
as if they are totally unmarked for place.[12]

The transparency argument is well supported for languages in which there is
only one coronal consonant or where only [+anterior] consonants exhibit a transparency effect, but the argument cannot be maintained in languages with more
than one coronal articulation and where all coronal consonants pattern together.
In PT nondental consonants such as retroflexes and palatals are classified as

[+coronal] and thus they are expected to pattern with dentals–alveolars, whereas AT combined with underspecification would classify them together with the consonants with an underlyingly specified Place Node. Given the fact that there has to be a Place Node for every nonanterior consonant, the data argue for PT rather than AT. Whether or not palatals should have a Coronal Node might be controversial (Avery and Rice, 1989; Keating, 1987), but there are certainly languages with more than one coronal articulation that involves nonpalatal articulation. If the transparency effect were really due to the lack of a Place Node, we would predict that palatals and retroflexes should not pattern with dentals–alveolars. However, palatal and retroflex consonants pattern with dental consonants rather than with the peripheral consonants, thus justifying the use of both values of the feature [coronal]. The intervocalic lenition in Tibetan discussed by Odden (1978) is one such case. There is a rule in Tibetan that changes the grave stops /p/, /k/, and /q/ to the corresponding voiced fricatives [β, γ, q] intervocalically. The fact that the nongrave consonants /t/, /ṭ/, /c/ and /kʸ/ remain unchanged not only argues against AT, where [−coronal] does not define a natural class, but also against an attempt to attribute the transparency effect to underspecification of the Place Node. This is because we cannot assume that retroflex, alveopalatal, and palatal consonants lack a Place Node like dental consonants.

Such facts show that it is not easy to determine a universally valid feature geometry for the Place Node. In the remainder of the article I show in detail two cases that seem to support contradictory theories.

3. THE CORONAL NODE IN SANSKRIT

In this section I propose an analysis for coronal assimilation and /n/-retroflexion in Sanskrit and argue that these phenomena are impossible to account for in PT without very ad hoc stipulations, but that they follow naturally from the representations assumed in AT.

3.1. Coronal Assimilation within AT

First, I look at one of the so-called internal and external sandhi processes. In these sandhi processes, one can observe an asymmetry in the direction of change. For instance, a segment assimilates to such marked features as [+voice] and [+nasal], as well as to the features that characterize retroflex and palatal segments. The unmarked value of each relevant feature, however, never plays a role in assimilation, a fact that supports the radical underspecification hypothesis. I limit my attention to place assimilation and show why it is necessary to have a Coronal Node as a distinct entity in the representations. Couched within the radical underspecification theory (Kiparsky, 1982:54–56; Archangeli, 1984;

Pulleyblank, 1986; Archangeli and Pulleyblank, forthcoming), various sandhi processes can be characterized as instances of spreading specified features to an unspecified slot (Cho, 1990). I show that the asymmetries found in place assimilation can be directly accounted for as autosegmental spreading in underspecified hierarchical feature representations once one assumes the Coronal Node.

The Sanskrit segmental inventory that is relevant for place assimilation is shown in (7).

(7)

	Labial	Dental	Retroflex	Palatal	Velar	Laryngeal
Stops	p	t	ṭ	c	k	
	ph	th	ṭh	ch	kh	
	b	d	ḍ	j	g	
	bh	dh	ḍh	jh	gh	
Nasals	m	n	ṇ			
Glides	v	l	r	y		
Fricatives		s	ṣ	ś		h

First, by adopting AT as the correct theory for Sanskrit, we arrive at the following segmental representation.

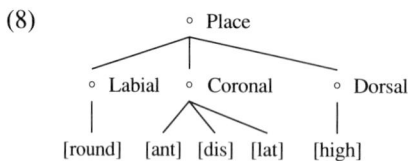

(8)

```
                    ○ Place
           ┌──────────┼──────────────┐
     ○ Labial     ○ Coronal      ○ Dorsal
        │          ╱  │  ╲           │
    [round]    [ant] [dis] [lat]  [high]
```

On the basis of the evidence from feature spreading and delinking, I assume that in underlying representations only one value of a given feature is present. Dental, retroflex, and palatal consonants are all characterized by a Coronal Node and they are differentiated from one another by the features [anterior] and [distributed], as shown in (9a).[13] We assume that dentals are maximally underspecified and the result is (9b).

(9) a. Fully Specified Matrix for Coronals

	Dental	Retroflex	Palatal
Ant	+	−	−
Dis	+	−	+

b. Underspecified Matrix

	Dental	Retroflex	Palatal
Ant		−	−
Dis		−	

Now let us see what kinds of coronal assimilations are found in Sanskrit and how they are accounted for in AT. First, the dental consonants (/t/, /n/, and /s/) assimilate to the following coronal consonant such as retroflex and palatal consonants and in all the other cases remain dental sounds. The consonants /t/ and /n/ also assimilate to /l/.[14] The relevant examples are illustrated in (10) (Whitney, 1889:66–68; Allen, 1962:83–84, 92).[15]

(10)   Sanskrit Coronal Assimilation

mahān + kaviḥ → mahānkaviḥ	'great poet'
mahān + bhāgaḥ → mahānbhāgaḥ	'illustrious'
tān + janān → tāñjanān	'those people'
tān + ḍimbhān → tāṇḍimbhān	'those infants'
trīn + lokān → trīllokān	'three worlds'
tat + dhaukate → taddhaukate	'it approaches'
ut + carati → uccarati	'rise'
etat + chattram → etacchattram	'this umbrella'
vidyut + jāyate → vidyujjāyate	'the dawn is born'
tat + labhate → tallabhate	'it takes'
tatas + ca → tataʃca	'and then'
pātas + ṭalati → pātaṣṭalati	'the foot is disturbed'

We should formulate the rule as spreading specified features from the neighboring Coronal Node, as formalized in (11). Dentals, which are unspecified for such coronal features as [anterior], [distributed], and [lateral], will acquire those features by a spreading mechanism. Dentals do not assimilate to noncoronals since the site of assimilation is the Coronal Node, not the Place Node.[16]

(11)   ○╴╴╴○ Place
           ╲╲╲╷
             ○ Coronal

In order for the rule to have the effect of referring only to the terminal features that define the Coronal Node, the formalization of the rule crucially relies on the presence of the Coronal Node for the triggering consonants. Contrary to the claim made by Avery and Rice (1989), the fact that the assimilation is limited to the Coronal Node does not in itself constitute evidence for the presence of a Coronal Node for dentals, since the target of assimilation could be totally unspecified and still undergo the rule. Also, there is no principle that guarantees their claim that when an articulator node is specified, only assimilation within the articulator will be found. If we formulate the rule as *spread the Coronal Node*, dentals will assimilate within the articulator node even if they are not specified for an empty Coronal Node. Since the rule is spreading the Coronal Node, it is crucial to refer to all the features under the Coronal Node as a set, but it is not necessary to posit the Coronal Node or the Place Node for the target, that is, dentals. Therefore, any of the representations in (12) will work for the target.[17]

(12) a. °   Root   b. °   Root   c. °   Root
                              | |
                           °   Place   °   Place
                                                      |
                                                     °   Coronal

In sum, it is necessary to refer to the Coronal Node as a functional unit and this is not possible to do within PT when it is combined with radical underspecification.

3.2. Coronal Assimilation within PT

Now let us try formulating the same assimilation rule within PT. The consonants are now distinguished not by the active articulator nodes like Labial, Coronal and Dorsal, but by such binary features as [ant], [dor] and [dist]. (13) represents one possible underspecified matrix within PT.

(13)

	Labial	Dental	Retroflex	Palatal	Velar
Ant			−	−	−
Dis		−			
Cor	−				−

Within PT one could formulate the place assimilation in such a way that only the features [anterior] and [distributed] spread. Even though such a rule ensures that dentals will assimilate to retroflexes and palatals, it also predicts that labials will assimilate to velars by acquiring the feature [−anterior] from velars. A technical solution to the problem of preventing labials from participating could be suggested, but the question remains as to why the features [anterior] and [distributed] pair up as a set to the exclusion of [coronal]. One such solution is to stipulate that only dentals assimilate due to their status as a maximally underspecified structure. I believe this move is undesirable because a rule has to refer to the absence of a structure, rather than to the presence of a structure. All these problems arise mainly because one cannot refer to the set of [+coronal] segments in underspecified representations within PT. PT, when combined with no underspecification or contrastive underspecification (Clements, 1988, Steriade, 1987c), can refer to the set of consonants designated by the feature [+coronal], but the prime virtue of radical underspecification disappears, that is, there is no way to explain the asymmetrical nature of assimilation. In radical underspecification the markedness relationships between consonants are expressed by means of underlying feature specifications, but in the other frameworks a totally different mechanism is called for to account for the special behavior of the dental consonant in many languages.

For the Sanskrit data, AT proves to be superior in that it explains why only certain features function as a unit and why the assimilation affects only the maximally unspecified dentals.

3.3. /n/-Retroflexion

Within PT it is also problematic to account for /n/-retroflexion without violating the locality condition that is well motivated in autosegmental phonology. The locality condition proposed by Poser (1985) and Steriade (1987a) dictates that rules cannot stipulate which segment class may or may not intervene between the target and the trigger. In general, rules can refer only to the target and the trigger, and they are subject only to positive, prosodically expressed locality conditions.

The nasal /n/ gets retroflexed when it follows a retroflex continuant. When the trigger is separated from the target by a coronal consonant, retroflexion is blocked. Within AT, /n/-retroflexion can be characterized as a rule that spreads the Coronal Node of a continuant (/ṣ/ and /r/) to an adjacent coronal nasal on the right projection (Whitney, 1889:65; Schein and Steriade, 1986:717–718), as shown in (14).[18]

(14)   a. /n/-Retroflexion

Application		No application	
iṣ-ṇā	'seek'	bhug-na	'bend'
pṛ-ṇā	'fill'	mṛd-nā	'be gracious'
vṛk-na	'cut up'	marj-āna	'wiping'
kṣubh-āna	'quake'	kṣved-āna	'hum'
kṛp-a-māna	'lament'	kṛt-a-māna	'cut'

b.

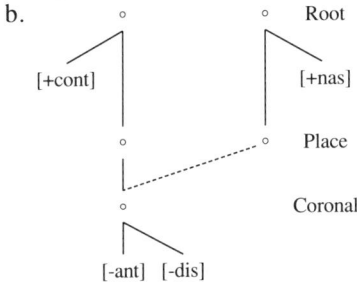

If a Coronal Node intervenes between the trigger and the target, the rule cannot apply since the trigger cannot spread the node across an intervening Coronal Node. In this sense, this rule requires the presence of a Coronal Node to account for the blocking effect. It is necessary to assume that all the relevant default rules have applied before /n/-retroflexion because not only palatals, laterals, and retroflexes but also dentals block the rule.[19]

Let us now analyze this process within PT. There is no concept of Coronal as a class node in the theory and it is impossible to explain why only coronals such as dentals, retroflexes, palatals, and laterals block the rule. In PT, they are all marked for [+coronal], and we can formulate the rule as applying across the [−coronal] specification. This formulation is problematic in two respects. First, it violates the locality condition in that there is an element ([−coronal]) that could optionally intervene between the target and the trigger. Second, even if the rule were formulable without being constrained by the locality condition, the fact that noncoronals are transparent to the application of the rule would remain arbitrary because it is stipulated without any motivation as part of the structural description of the rule. In this account, a hypothetical rule of /n/-retroflexion where coronals are transparent would be equally natural. On the other hand, in AT the fact that coronals function as blockers is directly derivable from the fact that the rule is spreading the Coronal Node onto the adjacent Place Node.

4. KOREAN PLACE ASSIMILATION

4.1. The Place Node under PT

The Korean consonantal inventory is shown in (15).

(15)

	Labial	Dental	Palatal	Velar	Glottal
Plain stops	p	t	c	k	
Aspirate stops	ph	th	ch	kh	
Tense stops	p'	t'	c'	k'	
Plain continuants		s			h
Tense		s'			
Nasals	m	n		ŋ	
Liquid		l			

In Korean we encounter the following place assimilation rules.[20]

(16) PLACE ASSIMILATION (Kim-Renaud, 1974; Cho, 1988)
    a. Dentals assimilate to labials, palatals, and velars.
    b. Labials and palatals assimilate to velars.

In Cho (1988), I attempted to explain why only certain types of assimilation are found in the language, and under what conditions such assimilatory processes take place. Given the assumptions set down by underspecified hierarchical segmental structure, the various seemingly unrelated rules can be collapsed into one single rule that spreads specified—and consequently marked—features to an adjacent, relatively unspecified segment.

It has been observed many times that /t/ is the least marked segment among Korean consonants. In (17) I list some peculiar characteristics of coronals, especially /t/, in addition to several assimilation processes involving place and manner (Kim, 1973:275–278; Kim-Renaud, 1974:231–240).[21]

(17) a. All coronal obstruents, regardless of their place and manner features
         are neutralized to /t/ in the coda position.
      b. In cluster simplification, coronal obstruents are deleted regardless of
         their position.
      c. In one type of compound tensification, coronals, but not labials and
         velars, undergo tensification (e.g., *il-pun* versus *il-t'o*).

Within PT, the following underspecified matrix distinguishes the four places
of articulation (Cho, 1988).

(18)

	Labial	Dental	Palatal	Velar
Ant			−	−
Cor	−			−

On these assumptions, the peculiar array of data can be represented as follows.
First, the dentals /t/ and /n/ assimilate to the following consonant in place.

(19) a. Korean Dental Assimilation
         pat + ko → pakko   'to receive and'
         kotpalo → kopparo   'straight'
         kət + ci → kəcci   'let us uncover'
         hankan → haŋkan   'the Han river'
         han + bən → hambən   'once'

      b.

Thus, any features under the Place Node spread; the rule is stated in (19b). For
labials the specified feature is [−coronal], for palatals it is [−anterior], and
velars are marked for both [−coronal, −anterior]. The reason why dentals cannot function as a trigger is obvious; they are unmarked for any feature and thus
cannot spread. This phenomenon of coronal assimilation is well attested cross-
linguistically (Sanskrit, English, Catalan, Japanese, etc.), but Korean also allows
noncoronals to assimilate, which provides a crucial test case for the two theories
of the Place Node.

Palatals and labials assimilate to velars, but velars never undergo assimilation
and there is no interaction between labials and palatals. Some examples and the
formalizations of the rules are given in (20).

(20) a. *nac + ko → nakko*   'to be low and . . .'
         kam + ki → kaŋ + ki   'a cold'
         əp + ko → əkko   'to bear on the back and . . .'

      b. 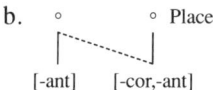   c.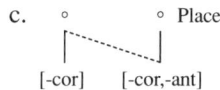

Now let us consider two questions: Why do velars never function as targets and why don't labials assimilate to palatals, and vice versa? The configurations shown by the velar–labial and labial–palatal sequences are represented in (21).

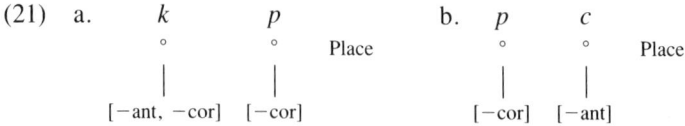

(21)   a.   *k*   *p*   b.   *p*   *c*

                  °   °   Place   °   °   Place

                  | | | |

           [−ant, −cor]   [−cor]   [−cor]   [−ant]

The reason why velars do not undergo the rule is obvious; they are more marked than any other segments and thus always trigger assimilation but never undergo the rule. I have to assume that labials and palatals do not interact in assimilation because they are marked for different unrelated features; labials are marked for [−coronal] and palatals are marked for [−anterior], and thus there is no inter-action between the two consonants.

The formulations introduced so far tell us two things. First, the choice of /t/ as the maximally underspecified segment requires that velars should be more marked than labials or palatals, which is confirmed by the assimilation processes in question. Second, there is something quite similar about the three rule for-mulations in (19b) and (20b–c): That is, assimilation is best characterized as the spreading of marked features to the less specified (rather than unspecified) coda consonant. This intuitive notion of more marked and less marked is formally de-fined as a subset relation, as shown below.

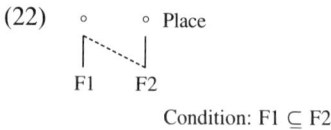

(22)   °   ° Place

          ⌐ ·····⌐

          F1   F2

              Condition: F1 ⊆ F2

Now Korean Place assimilation is collapsed as one feature-filling rule shown in (22), which spreads F2 onto the preceding Place Node when a set of features F1 in the Place Node is a subset of F2. The rule in (22) subsumes all the cases of Place assimilation. First, dentals that are totally unspecified assimilate to what-ever consonants follow them because zero-specification is the subset of any spec-ification. Second, each feature specification of labials and palatals is a subset of the specification of velars and is subsumed under (22). We have seen in this sec-tion that (22) owes its simplicity and generality to PT, where all places of artic-ulation are defined with a binary opposition so that the notion of markedness is derivable from the underspecified matrix. We see in the next section that AT, with its monovalent features, finds it difficult to classify the same segments along the markedness hierarchy.[22]

4.2. Korean Assimilation within AT

Iverson and Kim (1987:186–187) attempt to account for the assimilatory phe-nomenon within AT. First, within this account, the unspecified dentals acquire the Place Node by spreading. The assimilation of labials and palatals to velars should be accomplished by delinking followed by spreading. This is in direct contrast to the formulation in (22) in which no node or feature needs to be delinked.

(23) *p*   *k*   (24) *c*   *k*

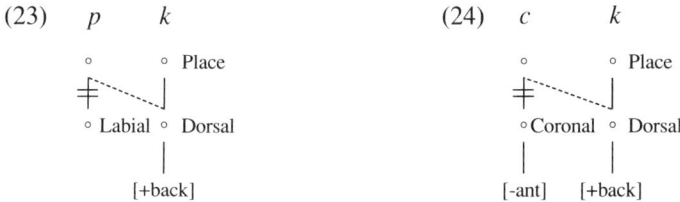

However, the reason why a velar triggers delinking as in (23) and (24) remains a mystery. I assume that the "feature-changing" operations always result from delinking followed by spreading (Poser, 1982; Kiparsky, 1985; Mascaró, 1987). Therefore, the delinking operation should be independently motivated and is not part of the assimilation proper. In many languages coda neutralization or delinking applies independently of spreading (Saltarelli, 1970).[23] In Korean, however, there is no independently motivated deletion, and delinking of a class node is a context-sensitive rule that applies only before a Dorsal Node.

Also, there is no explanation as to why there is no interaction between labials and palatals. In the feature makeup within PT, velars are more marked than labials and palatals and thus trigger spreading. In AT, there is no reason why labials and palatals should be less marked than velars. Assimilation of labials and palatals would be as natural as assimilation of velars to labials or palatals. The prediction of AT is limited to dentals, which are empty and thus will assimilate to any place. In summary, the articulator nodes assumed under AT make it impossible to explain why only certain assimilations are possible.

Before we leave this section, let us discuss an attempt to delimit the contrastive use of class nodes and see how such an attempt is related to our discussion of AT. Avery and Rice (1989) argue that class nodes can be underspecified and that this underspecification is determined by examining contrasts within a phoneme inventory of a given language. In particular, the node activation condition (NAC), stated in (25), universally determines the presence or the absence of a structure, in particular, a class node.[24]

(25) NODE ACTIVATION CONDITION

If a feature is distinctive for a class of segments in a phonological system, then the node that dominates that feature is said to be activated for that class of segments. Active nodes must be present in underlying representation. Inactive nodes are absent in underlying representation.

This delimitation is an attempt to constrain the power of underspecification by assigning a contrastive value to a class node only when it meets the NAC. For instance, the NAC forces specification of any class node that dominates terminal features that are distinctive in the phonology of a particular language. Even though the NAC is defined only on the basis of segment inventories and contrasts, the phonological processes in a given language, in particular, assimilation processes, are assumed to support the representations given by the NAC.

Unfortunately, this condition does not come cost-free; for instance, it depends on a rather arbitrary choice for assigning a structure to palatals. In Catalan, Avery and Rice assume that the Coronal Node is underspecified for palatals and is provided by a default rule. They adopt Keating's (1987) argument that the feature [high] for palatals is not dominated by an Articulator Node but instead links directly to the Place Node. Unlike Catalan, Sanskrit should attach the feature(s) for palatals under the Coronal Node since they participate in coronal assimilation and in /n/-retroflexion. Dentals assimilate not only to a retroflex but also to a palatal, and this assimilation is clearly limited within the Coronal Node. Therefore, the Coronal Node should be assigned to palatals. Similarly, palatals pattern with the other coronals (dentals and retroflexes and the lateral) in blocking /n/-retroflexion. To salvage the NAC, one has to assign a language-particular structure for palatals and assume that in some languages (e.g., Sanskrit) palatals pattern with dentals and contribute to activating a Coronal Node, while in others (e.g., Catalan and Korean) the features of palatals are defined in a different dimension from those of dentals and the other coronal consonants.

5. ON THE UNIVERSALITY OF THE ARTICULATOR NODES

We have seen in the above discussion that the two theories are independently motivated to account for two different languages. In Sanskrit, positing a Coronal Node as a distinctive entity is crucial for two otherwise unrelated phenomena: coronal assimilation and /n/-retroflexion. In a similar fashion, Korean phonology crucially relies on the cross-classifying function of terminal features that are not directly dependent on the Articulator Nodes, as evidenced in two different rules (place assimilation, /i/-rounding). Adoption of a universalist position seems too hasty at this point since a cluster of facts argue for one type of representation over the other in each language. At least, what is comforting is the fact that we do not need to posit two different representations for one language. If we take this parameterization seriously, we predict that every one of the phonological rules in a language should be consistent with a given structure for the Place Node. For instance, we predict that no phonological processes in Sanskrit refer to such features as [+anterior] or [−coronal] since natural groupings of segments defined by the Articulator Nodes are not compatible with those defined by these features.

Until further research reveals otherwise, I assume that the organization of the Place Node is determined once and for all in a given language, even though this position needs further confirmation. It might be still plausible that some processes are articulatorily defined in terms of the articulators, and that some other processes are acoustically defined differently in the same language, but I believe the way the Place Node is organized should not be process-dependent.

The question, however, remains as to how cross-linguistic variation should be accounted for in a principled manner. At this point we can offer only speculations. When we consider the multidimensional nature of speech sounds, it might be only natural to assume that some languages highlight one dimension over the other in organizing the sounds in the grammar. The facts of physics and physiology require us to define sounds in many different ways; for instance, articulatorily defined classes should be distinct from acoustically defined classes. We have to assume that place features are "more articulatorily organized" (in the sense that each articulator is assigned a more active role in organizing the sound system) in Sanskrit and other languages for which we have clear evidence for the Articulator Nodes, thus resulting in a hierarchical structure within the Place Node. On the other hand, a flat structure should be assumed for the Place Node for Korean as well as for other languages where [+anterior] and [−coronal] each define a natural class of segments.[25] If we continue on this speculation, a possible parameter would be the presence versus absence of some active articulators in the underlying representations. If a language does not select such articulators as Labial, Coronal, and Dorsal, the resulting structure would be what PT proposes, and if a language selects those articulators, then each articulator would define a monovalent set of segments as AT predicts.

ACKNOWLEDGMENTS

A shortened version of this article was presented at NELS 20. My sincere thanks go to S. Inkelas, M. Inman, P. Kiparsky, W. Leben, K. P. Mohanan, J. Paolillo, W. Poser, D. Zec, and to the editors of this volume for many helpful comments.

NOTES

[1] Mester (1986) argues that some properties of a feature geometry, in particular, dependency relations between features, vary from one language to another.

[2] In (1), and in all subsequent examples, cor = coronal, ant = anterior, dis = distributed, cont = continuant, lat = lateral, nas = nasal, and obs = obstruent.

[3] I do not review the arguments here because they are well represented in Sagey (1986) and McCarthy (1988) and also because almost all the recent work on feature geometry adopts AT.

[4] The position that the Articulator Nodes are universally specified in underlying representation (Clements, 1988 : 85) seems untenable when we consider a language like Hawaiian (Elbert and Pukni, 1979 : 12). In Hawaiian, there are no underlying coronal obstruents,

and there is no reason to assign a Coronal Node at any point in the derivation. One can assume that the velar place of articulation is the unmarked place, as evidenced by the fact that all of the English coronal consonants are realized as /k/ in the loan phonology.

[5] The particular choice of features like [anterior] and [coronal] is independent of the theory itself. I presently use these features because no other features have been proposed in the literature and substantial arguments have been accumulated for the feature [coronal], though the status of [anterior] is not clear (Kenstowicz and Kisseberth, 1979: 248–249).

[6] Chomsky and Halle (1968) proposed the feature "coronal," which corresponds closely to the feature "grave" of Jakobson *et al.* (1963) with some exceptions. The coronal feature primarily distinguishes dental, alveolar, and palato-alveolar consonants ([+coronal]) from labial, palatal, and velar consonants ([−coronal]). On the other hand, the feature grave is defined acoustically in order to distinguish peripheral sounds and labial and velar consonants ([+grave]) from the medial sounds, dentals, alveolars, palato-alveolars, and palatals ([−grave]). When faced with cross-linguistic evidence that palatals pattern with dentals or alveolars rather than with labials and velars, Halle and Stevens (1979) suggested that the feature coronal could be redefined both articulatorily and acoustically to incorporate palatals and modified the feature coronal to include palatals. Similarly, Lahiri and Blumstein (1984) proposed that palatals need to be grouped together with palato-alveolar, dental, alveolar, and retroflex consonants and that the Chomsky–Halle feature coronal needs to be revised with the same attributes as the Jakobson *et al.* feature grave. I follow this redefinition.

[7] Surely, the question remains as to how to account for the relative scarcity of examples where the feature [anterior] plays a crucial role of classifying segments. Further research might reveal more cases of the front–back distinction among consonants. Proponents of AT limit this feature to distinguishing among coronals.

[8] Becker (1978) claims that interchanges in point of articulation of labial and velar obstruents are always due to similarities in the spectral characteristics of the consonants involved.

[9] It is not clear what the proper relationship is between vowels and consonants that these analyses try to capture with the common feature [grave]. However, what is relevant for our purposes is the fact that peripheral consonants form a natural class.

[10] In the literature (Kim, 1973) *i*-umlaut is reported to apply just in case there is an intervening consonant that is either a labial or a velar. As shown in (6), it causes fronting of the back vowels /a/, /ə/, /o/, /i/, and /u/ before a following /i/ (e.g., *api* → *æpi, əmi* → *emi, aki* → *æki* but no umlaut in *kaci, əti,* or *məli*). In the standard dialect this process is highly morphologized. For the discussion of the Kyungsang dialect in which umlaut is more productive, see Hume (1989).

[11] See Avery and Rice's (1989) analysis of Ponapean for one such case.

[12] See also cases of coronal transparency in Paradis and Prunet (1989b). They observe that in Fula and Guere the Place Nodes of vowels treat intervening [+anterior] coronals as transparent and argue that the lack of a Place Node in coronals explains their transparency to vowels.

[13] In the chart in (9) only one type of stop series is represented, but place assimilation applies to all types of stop series (voiced, aspirated), nasals, and fricatives.

[14] There is yet another type of nasal that is often represented as /m̩/. This nasal assimilates to all places of articulation when followed by a stop, which is different from the

coronal assimilation we are discussing here. The assimilation of /m/ is really a two-step process of delinking a Place Node followed by an automatic spreading of the following Place Node.

[15] Postvocalic word-final fricatives become "visarga" (represented as ḥ), an aspirated continuant homorganic to the preceding vowel.

[16] I assume that the locus of the feature [lateral] is under the Coronal Node, as has been argued by Levin (1987). It may be possible to assume /l/ to be unspecified for the coronal features and to be specified as [−continuant] to contrast with /r/, as pointed out to me by the volume editors. However, in view of the fact that the two processes in Sanskrit (coronal assimilation and /n/-retroflexion) treat /l/ as a coronal consonant, both as a trigger and a blocker, /l/ is best characterized as [+lateral], which is dominated by the Coronal Node.

[17] The principle of simplicity would force us to choose (12a), the simplest structure, in the absence of any positive evidence for the Place Node and the Coronal Node.

[18] The sound ṛ represents a syllabic /r/.

[19] Paradis and Prunet (1989a:340−342) also argue that the Place Node of coronals must be absent in underlying representations but must be present very early in the derivation to block certain derivations.

[20] There are basically two kinds of assimilation processes, place assimilation and manner assimilation. It should be noted that place assimilation is an optional rule that can be suppressed depending on the style and the rate of speech, while manner assimilation is obligatory for some unknown reason.

[21] It is not clear how (17c) can be accounted for by assuming that /t/ is the least marked consonant.

[22] A similar strength hierarchy of consonants is observed by Menn (1975). She reports on a child acquiring English who has a stage in which dentals assimilate to labials and velars, and labials to velars, whereas velars never assimilate and labials do not assimilate to dentals. At present the implications of this phenomenon for language universals and feature geometry are not clear.

[23] Cho (1990) argues that consonant alternations in Hausa, Japanese, Italian, and Old Irish need not be analyzed as place assimilation but rather as syllable-controlled delinking, followed by an automatic spreading.

[24] The NAC is analogous to the contrastive use of the Tonal Node. Inkelas (1988) and Leben (1989) argue that the Tonal Node can function as a contrastive entity in the phonology and that there are real contrasts between the presence and the absence of class nodes, unmotivated in terms of other phonological feature differences.

[25] This reminds us of the configurationality parameter in syntax. The presence or the absence of a VP constituent determines if a language is configurational versus nonconfigurational (Whitman, 1986).

REFERENCES

Allen, W. (1962) *Sandhi*, Mouton, The Hague.

Archangeli, D. (1984) *Underspecification in Yawelmani Phonology and Morphology*, Doctoral dissertation, MIT, Cambridge, Massachusetts.

Archangeli, D. and D. Pulleyblank (forthcoming) *The Content and the Structure of Phonological Representations*, MIT Press, Cambridge, Massachusetts.

Avery, P. and K. Rice (1989) "Segment Structure and Coronal Underspecification," *Phonology* 6.2, 179–200.

Becker, L. (1978) "The Feature[s] [grave]," *Journal of Phonetics* 6, 319–326.

Cho, Y. Y. (1988) "Korean Assimilation," *Proceedings of WCCFL* 7, 41–52.

Cho, Y. Y. (1990) *The Parameters of Consonantal Assimilation,* Doctoral dissertation, Stanford University, Stanford, California.

Chomsky, N. and M. Halle (1968) *Sound Pattern of English,* Harper & Row, New York.

Clements, G. N. (1985) "The Geometry of Phonological Features," *Phonology Yearbook* 2, 223–250.

Clements, G. N. (1988) "Towards a Substantive Theory of Feature Specification," *Proceedings of NELS* 18, 79–93.

Collinder, B. (1965) *An Introduction to the Uralic Languages,* University of California Press, Berkeley and Los Angeles.

Elbert, S. and M. Pukni (1979) *Hawaiian Grammar,* University Press of Hawaii, Honolulu.

Ferguson, C. (1975) "'Short a' in Philadelphia English," in *Studies in Linguistics: In Honor of George L. Trager,* Mouton, The Hague.

Halle, M. and K. Stevens (1979) "Some Reflections on the Theoretical Bases of Phonetics," in B. Lindblom and S. Ohman, eds., *Frontiers of Speech Communication Research,* Academic Press, London.

Hume, E. (1989) "Front Vowels, Palatal Consonants and the Rule of Umlaut in Korean," *Proceedings of NELS* 20.

Hyman, L. (1973) "The Feature [grave] in Phonological Theory," *Journal of Phonetics* 1, 329–337.

Inkelas, S. (1988) "Tone Feature Geometry," *Proceedings of NELS* 18, 223–237.

Iverson, G. and K.-H. Kim (1987) "Underspecification and Hierarchical Feature Representation in Korean Consonantal Phonology," *Proceedings of CLS* 23, 182–198.

Jakobson, R., G. Fant, and M. Halle (1963) *Preliminaries to Speech Analysis,* MIT Press, Cambridge, Massachusetts.

Keating, P. (1987) "Palatals as Complex Coronals: X-ray Evidence," Paper presented at the 62nd annual meeting of the Linguistic Society of America.

Keating, P. (1988) *A Survey of Phonological Features,* Indiana University Linguistics Club, Indiana University, Bloomington.

Kenstowicz, M. and C. Kisseberth (1979) *Generative Phonology,* Academic Press, New York.

Kim, C.-W. (1973) "Gravity in Korean Phonology," *Language Research* 9, 274–281.

Kim-Renaud, Y.-K. (1974) *Korean Consonantal Phonology,* Doctoral dissertation, University of Hawaii, Honolulu.

Kiparsky, P. (1982) "Lexical Morphology and Phonology," in I. Yang, ed., *Linguistics in the Morning Calm,* Hanshin, Seoul, Korea.

Kiparsky, P. (1985) "Some Consequences of Lexical Phonology," *Phonology Yearbook* 2, 85–138.

Kiparsky, P. (1988) "Phonological Change," *Linguistics: The Cambridge Survey,* Vol. 1, Cambridge University Press, Cambridge, England.

Labov, W. (1981) "Resolving the Neogrammarian Controversy," *Language* 57, 267–308.

Lahiri, A. and S. Blumstein (1984) "A Re-evaluation of the Feature Coronal," *Journal of Phonetics* 12, 133–145.

Lass, R. (1976) *English Phonology and Phonological Theory,* Cambridge University Press, Cambridge, England.

Lass, R. and J. Anderson (1975) *Old English Phonology,* Cambridge University Press, Cambridge, England.

Leben, W. (1989) "Tonal Nodes and the Typology of Tone," Talk presented at the Phonology Workshop at Stanford University, Stanford, California.

Lee, B.-G. (1971) "A Reconsideration of NC/MH's Feature System," ms., Indiana University, Bloomington.

Levin, J. (1985) *A Metrical Theory of Syllabicity,* Doctoral dissertation, MIT, Cambridge, Massachusetts.

Levin, J. (1987) "A Place for Lateral in the Feature Geometry," Paper presented at the 62nd meeting of the Linguistic Society of America.

Mascaró, J. (1987) "A Reduction and Spreading Theory of Voicing and Other Sound Effects," ms., Universitat Autonoma de Barcelona.

McCarthy, J. (1988) "Feature Geometry and Dependency," *Phonetica* 43, 84–108.

Menn, L. (1975) "Counterexample to 'Fronting' as a Universal of Child Phonology," *Journal of Child Language* 2, 293–296.

Mester, A. (1986) *Studies in Tier Structure,* Doctoral dissertation, University of Massachusetts, Amherst.

Odden, D. (1978) "Further Evidence for the Feature [grave]," *Linguistic Inquiry* 9, 141–144.

Paradis, C. and J.-F. Prunet (1989a) "Markedness and Coronal Structure," *Proceedings of NELS* 19, 330–344.

Paradis, C. and J.-F. Prunet (1989b) "On Coronal Transparency," *Phonology* 6.2, 317–348.

Poser, W. (1982) "Phonological Representations and Action-at-a-Distance," in H. van der Hulst and N. Smith, eds., *The Structure of Phonological Representations,* Part 2, pp. 121–158. Foris Publications, Dordrecht.

Poser, W. (1985) "There is No Domain Size Parameter," *GLOW Newsletter* 14, 66–67.

Pulleyblank, D. (1986) *Tone in Lexical Phonology,* NLLT Collection, Reidel, Dordrecht.

Sagey, E. (1986) *The Representation of Features and Relations in Non-linear Phonology,* Doctoral dissertation, MIT, Cambridge, Massachusetts.

Saltarelli, M. (1970) *A Phonology of Italian in Generative Grammar,* Mouton, The Hague.

Schein, B. and D. Steriade (1986) "On Geminates," *Linguistic Inquiry* 17, 691–744.

Steriade, D. (1987a) "Locality Conditions and Feature Geometry," *Proceedings of NELS* 17, 595–617.

Steriade, D. (1987b) "On Class Nodes," ms., MIT, Cambridge, Massachusetts.

Steriade, D. (1987c) "Redundant Values," *Proceedings of CLS* 23, 339–362.

Vago, R. (1976) "More Evidence for the Feature [grave]," *Linguistic Inquiry* 7, 671–674.

Whitman, J. (1986) "Configurationality Parameters," in T. Imai and M. Saito, eds., *Issues in Japanese Linguistics,* Foris Publications, Dordrecht.

Whitney, W. D. (1889) *Sanskrit Grammar,* Harvard University Press, Cambridge, Massachusetts.

THE UNDERSPECIFICATION OF CORONALS: EVIDENCE FROM LANGUAGE ACQUISITION AND PERFORMANCE ERRORS

JOSEPH PAUL STEMBERGER *
CAROL STOEL-GAMMON [†]

*Department of Linguistics
University of Minnesota
Minneapolis, Minnesota 55455

[†]Department of Speech and Hearing Sciences
University of Washington
Seattle, Washington 98195

1. INTRODUCTION

Coronals often take part in phonological patterns that are different from those of other places of articulation.[1] For example, in many languages coronals assimilate to other places of articulation even though velars and labials do not assimilate. Such behavior has been used to argue that coronals are not specified for place of articulation in underlying forms.

Arguments for underspecification in coronals are generally based on phonological evidence in adult grammars, and it is a legitimate question as to whether actual speakers of a language use underspecified representations on-line during language production and perception.[2] There are two parts to this question. First, do coronals behave differently from other places of articulation in performance? Second, must such behavior be attributed to underspecification rather than to known performance factors (such as phone frequency)? The answer to both questions appears to be yes. In (1), we present the phonemic inventory of

Phonetics and Phonology, Volume 2
The Special Status of Coronals

English, from which most of our data come, with the place feature specifications that we assume are present in underlying representations.

(1)

	p	b	f	v	m	k	g	ŋ	t	d	s	z	n	θ	ð	š	ž
Labial	√	√	√	√	√												
Dorsal						√	√	√									
Coronal														√	√	√	√
Anterior														−	−		
Distributed																+	+

Some researchers have questioned whether underspecification should be present in the cognitive systems of real speakers. Christdas (1988:85) and Mohanan (1989) point out that, while simplifying lexical entries, underspecification also increases the on-line application of processes and cannot be viewed as an overall simplification of the phonological system. We agree with this point, but there are other reasons why underspecification might be present in performance. The most likely reason is the way that underspecification interacts with nonlinguistic factors such as frequency. Kiparsky (1985:97) proposes that the underspecified value of a feature should be the universally unmarked one (though Archangeli, 1984:56, argues that this is just a tendency). Jakobson (1968) notes that unmarked elements tend to be more frequent than marked elements within a particular language. Studies of phoneme frequencies in English consistently show that alveolars are more common than other places of articulation, both as a class and for most minimal contrasts such as /t/-/p/ and /s/-/f/ (e.g., Denes, 1963: 894). The use of underspecification with a default feature-filling rule amounts to extracting the most frequent value of a feature for a given class of segments and building a bias into the language system to use that value of the feature unless it is specifically contradicted by other phonological information. Frequency is important in many aspects of cognition, and frequency biases are often built into psycholinguistic models (e.g., Morton, 1969:167; Forster, 1979; McClelland and Rumelhart, 1981:379). We suggest that underspecification is another way to effect a frequency bias.

This brings in a new motivation for underspecification that remains to be examined in detail. If frequency does underlie underspecification, then languages with different statistics for phoneme frequency should use different underspecified feature values. Conversely, if we examine languages that have different underspecified feature values, as revealed by standard phonological argumentation, we should find that it is the most frequent feature value in the language that is underspecified in every case. Determining whether these predictions are true is an interesting direction for future research.

Our findings here suggest that [coronal] is underspecified in performance. We argue that performance factors (in particular, phone frequency and the order of acquisition of consonants in English) cannot account for the facts. Markedness without underspecification does not currently work. We also argue that Archangeli's (1984) notion of distinctness in phonological representation is incorrect.

2. SOMETHING VERSUS NOTHING

Before discussing our data, it is useful to show the consequences that should derive from underspecification. Consider the representations in (2).

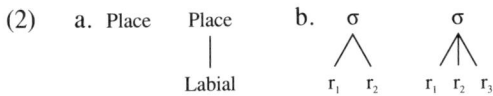

(2)   a. Place   Place   b.   σ   σ
                    | /\   /|\
                  Labial r_1 r_2 r_1 r_2 r_3

In (2a), we contrast presence versus absence of an Articulator Node (in, for example, /t/ versus /p/). In (2b), we contrast presence versus absence of a whole segment, that is, of a Root Node (in, for example, /bi/ versus /bri/). In both cases, there is a phonological element present that corresponds to nothing in the other item. It is very important that the presence of a segment in a sequence is encoded in essentially the same way as the presence of a specified unit on a particular tier. Because of this similarity in their representations, we might expect phenomena of language performance that are sensitive to whether or not a segment is present to also be sensitive to whether or not a feature is specified.

It is thus informative to examine the behavior of consonant clusters. Stemberger and Treiman (1986) explored the behavior of consonant clusters in language production in English in detail, using (1) spontaneous errors from a corpus of 7,500 errors collected by Stemberger from natural speech situations and (2) errors induced in a laboratory setting using the SLIPS procedure (Motley and Baars, 1975).[3] The SLIPS procedure uses phonological priming to bias subjects toward a particular type of error. Consider the example in (3).

(3)   Bias pair   *PLUSH   PUB*
      Bias pair   *PLUG   PUFF*
      Target pair   *PUCK   PLUMP*
      Cue to speak   ?

The pairs of words are presented visually on a computer screen, one pair at a time. Subjects read the pairs silently. When the cue to speak appears, they have to say aloud the last pair of words that they saw (the target pair), as quickly as possible. The target pair is preceded by two bias pairs. The bias pairs set up a bias for the words to begin in a particular way. In (3), the bias is for the first word to begin with /pl/ and the second word to begin with /p/—the reverse of the order in the target pair. This technique induces subjects to produce errors where the sounds are in the primed order rather than in the target order in one word or both (i.e., *PLUCK PLUMP, PUCK PUMP,* or *PLUCK PUMP*).

Stemberger and Treiman report a strong bias for speakers to add consonants to words. For example, for (3), the most common type of error was to add the /l/ to the other word, yielding *PLUCK PLUMP.*[4] It was less common for the /l/ to be lost, to yield *PUCK PUMP.* Stemberger (in press-a), on the basis of a further experiment on clusters, argues that a high rate of exchange errors (where a consonant is lost from one word and added to the other) should often be observed; this high rate derives from the fact that loss errors are often commuted into exchange errors, raising the rate of exchange errors. He argues that a high rate of exchange errors is itself indicative of a strong bias toward adding consonants.[5]

These characteristics hold only for *contextual* errors, that is, errors that involve the interaction of two phonological elements that are present in a word or phrase, as above. Stemberger (1990) reports that *noncontextual* or *no-source* errors, that is, errors that involve only a single phonological unit where the error does not "borrow" any nearby phonological units (e.g., with *GRIN PLUCK* realized as *GRIN PUCK*), show the opposite bias: Consonants are generally lost out of clusters to yield singletons, only rarely being added to singletons to yield clusters. Thus, when something competes with nothing, nothing will win in isolation, but support from a neighboring word will make something win. It should be emphasized that these biases are present only when something competes with nothing, never when something competes with something else.

If alveolars are underspecified for [coronal] in English, they contain nothing that can be brought into competition with something in contextual errors. Since nothing in /t/ contrasts with [labial] in /p/, we expect either a bias to replace /t/ with /p/ (which involves replacing nothing with [labial]), a very high rate of exchange errors, or both, since this is what happens when something competes with nothing in consonant sequences. In contrast, with [labial] in /p/ versus [dorsal] in /k/, we expect that /p/ will substitute for /k/ as often as the reverse (barring the effects of other performance factors), and that there will be a relatively low rate of exchange errors.[6]

The bias to add elements in context seems to be a general property of underspecification. Kiparsky (1985:98) and Archangeli (1984:36) have proposed that, in the unmarked case, assimilations will involve underspecified segments linking to a feature specified in another segment, as part of a general goal of filling in features. In language production, this bias holds not only at the feature level but with whole segments as well. The bias toward exchange errors is a consequence of underspecification that seems to be entirely a performance phenomenon (possibly because exchange between nonadjacent elements is common in performance but rare in phonological processes).

3. CORONALS IN SPEECH ERRORS

We can now examine the behavior of coronals in adult speech errors. In every case, we find that the predictions made on the basis of consonant clusters hold for substitutions involving obstruents and nasals of different places of articulation.

Shattuck-Hufnagel and Klatt (1979:46) reported a bias for alveolars to be replaced by another place of articulation in speech errors made by adult native speakers of English; the observed number (N) of errors of a given type in their corpus is given in parentheses:[7]

(4)   a. *And **SHO** she just cashed it.* [*so*]   ($N = 68$)
      b. *. . . seventy percent to **SO**—to **show** that . . .*   ($N = 33$)

They reported that, in general, segment A and segment B showed symmetrical substitution patterns (i.e., A substituted for B as often as B substituted for A), with one exception: Alveolars tended to be replaced by palato-alveolars more often than the reverse. They suggested that this might be related to the postlexical rule of palatalization in English but were not explicit about how it might be related.

Levitt and Healy (1985:723) addressed whether this bias was present, using the SLIPS technique. Unfortunately, they obtained no reliable difference in contextual errors; null results are difficult to interpret, and we cannot conclude that no bias was present. In noncontextual errors, they found a bias in the opposite direction: Palato-alveolars tended to be replaced by alveolars more often than the reverse. They concluded that there was no bias toward palato-alveolars. However, since noncontextual errors involving consonant clusters generally involve the loss of a consonant, noncontextual substitution errors should mostly involve the loss of specified features; hence, palato-alveolars should tend to be replaced by alveolars, as observed.

Stemberger (in press-a) also examined this issue using the SLIPS technique. He obtained the following results:

(5)

Sample stimulus	Alveolar → palatal	Palatal → alveolar	Exchange
SHUCK SIFT	22	8	12
CHUCK TAP	14	1	6
JOT DANE	5	5	6

There is clearly a bias to replace alveolars with palato-alveolars in contextual speech errors.

Shattuck-Hufnagel and Klatt claimed that there were no other biases, implying that there was no bias for alveolars to be replaced by velars or labials. However, this may have been due to the small numbers of errors involving particular segments. Shattuck-Hufnagel and Klatt examined the question for individual pairs of phonemes rather than for classes of phonemes, and there are simply too few errors involving most pairs of phonemes to allow us to see if a bias is present. Biases are in general easier to observe as more errors are involved. We can obtain larger numbers by comparing classes of phones, that is, by summing all the individual minimal contrasts to compare alveolars as a class with labials as a class. The results of these comparisons are given for Shattuck-Hufnagel and Klatt's (1979) MIT corpus in (6), for Stemberger's (in press-a) corpus in (7), and for Berg's (1988:48) German corpus in (8). The level of statistical significance, using a two-tailed sign test (which tests whether the distribution of numbers in two groups differs from a 50–50 split), is provided in the rightmost column; non-significant differences are labeled "n.s."

(6)   MIT Corpus

	Alveolar → other	Other → alveolar	p
Palato-alveolar	96	54	<.001
Labial	100	88	n.s.
Velar	36	36	n.s.
Interdental	30	24	n.s.

(7)   Stemberger Corpus

	Alveolar → other	Other → alveolar	p
Palato-alveolar	80	51	<.02
Labial	75	82	n.s.
Velar	63	33	<.01
Interdental	30	16	<.10

(8)   Berg Corpus

	Alveolar → other	Other → alveolar	p
Palato-alveolar	50	26	<.01
Labial	79	39	<.05
Velar	67	39	<.05

The results are somewhat inconsistent. All contrasts show a significant bias toward other places of articulation in at least one corpus, but there are some cases where no differences are found. Again, null results are hard to interpret, and the presence of significant differences *somewhere* must be accepted.

Stemberger (in press-a) carried out experiments with other places of articulation in an effort to provide experimental evidence for these other biases, using the SLIPS procedure. He began with two contrasts: velar versus alveolar and velar versus labial:

(9)

	Sample Word Pairs	X → Velar	Velar → X	Exchange
Alveolar	*DULL GUNK*	2	4	13
Labial	*POT COD*	6	8	7

In the few nonexchange errors involving alveolars and velars in (9), substitution is symmetrical, as is the case in the larger number of nonexchange errors involving labials and velars. There is a striking difference in the relative proportions of exchange errors, however: 68.4% of the errors involving alveolars versus velars, 33.3% of the errors involving labials versus velars.

A second experiment also examined two contrasts: labial versus alveolar and labial versus velar:

(10)

Word Pair	Contrast	X → Labial	Labial → X	Exchange
Alveolar stops				
PUB TUCK	p/t	6	5	22
DANE BALE	b/d	13	9	16
		19	14	38
Other alveolar				
MASH NAP	m/n	29	14	17
FOE SOLE	f/s	5	1	3
VEAL ZEST	v/z	6	3	2
		40	18	22
Total alveolar		59	32	60
Velar stops				
POT COD	p/k	4	12	12
BAIT GUIDE	b/g	12	6	9
		16	18	21

There is a bias for alveolars to be replaced by labials, stronger on nasals and fricatives than on stops. For stops, there is instead a high exchange rate, with no real difference between voiced and voiceless stops. For the velar–labial contrasts as a whole, there is a low exchange rate (significantly lower than for alveolar–labial stop contrasts) and no asymmetry of substitutions.[8] The lack of asymmetry of substitution errors between velars and labials is deceptive, however. Examining the p/k and b/g contrasts separately, we see that there is a bias toward velars for the voiceless stops, but a bias toward labials for the voiced stops (a significant difference), with the same low rate of exchanges for both contrasts. While all alveolars interact with labials in one of two fashions (a bias toward the labials or a high exchange rate), different velars behave differently with respect to labials—a fact that has particularly interesting implications for accounts that do not assume underspecification for [coronal], as we see below.

The observed differences are not limited to speech errors made by adults. Stemberger (1989) examined a corpus of speech errors made by his two oldest children (the oldest age included was 6 years, 9 months). These errors were similar to adult speech errors, being nonsystematic deviations from both the adult target and the child's usual "systematic errors" in the pronunciation(s) of the words involved. All were observed after the contrast between the two segments was produced accurately in the environment in which each error occurred. Examples and results are shown in (11) and (12), using a two-tailed sign test.

(11)   a. *Morgan, get out of the **GITCH**. [ditch]*
       b. *I want you **POO**—to play with me.*

(12)

Substitution	N	Substitution	N	p
alveolar → velar	24	velar → alveolar	6	<.005
alveolar → labial	30	labial → alveolar	15	<.025
alveolar → palato	14	palato → alveolar	2	<.05
alveolar → interdental	2	interdental → alveolar	0	n.s.
labial → velar	9	velar → labial	5	n.s

We find the predicted asymmetries between alveolars and other places of articulation, but no bias between labials and velars, just as in adult speech.

Alveolars are thus special. They show a bias to be replaced by other places of articulation. They often show a higher rate of exchange errors than other places of articulation do. These differences are as predicted by underspecification.

4. CORONALS IN CHILD PHONOLOGY

There are three types of evidence from child language that might be considered a priori to show that coronals are special: relative order of acquisition, behavior in harmony processes (assimilation at-a-distance), and fusions (where two adjacent consonants are merged into a single consonant). We might expect coronals to be acquired first and to be more prone to assimilation in harmony.

Relative order of acquisition turns out to be unrevealing. Of the three main places of articulation, velars are acquired last by most children. However, studies have found no differences between alveolars and labials, in any position in the syllable (Stoel-Gammon, 1985:509; Vihman, Ferguson, and Elbert, 1986:26).

Some children master coronals (usually as dentals) first, but others do the opposite. Coronals are not special in this way.[9]

Place of articulation can be examined in consonant harmony, which is common in child language and usually involves two nonadjacent consonants in the same word:

(13)   a. [gak] 'duck' (velar harmony)
       b. [bup] 'book' (labial harmony)

We predict that harmony processes should show a bias toward replacing underspecified elements with specified elements: Most children should assimilate alveolars to velars and labials; few should do the reverse. We make this prediction for two reasons: (1) Such an asymmetry is present in speech errors, and (2) we take the unmarked assimilation to involve linking (structure-building) with no delinking (which would be structure-changing). In contrast, harmony involving two specified features should be equally common in both directions (velars to labials, or vice versa).

The question of whether there are general biases across children in consonant harmony has been asked before. Smith (1973:163) suggests that there are no biases across children. Lewis (1936:183) proposed that newly learned sounds assimilate to sounds that have been in the child's system longer. Menn (1976) and Cruttendon (1978:373) suggest that alveolars assimilate to velars and labials, velars and labials never assimilate to alveolars, and velars and labials show assimilation in one direction only.[10] They differ on the interaction of velars and labials, with Menn stating that labials assimilate to velars but Cruttendon stating that velars assimilate to labials. No real explanation was given for these biases. Menn puts the segments in a "strength" hierarchy and says that weak segments harmonize to stronger ones—an inherently circular description, since no independent evidence was given to justify the hierarchy. Cruttendon suggests that alveolars are more difficult to produce from a motor point of view than velars or labials, and that the bias is toward easier articulations. There are no phonetic data to support the difficulty of alveolars, however, and their commonness in babbling (Locke, 1983) and early words (e.g., Stoel-Gammon, 1985:507) suggest they are motorically easy.

There is also a drawback inherent in the single-subject studies that have so far been done. Child phonology is quite complex and subject to a variety of factors, leading to a great deal of variability between children. Different factors can lead to opposite biases in different children. We need to be certain that the pattern shown by a given child is representative of children as a whole and then determine what factor underlies it. To test this hypothesis adequately, we must examine data from many children. Our study was based on data from 51 children acquiring English. The children fell into two groups. The first group was made up of 33 children studied longitudinally from the age of 9 months to 2 years by the second author, with a focus on lexical items and phonetic segments. (See Stoel-Gammon, 1985:506, for details.) The second group was made up of 18 children on whom enough detailed information was available to be of use to us, from the literature and from unpublished diary studies. (See Stemberger and Stoel-Gammon, 1989, for a full description.)

We first identified a child's nonassimilatory substitutions. We then looked for harmony, eliminating any cases that could be attributed to nonassimilatory processes (following Vihman, 1978:289). For example, if a child replaced velars with alveolars everywhere (as in [da:] 'cow'), a pronunciation such as [dejt] 'Kate' was analyzed not as alveolar harmony but rather as nonassimilatory velar fronting. We excluded a few cases of nonharmonic assimilation between adjacent segments (e.g., the assimilation of /p/ to [k] after the vowel [ow] by six children, involving the dorsal features of [w]). We excluded all cases of full and partial reduplication, where a wide variety of consonants assimilate to a wide variety of consonants regardless of phonetic similarity.

We report here on the nonassimilatory processes as well as on harmony, since they provide a control on the interpretation of harmonies. In order to rule out nonlinguistic explanations for these data in particular, it is crucial that there not be general biases toward, for example, velars that show up in all processes in the child's speech.

The results are given in (14) for alveolar versus velar.

(14)

Substitution	Harmony	Nonassimilatory
Alveolar → velar	19	1
Velar → alveolar	1	24
Bidirectional	3	3

Harmony was classed as *bidirectional* if an alveolar assimilated to a velar in some words (e.g., *dog*), but a velar assimilated to an alveolar in other words (e.g., *Kate*); for most of these children, only regressive assimilation was present, and the order of the two consonants in the word determined which consonant underwent assimilation. As expected from the literature, there is a strong bias toward replacing velars with alveolars in nonassimilatory substitutions ($p <$ .001), but a bias toward velars in harmony ($p < .001$).[11] Note that in all but one instance where velars are assimilated to alveolars, the harmony is actually bidirectional.

The results are given in (15) for alveolar versus labial.

(15)

Substitution	Harmony	Nonassimilatory
Alveolar → labial	18	1
Labial → alveolar	2	4
Bidirectional	4	2

There is a bias toward replacing alveolars with labials in harmony ($p < .01$), as strong as with velar harmony. There were few cases of nonassimilatory substitutions. In all but two cases of harmony where a labial is assimilated to an alveolar, the harmony is bidirectional.

The results are given in (16) for velar versus labial.

(16) Substitution	Harmony	Nonassimilatory
Labial → velar	5	1
Velar → labial	9	1
Both directions	4	0

Nonassimilatory substitutions are very rare. There is no asymmetry of substitution for harmony processes; it is as likely that velars will assimilate to labials as it is the reverse.[12] Since the small difference that is present is for velars to become labials, however, any hypothesis that predicts that labials should tend to become velars is falsified.

There is a third likely source of data in child language that bears on the same issues. In some children's speech, the two consonants in a consonant cluster can be fused into a single segment. When the cluster is /sp/, the usual fusion seems to be [f] (e.g., [fat] 'spot'), combining the manner of /s/ with the place of /p/, that is, combining the specified features of the two segments. We know of seven children where this was the case (three children in our longitudinal sample, three discussed in Ringo, 1985, and one in a pilot experiment with Karen Pollack). We know of no instance in which the opposite happened, where the child combined the underspecified feature values to yield [t]. The fusion yields [f] significantly more often than [t], using a two-tailed sign test. This agrees well with the harmony data and is what might be expected on the basis of underspecification.[13]

5. OTHER EXPLANATIONS

The data discussed above, from speech errors and from child consonant harmony, demonstrate that alveolars behave differently from other places of articulation. Underspecification of [coronal] predicts the results nicely. However, we have not made a case for underspecification as the *only* possible explanation. We can think of three other alternatives: the order of acquisition of the consonants involved, the frequencies of the consonants involved, and markedness without underspecification. None of these alternatives succeeds.

First, consider the finding that alveolars tend to be replaced by other places of articulation. Since alveolars are the most frequent place of articulation, we can account for this by assuming a bias toward less frequent phonemes. Since alveolars are the unmarked place of articulation, we can account for it by assuming a bias toward more marked phonemes. Order of acquisition, however, fails. If we assume a bias toward later-learned phonemes (contra Lewis, 1936), we account for the bias to replace alveolars with velars and palato-alveolars. However, since alveolars and labials are acquired at about the same time, we cannot account for the bias to replace alveolars with labials.

Second, consider the results involving the interaction of labials and velars. For child consonant harmony, there was no reliable difference. For speech errors, voiceless stops were biased toward velars, but voiced stops were biased toward labials. These results are again problematic for order of acquisition; since labials, much like alveolars, are acquired before velars, we would expect a general bias for labials to assimilate to velars. These results are straightforward for a frequency account, however, as long as we assume a bias for phonemes to be replaced by a phoneme of higher frequency; /b/ is more frequent than /g/, and /k/ is more frequent than /p/ (e.g., Denes, 1963:894). Thus, the biases toward /k/ and /b/ can be attributed to phone frequency. These results at first appear surprising from the point of view of markedness. We usually assume that one place of articulation is unmarked relative to another, and this interaction with voicing looks odd. However, Gamkrelidze (1975) proposed just such an interaction. He showed that languages that lack one stop in a series will lack voiceless /p/ but voiced /g/, suggesting that, relative to labials, velars are marked in the voiced series but unmarked in the voiceless series. Our results would thus involve a markedness bias for the labial–velar contrasts, giving a bias toward unmarked /k/ and /b/ from marked /p/ and /g/.

When we put all our results together, however, we find that none of these explanations is consistent with the data. Order of acquisition cannot account for much of the data. For frequency, we must assume a bias toward *less* frequent phonemes when alveolars interact with other places of articulation, but a bias toward *more* frequent phonemes when labials and velars interact. Similarly, for markedness, we must assume a bias toward *more* marked phonemes when alveolars are involved, but a bias toward *less* marked phonemes when labials and velars interact. While it is always possible in a complex world that the cognitive system underlying phonology uses completely different principles for encoding and/or utilizing the phoneme frequency and markedness of alveolars versus other places of articulation, it seems highly unlikely. Arbitrarily stipulating the differences needed is also quite unenlightening. Why should alveolars be special in this way, reversing the usual effects of frequency and/or markedness?

Even if we were to opt for such a complex position, we would run into difficulties. An "antifrequency" bias for alveolars would be impossible to include in models of language processing. There are powerful effects toward more frequent elements in most cognitive domains, including phonological processing and specifically relating to alveolars (Blumstein, 1973; Levitt and Healy, 1985:723).

Frequency effects are usually accounted for by giving the more frequent item a greater level of strength (e.g., Morton, 1969). A similar bias toward the less frequent element is impossible to build in, since an item of low frequency cannot simultaneously be of lesser strength than one of high frequency *and* of greater strength. An "antimarkedness" bias for alveolars runs into the same difficulty, since unmarked elements tend to be more frequent within a language than marked elements. An antimarkedness bias thus subsumes an impossible antifrequency bias. There are thus good theoretical reasons to reject these alternatives even if they were adequate to account for our data.

We claim that (unmarked) coronals are the underspecified place of articulation in English, as in many other languages. This may derive from the fact that alveolars are the most frequent consonants in English, with underspecification being one way in which the system can be biased toward frequent outcomes. Thus, while phone frequency itself cannot account for the data, it may do so indirectly if it underlies the presence of phonological underspecification in the language system. It is possible that it is not phone frequency in speech that is relevant but rather frequency in prelinguistic babbling: Alveolars are more common in babbling than labials or velars (Locke, 1983), though it is not yet known why. It is also possible that children may learn which value is underspecified on the basis of phonological processes observable in adult speech, since adult English has processes to assimilate alveolars to other places of articulation but not the reverse. It is improbable that such knowledge can be attributed to 18-month-olds, but the possibility cannot be ruled out. Lastly, it is possible that the underspecification of alveolars–dentals for [coronal] is innate. Which source of the underspecification of coronals is correct must be determined by future research, but we favor the phone-frequency explanation.

Some children show harmony in the unpopular direction, with alveolars replacing velars or labials. Do these children have velars or labials underspecified, with alveolars specified for place of articulation? This is possible, but not necessary. Most of these children show bidirectional harmony and may simply be assimilating the entire Place Node (assuming that the Place Node is present even when it dominates no Articulator Nodes):

(17) sl_1 sl_2

       pl_1 pl_2

       |

       Labial

For the few children who only assimilate alveolars to velars or labials, there are three possibilities. (1) The child might be deleting the Labial Node near a similar segment that does not have any elements dominated by the Place Node (or that lacks a Place Node):

(18)   pl$_1$ pl$_2$

                          |

        Labial → ∅ / _____

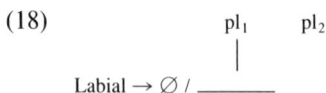

No true assimilation (spreading of nodes) is actually present. This requires that we can explicitly refer to the absence of features in the environment of a rule; Archangeli (1984:47) suggests that this is impossible, since, for example, [labial] and [ ] are not distinct. (2) Assimilation might be taking place at a late point in processing, after default features have been filled in:

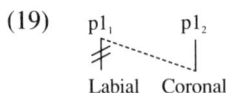

(19)   pl$_1$ pl$_2$

        Labial   Coronal

(3) The odd direction of assimilation may be due to one of the other factors above. For example, in a given child's speech, velars may assimilate to alveolars because alveolars were acquired earlier or are more frequent; indeed, harmony may be the lingering reflex of an earlier nonassimilatory process (Vihman, 1978: 305). We are not denying the importance of these factors or their presence in a minority of cases, just the idea that they alone can account for the facts of consonant harmony.

6. DISCUSSION AND CONCLUSIONS

We have examined error phenomena involving the interaction of coronals with other places of articulation. We have shown that there are systematic biases, such that alveolars tend to be replaced by all other places of articulation (including marked coronals: palato-alveolars and interdentals) and such that alveolars tend to be involved with high rates of exchange errors. In contrast, two specified feature values (as in marked coronals, labials, and velars) are assimilated in a symmetrical fashion (or biased as predicted by other factors such as phone frequency) and show low rates of exchanges. We have considered a number of possible explanations for the data, but only phonological underspecification succeeds.

Recently, some phonologists have begun to argue against the "radical" version of underspecification assumed here. Steriade (1987) and Mester and Itô (1989) argue for a lesser degree of underspecification, where only redundant features are left blank. In English, [coronal] would be specified for obstruents and /n/ because place of articulation is contrastive. The only alveolars for which it would be underspecified are /l/ and /r/; since the only liquids in English are alveolars, their place of articulation is not contrastive.

In order to handle the types of data for which underspecification has been used, such as a special tendency for unmarked elements to assimilate to other elements or a special tendency to be invisible to assimilation processes between other segments, Mohanan (1989) suggests that we can make use of a theory of markedness and naturalness to describe such properties. While this is the case for phonological phenomena in grammars, it should be noted that it is a purely descriptive analysis; in no sense can one say that one has "explained" the tendency of coronals to assimilate by stipulating that they tend to assimilate. Underspecification, in contrast, predicts this to be likely, since there is a well-formedness condition on the output of the grammar that requires that features be filled in, at least for primary place and manner features.

Markedness also does not provide a viable explanation for the data explored here. It would appear that we must assume a bias toward marked segments when alveolars are involved, but a bias toward unmarked segments otherwise. The only way for simple markedness without underspecification to account for this data would be to assume that /p/ is marked relative to /k/, and /g/ is marked relative to /b/. However, this would conflict with information from the segmental inventories of languages, which has more traditionally been linked to markedness. If it could be maintained, however, that this "markedness" is specific to English and may conflict with a default universal markedness, then the data could be accommodated. Whether such a scheme would really work, and whether there is any independent source of data that could be used to argue for it, must await a serious formal attempt to develop such a theory of markedness.

We noted above that some children assimilate velars and labials to alveolars, and that in speech errors a /k/ can be replaced by a /t/. This causes problems for one possible view of underspecified elements: that they are inaccessible to phonological processes (and cognitive processing) (Archangeli, 1984). In these cases, it is clear that speakers are recognizing that alveolars are distinct from labials, for example, and contrast with them. But if [coronal] is absent and inaccessible, how can the speaker tell? Mester and Itô (1989) use just such an argument to argue against radical underspecification. They show that several languages have restrictions on underlying representations and very early phonological rules that refer to the place of articulation of coronals: (1) Homorganic consonants (including coronals) cannot co-occur in a root in Semitic or Javanese, and (2) an early (lexical) rule in Japanese links palatalization preferentially to coronals (which may be considered a problem for underspecification if we assume that feature-filling rules apply only postlexically). Thus, coronals must be distinct from other places of articulation from the beginning of a derivation.

We suggest that Archangeli's view of how to determine when two representations are distinct is wrong. In underlying forms, the phonological information of /t/ is different from that of /p/, because there is a blank that corresponds to [labial]. Morpheme structure conditions can determine that /t/ and /p/ are different in that way, and that /t/ and /d/ seem to be of the same place of articulation. Early rules can discriminate /t/ from /p/. In actual processing during language production, the cognitive systems of English speakers treat /t/ and /p/ as distinct. There is a bias to assimilate the /t/ to the /p/, deriving from underspecification, but the reverse can happen also, due to performance factors that underlie all errors and child phonology phenomena such as consonant harmony. Abandonment of the concept of distinctiveness, as laid out by Archangeli (or supplementing it with the property of *identity*), allows us to handle our data here and makes phenomena in adult grammars, such as Mester and Itô discuss, appear quite reasonable and well behaved. There are no strong arguments in the literature that underspecification *should* render /t/ and /p/ completely indistinct for all purposes, and any such argument would argue against contrastive underspecification and for radical underspecification, in any event. Radical underspecification is the best approach for performance data and for traditional grammatical evidence.

Coronals behave quite specially in language performance, and phonological underspecification of place features appears to be the best explanation for this special behavior. Markedness without underspecification cannot account for our findings and, indeed, conflicts with the way that phoneme frequency is encoded in cognitive models of performance. The possible relationship between underspecification and phone frequency that we have suggested adds a new argument for underspecification in a language, and it is of interest to see if this agrees with other arguments for underspecification. We have provided empirical evidence for the psychological validity of the underspecification of [coronal] in English. Cross-linguistic psycholinguistic studies are needed to see if this underspecification is universal.

ACKNOWLEDGMENTS

This work was supported in part by NSF Research grant #BNS-8710288 to Joseph Paul Stemberger and by Department of Education Grant #G00-8002238 to Carol Stoel-Gammon.

NOTES

[1] By "coronal" we mean here the unmarked coronal in the language, usually dental or alveolar, rather than marked coronals such as interdentals, palato-alveolars, retroflexes, and palatals.

[2] Processes apply on-line if the speaker applies them in the course of a derivation in actual performance. They are off-line if they function as redundancy rules in the lexicon.

[3] All speech errors discussed .n this paper involve the interaction of phonological elements in two different words.

[4] The order of the primed sequences was varied so that the consonant cluster in the target pair appeared in the first word of the pair as often as in the second word of the pair.

This was true of all the experiments reported here; segments always appeared equally often in both orders. The order of the two segments made no difference.

[5] It might be possible that high exchange rates are expected whenever there is a bias for one thing to be involved more in errors than the other. However, experiments have thus far found low exchange rates for frequency-related biases. Further research is needed to determine whether high exchange rates result only from the addition bias.

[6] This expectation presumes, of course, that stops in English cannot be *both* [labial] and [dorsal].

[7] Shattuck-Hufnagel and Klatt combined contextual and noncontextual errors in their analyses.

[8] Errors involving velars were intended to be compared just to the subset of data involving alveolar stops, as these are phonologically closest. We do not want to contend with possible differences that might derive solely from nasals and fricatives showing different effects.

[9] Jakobson (1968) claims that labials are acquired first, but this does not seem to be true in general. Though Ingram (1988) argues that the data are consistent with Jakobson's position, he also notes that they are not compelling.

[10] There are no data regarding harmony between alveolars and either palato-alveolars or interdentals. Marked coronals are generally not acquired until long after the ages for which we have data in this study (e.g., Stoel-Gammon, 1985), by which time harmony has become rare, though we would expect that alveolars tend to assimilate to marked coronals.

[11] All statistical tests in this section used a two-tailed sign test over subjects, excluding ties (i.e., bidirectional harmony).

[12] The lack of a significant asymmetry does not derive from smaller numbers. The proportion of labial–velar harmonies involving labials assimilating to velars (38.5%) is much higher than with the minority harmony processes in the velar–alveolar cases (5%) and the labial–alveolar cases (10%); this would miss significance even with equivalent numbers.

[13] However, there are cases (e.g., Stemberger's second daughter) where /sk/ is apparently fused to [t] (e.g., [tʰip] 'skip'), possibly related to the absence of [x] from the phonetic inventory of English. Perhaps the most common type of fusion occurs with /sn/ and /sm/ clusters, which become voiceless nasals (combining the unmarked voicing of the fricative with the nasal). We believe that such fusions result from performance factors (Stemberger, in press-b).

REFERENCES

Archangeli, D. (1984) *Underspecification in Yawelmani Phonology and Morphology,* Doctoral dissertation, MIT, Cambridge, Massachusetts.

Berg, T. (1988) *Die Abbildung des Sprachproduktionsprozesses in einem Aktivationsflussmodell,* Niemeyer, Tübingen.

Blumstein, S. (1973) *A Phonological Investigation of Aphasia,* Mouton, The Hague.

Christdas, P. (1988) *The Phonology and Morphology of Tamil,* Doctoral dissertation, Cornell University, Ithaca, New York.

Cruttendon, A. (1978) "Assimilation in Child Language and Elsewhere," *Journal of Child Language* 5, 373–378.

Denes, P. B. (1963) "On the Statistics of Spoken English," *Journal of the Acoustical Society of America* 35, 892–904.

Forster, K. I. (1979) "Accessing the Mental Lexicon," in E. Walker, ed., *Explorations in the Biology of Language*, pp. 139–174, Bradford Books, Montgomery, Vermont.

Gamkredlidze, T. V. (1975) "Correlation of Stops and Fricatives in a Phonological System," *Lingua* 35, 231–261.

Ingram, D. (1988) "Jakobson Revisited: Some Evidence from the Acquisition of Polish," *Lingua* 75, 55–82.

Jakobson, R. (1968) *Child Language, Aphasia, and Phonological Universals*, Mouton, The Hague.

Kiparsky, P. (1985) "Some Consequences of Lexical Phonology," *Phonology Yearbook* 2, 83–138.

Levitt, A. G. and A. F. Healy (1985) "The Roles of Phoneme Frequency, Similarity, and Availability in the Experimental Elicitation of Speech Errors," *Journal of Memory and Language* 24, 717–733.

Lewis, M. M. (1936) *Infant Speech: A Study of the Beginnings of Language*, Harcourt Brace, New York.

Locke, J. L. (1983) *Phonological Acquisition and Change*, Academic Press, New York.

McClelland, J. L. and D. E. Rumelhart (1981) "An Interactive Activation Model of Context Effects in Letter Recognition. Part 1. An Account of Basic Findings," *Psychological Review* 88, 375–407.

Menn, L. (1976) *Pattern, Control, and Contrast in Beginning Speech: A Case Study in the Development of Word Form and Word Function*, Doctoral dissertation, University of Illinois, Champaign.

Mester, R. A. and J. Itô (1989) "Feature Predictability and Underspecification: Palatal Prosody in Japanese Mimetics," *Language* 65, 258–293.

Mohanan, K. P. (1989) "On the Bases of Underspecification," ms., Stanford University, Stanford, California.

Morton, J. (1969) "The Interaction of Information in Word Recognition," *Psychological Review* 76, 165–178.

Motley, M. T. and B. J. Baars (1975) "Encoding Sensitivities to Phonological Markedness and Transition Probability: Evidence from Spoonerisms," *Human Communication Research* 2, 351–361.

Ringo, C. C. (1985). *The Nature of Change in Phonological Development: Evidence from the Acquisition of /s/ + Stop and /s/ + Nasal Clusters*, Doctoral dissertation, Brown University, Providence, Rhode Island.

Shattuck-Hufnagel, S. and D. Klatt (1979) "The Limited Use of Distinctive Features and Markedness in Speech Production: Evidence from Speech Errors," *Journal of Verbal Learning and Verbal Behavior* 18, 41–55.

Smith, N. (1973) *The Acquisition of Phonology*, Cambridge University Press, Cambridge, England.

Stemberger, J. P. (1989) "Speech Errors in Early Child Language Production," *Journal of Memory and Language* 28, 164–188.

Stemberger, J. P. (1990) "Wordshape Errors in Language Production," *Cognition*, 35, 123–157.

Stemberger, J. P. (in press-a) "Apparent Anti-Frequency Effects in Language Production: The Addition Bias and Phonological Underspecification," *Journal of Memory and Language*.

Stemberger, J. P. (in press-b) "A Connectionist View of Child Phonology: Phonological Processing without Phonological Processes," in C. Ferguson, L. Menn, and C. Stoel-Gammon, eds., *Phonological Development: Theories and Applications*, York Press, Parkton, Maryland.

Stemberger, J. P. and R. Treiman (1986) "The Internal Structure of Word-Initial Consonant Clusters," *Journal of Memory and Language* 25, 163–180.

Stemberger, J. P. and C. Stoel-Gammon (1989) "Consonant Harmony and Underspecification in Child Phonology," ms., University of Minnesota, Minneapolis.

Steriade, D. (1987) "Redundant Values," *Proceedings of CLS* 23, 339–362.

Stoel-Gammon, C. (1985) "Phonetic Inventories, 15–24 Months: A Longitudinal Study," *Journal of Speech and Hearing Research,* 28, 505–512.

Vihman, M. M. (1978) "Consonant Harmony: Its Scope and Function in Child Language," in J. H. Greenberg, ed., *Universals of Human Language,* Vol. 2: *Phonology.* Stanford University Press, Stanford, California.

Vihman, M. M., C. A. Ferguson, and M. Elbert (1986) "Phonological Development from Babbling to Speech: Common Tendencies and Individual Differences," *Applied Psycholinguistics* 7, 3–40.

ON THE SPECIAL STATUS
OF CORONALS IN APHASIA

RENÉE BÉLAND *
YVES FAVREAU †

*Laboratoire Théophile Alajouanine
Montréal, Québec H3W 1W5, Canada*

†*Laboratoire Théophile Alajouanine and
Université de Montréal
Montréal, Québec H3W 1W5, Canada*

1. INTRODUCTION

Current research in phonological theory indicates that the coronal segments behave differently from labials and velars in harmony and assimilation processes. Avery and Rice (1988:104–105) and Paradis and Prunet (1989) have proposed that coronal segments are characterized by the absence of a Place Node in their representation. Aphasic speech constitutes an important source of data for testing linguistic theories.[1] The special status of coronals in aphasic speech has been pointed out in a study by Puel, Nespoulous, Bonafé, and Rascol (1980:253). Their analysis of substitution errors produced by a pure anarthria patient indicates that alveodental segments were by far the most frequent substitute segments.[2] In particular, the alveodentals /t/, /d/, /s/, and /z/ were significantly more frequent in the aphasic speech output than in the stimuli set. They interpreted this effect as a "frequency effect," the coronal segments being the most frequent phonemes in the French language (Lafon, 1963). They suggested that a comparison of substitutions produced in any other language, in which coronal segments do not represent the most frequent segments of the phoneme inventory,

201

would permit them to decide if the tendency to replace segments by alveodental segments results either from inertia of the phonological system or from inertia of the articulators. Given that most languages have dentals in their phonemic inventory (Zipf, 1949; Kean, 1975), they favored the second hypothesis. One major conclusion of this study was that place of articulation constitutes the most vulnerable feature in substitutions produced by this anarthric patient.

Kilani-Schoch (1982:157) analyzed the spontaneous speech of a French aphasic subject and reported that the coronals /l/, /r/, and /s/ are more likely to be omitted or syncopated than any other segment. Ardila, Montañes, Caro, Delgado, and Buckingham (1989:174) reported that the feature [grave/compact] (Jakobson, Fant, and Halle, 1963) is one of the features most frequently involved in substitutions produced by native Spanish-speaking aphasics ([−grave] consonants are [+coronal] in Chomsky and Halle, 1968). This was observed in all four aphasic groups: Broca, Wernicke, Conduction, and Anomic. Unfortunately, the authors do not report the direction of the tendency and therefore it is not possible to determine if there were more substitutions going from a [+coronal] toward a [−coronal] segment or the reverse, more [−coronal] segments being replaced by [+coronal] segments. Ferreres (forthcoming) reported the following distribution of coronals, labials, and velars in a total of 9,657 segments produced by normal native Spanish speakers in spontaneous speech: coronals = 69.62%, labials = 18.45%, and velars = 11.21%. The most frequent phoneme is /s/, and the least frequent is /ñ/. Analysis of substitution errors produced by 11 Spanish native speakers suffering from Broca's aphasia indicates a negative correlation between the incidence of substitution for a segment and its relative frequency of occurrence in normal subjects' spontaneous speech. Velars and labials are more affected by substitutions than are coronals. These studies on aphasic speech (Spanish and French) indicate that coronal segments behave differently from other segments, whether in segmental substitution, in syncopation, or in addition.

In this article, we analyze phonemic paraphasias in order to assess the special behavior of coronals in French-speaking aphasics.[3] Our objective is to test theoretical assumptions about the internal representations of coronal segments and about their underspecified nature. Analyses are conducted on (1) substitutions (nonassimilatory processes), (2) consonant harmonies, (3) consonant epentheses, (4) syncopations, and (5) vowel spreadings. We use a probabilistic approach, that is, our statistical tests take into account both the relative distribution of the coronal segments in our stimuli sets and the relative distribution of coronal segments in the French consonant inventory (there are 9 coronals, 5 labials, and 3 velars). For instance, the chance of a coronal segment being substituted depends on the number of coronal segments in the stimuli sets. The probability of a coronal segment being used as an epenthetic segment is higher (52% or 9/17) than the probability of a labial (29% or 5/17) or of a velar (17% or 3/17) given that coronals represent more than half (9/17) of the total consonant inventory of the

French language. Our analyses indicate that coronals behave differently from labials and velars in substitutions, consonant epentheses, syncopations, and vowel spreadings even when the higher frequency of coronals is taken into account.

2. METHOD

Phonological disturbances are part of the semiology of most, if not all, aphasic syndromes. Data presented in this article come from two corpora collected from subjects with Broca's, Wernicke's, conduction, and mixed aphasia and from normal control subjects.[4]

2.1. Corpus A (Béland, 1985)

A total of 29 aphasic subjects (7 Broca's, 10 Wernicke's, 6 conduction, and 6 mixed) with left cerebral lesions were selected for this study. All subjects (native French speakers) were paired with a normal control subject with respect to age, sex, and educational level. A repetition task and a reading-aloud task of 321 word stimuli were administered to the 58 subjects. The stimuli were selected on the basis of length (four phonemes) and syllabic structure. The list included examples of the 12 possible combinations of C and V present in French: CVCV, VCVC, CCVC, CVCC, CCCV, VCCC, VVCV, CVVC, VVCC, VCCV, and CCVV. The words were also selected for their segmental content, and the distribution of each consonant segment was controlled. A total of 4,286 simple errors (that is, errors in which one and only one target segment is omitted, substituted, or added) were collected from aphasic subjects (repetition = 1,850, oral reading = 2,436), and 1,289 from control subjects (repetition = 766, oral reading = 523). Control subjects produced overall six times less errors than aphasic subjects, but the distribution and the nature of the errors are similar to those of errors produced by aphasic subjects. For this reason, analyses are not conducted separately on aphasic data and on control subjects' data.

2.2. Corpus B (Favreau, 1989)

Four aphasic subjects (2 Wernicke's, 1 conduction, and 1 mixed) matched for age, sex, and schooling with four control subjects were submitted to a repetition task comprising a total of 144 stimuli. Two-thirds of the stimuli (96) were real words and one-third (48) was nonsense words. Words were selected for their frequency of occurrence (low and high frequencies according to Pérennou and de Calmès, 1987) and for their syllabic structure.[5] Nonsense words had identical phonological characteristics to those of real words.[6] The purpose of employing nonwords in the stimuli set was twofold. First, we wanted to set the phonological structure of stimuli apart from other lexical attributes such as lexical frequency, grammatical function, or semantic features. We know from the psycholinguistic literature (Hudson and Bergan; 1985, McCarthy and Warrington, 1984:469–472; Seidenberg and McClelland, 1987; Favreau, Nespoulous, and Lecours, forthcoming) that such characteristics play an important role in on-line oral word production. In nonword stimuli, such lexical factors cannot interfere with the phonological structure. Our second motivation for the introduction of nonword stimuli in Corpus B was the impossibility of subjects using internal feedback for their production. The absence of underlying representations for nonwords forced the speakers to use different strategies for the oral reproduction of such stimuli. Our hypothesis was that the absence of underlying representation favors the emergence of "pure" phonological processes.[7] A total of 362 simple errors were collected: 343 from aphasics and 19 from control subjects. As in Corpus A, no distinction was made between errors produced by aphasics and those produced by normals.

3. SEGMENTAL REPRESENTATION

In this article we assume the simplified feature geometry model presented in (1).

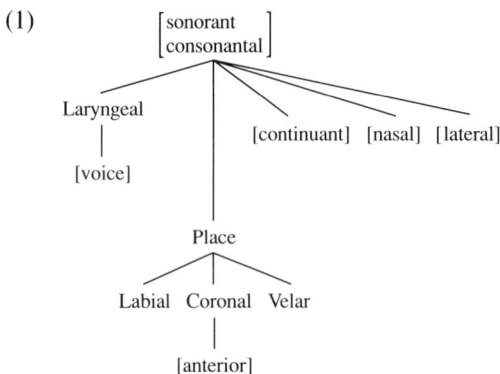

(1)

$$\begin{bmatrix} \text{sonorant} \\ \text{consonantal} \end{bmatrix}$$

Laryngeal

[continuant] [nasal] [lateral]

[voice]

Place

Labial Coronal Velar

[anterior]

The simplified version presented in (1) is quite similar to the one assumed by Sagey (1986), Avery and Rice (1988:101), Paradis and Prunet (1989), and others. The Root Node, composed of the features [sonorant] and [consonantal], dominates the Laryngeal and Place Nodes, as well as the terminal features [continuant], [nasal], and [lateral]. The Place Node dominates the Labial, Coronal, and Velar articulator nodes. The Laryngeal Node dominates the feature [voice] and the Coronal Node dominates the feature [anterior]. In French, this feature is distinctive in the representation of the fricative coronals /s/ and /z/ ([+anterior]) and /ʃ/ and /ʒ/ ([−anterior]): We assume that only marked features are present in underlying representations (URs), for instance, the features [+voice] and [−anterior], but not [−voice] or [+anterior], appear in URs.

4. SUBSTITUTIONS AND CONSONANT HARMONIES: PREDICTIONS

A special status has been attributed to coronals by a number of linguists. Kean (1975) considers coronals as the least marked consonants. Kiparsky (1985:97) argues that the feature value [+coronal] can be absent in underlying representations. Archangeli and Pulleyblank (1989:204–208), Kiparsky (1982), and Paradis and Prunet (1989), among others, adopt a radical underspecification approach, in which only nonredundant values are present underlyingly. Within such an approach, /ʃ/ and /ʒ/ are the only coronals in the French language with a Place Node in UR. On the other hand, Clements (1987), Mester and Itô (1989: 276–282), Steriade (1987), and others adopt a contrastive underspecification approach; they consider that feature values are present underlyingly only if they are necessary to distinguish at least two segments in URs. Avery and Rice (1988: 105), who also assume a model of contrastive underspecification, argue that when a feature is distinctive for a given pair of phonemes in a language, the node that dominates this feature is present in the UR of both phonemes, but only the feature with a marked value is present. As the feature [anterior] is distinctive for the pairs /s/:/ʃ/ and /z/:/ʒ/ of the consonant inventory of French, fricative coronals /s/ and /z/ as well as /ʃ/ and /ʒ/ would have a Place Node and a Coronal Node.

In both types of underspecification, some coronal segments lack a Place Node in their respective representations. We hypothesize that these segments behave differently from labials and velars in substitutions. We first compare the substitutions of coronals with those of labials and velars, then we look at the directionality of consonant harmonies in stimuli, including two consonants of different places of articulation.

4.1. Distributions of Substitutions in Corpora A and B

The percentages of coronals, labials, and velars in stimuli sets of both corpora and the frequency of substitutions involving these three classes are given in (2).

(2) a. Corpus A (321 word stimuli)

Distribution in word stimuli	Distribution of substituted segments
coronals = 420 (61.6%)	coronals = 295 (57.5%)
labials = 191 (28%)	labials = 147 (28.6%)
velars = 71 (10.2%)	velars = 71 (13.8%)

b. Corpus B (144 stimuli)

Distribution in word stimuli	Distribution of substituted segments
coronals = 148 (61.6%)	coronals = 70 (64.2%)
labials = 64 (26.8%)	labials = 23 (21.10%)
velars = 28 (11.6%)	velars = 16 (14.9%)

Distribution in nonword stimuli	Distribution of substituted segments
coronals = 73 (60.8%)	coronals = 19 (57.5%)
labials = 38 (31.6%)	labials = 13 (39.39%)
velars = 9 (7.5%)	velars = 1 (3.03%)

Coronal segments have the highest percentages in all stimuli sets. Such a distribution introduces a bias toward coronal segments that are more likely to be involved in substitutions. A statistical chi-square test (χ^2) performed on the distributions in (2) indicates that coronals are in fact substituted more often than other consonants but, in the case of Corpus A, significantly less than expected given their frequency in the test ($\chi^2 = 3.63$, d.f. $= 1$, $p < .05$).[8] In Corpus B, the frequency of substitution of coronals is not significantly different from the expected one. (For words, $\chi^2 = 0.349$, d.f. $= 1$, $p < .90$; for nonwords, $\chi^2 = 0.13$, $p < .90$.) The number of substitute candidates is also uneven for the three Articulator Nodes. The French phoneme inventory comprises 9 coronals, (/t/, /d/, /n/, /s/, /z/, /ʃ/, /ʒ/, /l/, and /r/), 5 labials (/p/, /b/, /m/, /f/, and /v/), and 3 velars (/k/, /g/, and /ɲ/).[9] If substitutions were randomly produced, the substitute for a coronal should be a coronal as often as it is a labial or a velar (5 labials + 3 velars = 8 segments), since when a coronal is the target, the 8 remaining coronals of the inventory are available as substitutes. The respective distributions of substitute consonants for coronal, labial, and velar targets that should be expected if substitutions were randomly produced are given in (3), (4) and (5).

(3) Distribution of substitute segments for coronal targets if substitutions were randomly produced:
     coronals > coronals = 50%
     coronals > labials   = 31.25%
     coronals > velars   = 18.75%

(4) Distribution of substitute segments for labial targets if substitutions were randomly produced:
     labials > labials   = 25%
     labials > coronals = 56.25%
     labials > velars   = 18.75%

(5) Distribution of substitute segments for velar targets if substitutions were randomly produced:

velars > velars   = 12.5%
velars > coronals = 56.25%
velars > labials   = 31.25%

The observed and expected distributions for all the possible types of substitutions are given in matrix (6) for Corpus A and in matrix (7) for Corpus B.

(6) a. Observed distribution of substitutions in Corpus A [10]

	Coronals	Labials	Velars	Total
Coronals	230 (44.8%)	42 (8.18%)	23 (4.48%)	295
Labials	39 (7.6%)	96 (18.71%)	12 (2.3%)	147
Velars	32 (6.23%)	14 (2.7%)	25 (4.87%)	71
Total	301 (58.6%)	152 (29.6%)	60 (11.6%)	513

b. Expected distribution in Corpus A

	Coronals	Labials	Velars	Total
Coronals	147 (28.7%)	93 (17.9%)	55 (10.8%)	295
Labials	83 (16.1%)	37 (7.15%)	28 (5.4%)	147
Velars	40 (7.8%)	22 (4.3%)	9 (1.7%)	71
Total	270 (52.6%)	152 (29.6%)	92 (17.9%)	513

(7) a. Observed distribution of substitutions in Corpus B: Word stimuli

	Coronals	Labials	Velars	Total
Coronals	51 (41.6%)	11 (10.1%)	8 (7.1%)	70
Labials	8 (7.1%)	11 (10.1%)	4 (5.55%)	23
Velars	9 (8.25%)	5 (4.6%)	2 (1.8%)	16
Total	68 (62.4%)	27 (24.8%)	14 (12.8%)	109

b. Expected distribution in Corpus B: Word stimuli

	Coronals	Labials	Velars	Total
Coronals	35 (32.1%)	22 (20.1%)	18 (12%)	70
Labials	13 (11.9%)	6 (5.3%)	4 (4%)	23
Velars	9 (8.2%)	5 (4.6%)	2 (1.8%)	16
Total	57 (52.2%)	33 (30%)	24 (17.8%)	109

c. Observed distribution of substitutions in Corpus B: Nonword stimuli

	Coronals	Labials	Velars	Total
Coronals	10 (30.3%)	4 (12.1%)	5 (15.15%)	19
Labials	6 (18.2%)	7 (21.2%)	0	13
Velars	1 (3%)	0	0	1
Total	17 (51.5%)	11 (33.35%)	5 (15.15%)	33

d. Expected distribution in Corpus B: Nonword stimuli

	Coronals	Labials	Velars	Total
Coronals	9.5 (28.8%)	6 (18%)	3.5 (10.8%)	19
Labials	7 (22.2%)	3.25 (9.85%)	2.5 (7.4%)	13
Velars	0.6 (1.7%)	0.3 (1%)	0.2 (.5%)	1
Total	17.1 (52.7%)	9.8 (28.7%)	6.2 (18.6%)	33

The expected value for each of the nine types of substitutions is determined by taking into account both the frequency of the collected substitutions in each of the nine types and the probability for a segment to be used as a substitute.[11]

In Corpus A, substitutions of coronals for coronals are 1.56 times more frequent than expected (230 substitutions observed, 147.2 expected), while substitutions of labials for labials (96 observed, 36.7 expected) and velars for velars (25 observed, 8.7 expected) are, respectively, 2.62 times and 2.87 times more frequent than expected.

In Corpus B, for the word stimuli, substitutions of coronals for coronals are 1.46 times more frequent than expected (51 substitutions observed, 35 expected), while substitutions of labials for labials are 1.9 times more frequent than expected; the frequency of substitutions of velars for velars is the one expected (2 observed, 2 expected). For the nonword stimuli, the frequency of substitutions of coronals for coronals is very close to the one expected (10 observed, 9.5 expected), but the substitutions of labials for labials are 2.15 times more frequent than expected (7 observed, 3.25 expected); the frequency of substitutions of velars for velars is close to the one expected (none observed, 0.2 expected).

A class effect, that is, the tendency for substitute and substituted segments to share the same surface Place Node, is thus present in consonant substitutions of our corpora, for coronals, labials, and velars. However, this effect is not as strong for coronals as it is for labials and velars in Corpus A. In Corpus B, the class effect is also not as strong for coronals as it is for labials; it is not observed for velars, but this is probably due to the small number of velar substitutions (a total of 17 substitutions).

We suggest that the coronal targets are more likely to be replaced by segments of other Place Nodes because they lack a Place Node in their underlying representation. The replacement of a coronal by a labial or a velar is the result of a specification process: The empty Place Node is filled in by a node dominating either a Velar or a Labial Node.

In the case of nonwords, we observed that the number of intercoronal substitutions corresponds to the expected frequency. This observation must be taken cautiously because of the small number of examples involved. However, the tendency to specify a Place Node when none is present in UR seems to be enhanced when no permanent underlying representation is available. The /t/ of the nonword stimulus /topy/, for example, is replaced by /k/ (/topy/ > [kopy]) because it is interpreted as a "flaw" in the underlying representation, further repaired by adding a Place Node that dominates a Velar Node. Further experiments on non-word stimuli will permit us to determine the extent of this specification process.

In summary, with the exception of nonword stimuli, only substitutions in which the substituted and the substitute consonants share a same Articulator Node are more frequent than expected. The place of articulation remains un-changed in most substitutions, whatever the target. However, this class effect is not as strong for coronal targets as it is for velars and labials, presumably because of the absence of a Place Node in the former.

4.2. Consonant Harmony

A number of substitution errors correspond to consonant harmony processes. In these substitutions, one of the target segments is substituted for another seg-ment of the stimulus (e.g., /swaf/ *soif* 'thirst' > [fwaf], in which the target /s/ is replaced by /f/). These substitutions are examples of total segmental assimila-tion. In the cases of consonant harmony, Stemberger and Stoel-Gammon (this volume) report a strong tendency for anterior coronals to assimilate to either la-bials, nonanterior coronals, or velars in normal speech errors. They interpret this tendency as evidence of the underspecification of coronals, arguing that noth-ing can spread from the underspecified segment, while something can spread from the specified segment. For example, if both a /d/ and a /g/ occur in a same phonological unit, they are more likely to become /g/ than /d/ (e.g., *dog* > *gog*, not *dod*).

In our corpora, a total of 110 substitutions are consonant harmonies (contin-uancy assimilations: 17; nasality assimilations: 10; voicing assimilations: 41; and place assimilations: 42). Distribution of the substitutions of the place assimilatory type collected from Corpus A and Corpus B are given in (8).

(8) Distribution of Place Assimilation Examples from Corpora A and B

Coronal > Labial	Labial > Coronal	Velar > Labial	Labial > Velar
$t > b = 0$	$b > t = 2$	$k > p = 2$	$p > k = 0$
$t > m = 4$	$m > t = 0$	$g > m = 1$	$m > g = 0$
$t > v = 1$	$v > t = 0$	Total $= 3$	Total $= 0$
$d > m = 1$	$m > d = 0$		
$s > f = 3$	$f > s = 5$	Coronal → Velar	Velar → Coronal
$l > v = 2$	$v > l = 0$	$t > k = 5$	$k > t = 8$
$r > p = 2$	$p > r = 0$	$d > k = 1$	$k > d = 0$
$\int > p = 0$	$p > \int = 3$	Total $= 6$	Total $= 8$
$ʒ > b = 0$	$b > ʒ = 1$		
$ʒ > v = 0$	$v > ʒ = 1$		
Total $= 13$	Total $= 12$		

The number of examples in which coronals assimilate to velars (e.g., /tYrk/ *Turc* 'Turkish' > [kYrk]; /kYlt/ *culte* 'cult' > [kYlk]) is about the same as the number of examples in which the harmony process goes in the opposite direction (e.g., /talk/ *talc* 'talc' > [talt]) (coronals > velars = 6; velars > coronals = 8). In the same way, coronals assimilate to labials (e.g., /zwav/ *zouave* 'fool' > [vwav]) as often (12 examples) as labials assimilate to coronals (13 examples) (e.g., /swaf/ *soif* 'thirst' > [swas]). In three examples, a labial assimilates to a velar (/kɔpɛ̃/ *copain* 'friend' > [pɔpɛ̃] (produced by two aphasic subjects); /gamɛ̃/ *gamin* 'kid' > [mamɛ̃]); we have no examples of velars assimilating to labials. The small number of examples collected does not allow us to draw conclusions about the assimilation process involving those two places of articulation.

In all the cases involving coronals, there does not seem to be any relation between underspecification and directionality of the assimilation process. We have seen in the beginning of Section 3, however, that in Avery and Rice's version of contrastive underspecification, in addition to the nonanterior coronals /ʃ/ and /ʒ/, anterior fricative coronals /s/ and /z/ have a Place Node in UR. For consonant assimilations involving a coronal and a labial, the isolation of fricative coronals reveals a different picture, as seen in (9).

(9)

	Coronal > labial	Labial > coronal
Coronals /t, d, n, l, r/	10	2
Coronals /s, z/	3	5
Coronals /ʃ, ʒ/	0	5

Our data on consonant harmonies support Stemberger and Stoel-Gammon's hypothesis for examples involving the coronals /t, d, n, l, r/. Assimilation of the coronals /t, d, n, l, r/ to a velar is five times more frequent than the opposite assimilation (10 versus 2). When the coronals /s, z/ or /ʃ, ʒ/ are involved, assimilation of the labial to the coronal is more frequently observed (e.g., /swaf/ *soif* 'thirst' > [swas]). The contrastive underspecification approach in which a Place Node is present for all fricative coronals (/s/, /z/, /ʃ/, /ʒ/) accounts for the tendency observed in our data. The fricative coronals behave like node-specified segments in that there is a node exchange between the Labial and the Coronal Nodes (the replacement of a labial by a coronal can also result from a delinking process affecting the Place Node). The no–Place Node coronals /t/, /d/, /l/, /n/, and /r/, on the contrary, assimilate to the labials. There is thus an asymmetry between the labials and the velars when these consonants co-occur with a coronal. Coronals /t/, /d/, /n/, /l/, and /r/ frequently assimilate to labials (coronal > labial = 10; labial > coronal = 2), whereas velars assimilate to those coronals as much as coronals assimilate to velars (velar > coronal = 8; coronal > velar = 6).

5. CONSONANT EPENTHESIS AND SYNCOPATION PROCESSES

In this section, we analyze examples of syncopation and consonant epenthesis produced by aphasics and control subjects. We are interested in the nature of the consonant epenthetic segments and the nature of the syncopated segments. Both phenomena, syncopation and epenthesis, must be connected in some way. Our hypothesis is that the favorite epenthetic segments should also be the favorite syncopated segments. We assume that epenthetic segments or default segments are less marked.

In aphasic speech, a large number of syncopation examples affect branching onset or codas; for instance, branching constituents such as *br-* and *tr-* are reduced to the obstruents *b-* and *t-* (Béland, 1987:213; Valdois, 1987:214–244). These syncopations are not analyzed in the present study since we are only interested in those that apply in the same contextual environments as epenthesis. We limit our analyses to the word-initial, intervocalic, and word-final positions. First, in Section 5.1, we present the distribution of consonant epenthetic segments and compare it with the one that would be expected if epenthetic segments were randomly selected from the French consonant inventory. Then, in Section 5.2, we present the distribution of syncopated segments of each class in the three positions. Finally, in Section 5.3, we compare the two phenomena with regard to the behavior of coronals.

5.1. Coronals as Epenthetic Consonants in Aphasia and Normal Speech Errors

In a maximal underspecification approach, only nonredundant feature values are present underlyingly. According to Archangeli (1984:58), redundant feature values are those corresponding to the default segment, that is, the epenthetic segment of the phoneme inventory. In the absence of an epenthetic segment in a language, the default segment corresponds to the universally unmarked segment. The French vowel inventory includes the epenthetic vowel schwa, but there is no obvious epenthetic consonant segment. According to Archangeli (1984) and Grignon (1984:174), the default consonant segment in the French phoneme inventory would be /t/, the universally unmarked segment. We should then expect this default segment to be used by aphasic and control subjects as an epenthetic segment. According to Piggott and Singh (1985:416), in an intervocalic context epenthetic segments are usually glides. Whatever epenthetic segments we find in our data, our hypothesis is that their nature is derivable from the structural characteristics of the feature geometry and from an adequate underspecification theory. In particular, given their underspecified nature, we expect the coronals to play an important role in epenthetic processes.

Analyses were conducted on epenthesis examples produced by control and aphasic subjects, for both word and nonword stimuli. We distinguished three contexts for consonant epenthesis: (1) insertion of a consonant segment between two vocalic nuclei (e.g., /dœɔr/ *dehors* 'outside' > [dœlɔr]) or between a surface glide and a vowel (e.g., /Ynjɔ̃/ *union* 'union' > [Ynitɔ̃]), (2) insertion of a consonant segment in a word-initial position (e.g., /Yblo/ *hublot* 'porthole' > [tYblo]) for stimuli with an empty onset in the first syllable, and (3) insertion of a consonant segment in a word-final position (e.g., /aspɛ/ *aspect* 'aspect' > [aspɛn]). The distributions of epenthetic segments found for the three contexts are given in Table 1.

In order to show the special behavior of coronals in consonant epenthesis, we compare in (10) the observed frequency of epenthetic labials, coronals, and velars in the three contexts to the expected distribution if epenthetic segments were randomly selected from the French consonant inventory.

(10)   Expected and observed frequencies of labials, coronals, and velars in epenthesis

	Labials	Coronals	Velars
Expected	29.4%	52.9%	17.6%
Observed			
Word-initially	22.4% (11)	73.5% (36)	4.1% (2)
Intervocalically	7.0% (3)	81.3% (35)	11.6% (5)
Word-finally	7.3% (3)	81.3% (35)	7.3% (3)
Total	12.8% (17)	79.7% (106)	7.5% (10)

In (10), epenthesis examples that correspond to verbal formal paraphasias, assimilations, or /ʔ/ and /h/ epentheses are not taken into account. The expected percentage of coronals is determined by the number of coronals in the French consonant inventory (9 coronals on a total of 17 segments, 9/17 = 52.9%). In word-initial position, the observed distribution of epenthetic segments is significantly different from the expected one (χ^2 = 9.819, d.f. = 2, p < .01). The proportion of coronals is higher than expected (observed = 36 [73.5%], expected = 26 [52.9%]), whereas the proportion of labials and velars is lower than expected. In the intervocalic context, the distribution is also significantly different from the expected one (χ^2 = 14.821, d.f. = 2, p < .01). Coronals are inserted in the intervocalic position with a greater frequency than expected if segments were randomly selected from the consonant inventory. Labials are produced less than expected, while velars are close to chance level (the χ^2 is only 0.873, p < .70). Valdois (1987:109) has reported this same tendency in her analysis of aphasic speech: The coronals /l/, /r/, /n/, /s/, /ʃ/, and /ʒ/ are found in 27 of the 28 collected examples.

In word-final position, the observed distribution is also significantly different from the expected one (χ^2 = 17.467, d.f. = 2, p < .001). The number of coronals inserted in this position is higher than expected, while the number of velars and labials is lower than expected. Mohanan (1989) argues that productively

TABLE 1

DISTRIBUTION OF CONSONANTAL EPENTHETIC SEGMENTS IN CORPORA A AND B[a]

Intervocalic context		Word-initially	Word-finally
Coronals	$t = 7$ (2 ass)	$t = 11$	$t = 3$
	$d = 1$	$d = 5$	
	$n = 5$ (2 ass)	$n = 6$ (1 ass)	$n = 3$
	$l = 24$ (5 ass)	$l = 12$ (2 ass)	$l = 1$
	$r = 7$ (1 ass)	$r = 1$	$r = 11$
	$s = 2$ (2 ass)	$s = 2$	$s = 9$ (1 ass)
	$\int = 2$ (2 ass)	$ʒ = 4$ (2 ass)	$z = 5$
	$ʒ = 1$		$\int = 5$ (1 ass)
Labials	$p = 1$ (1 ass)	$p = 4$ (1 ass)	$p = 1$
	$b = 1$		
	$m = 1$ (vfp)	$m = 6$	$m = 1$
	$v = 3$ (1 vfp)	$v = 1$ $f=1$	$v = 1$
Velars	$k = 5$	$k = 3$	$k = 2$
Laryngeals	$ʔ = 11$	$ʔ = 1$	
	$h = 19$[b]	$h = 13$	

[a] Ass = assimilation; the epenthetic segment is a copy of a segment of the word stimulus (e.g., /laik/ *laïc* 'civil' > [lalik]). vfp = verbal formal paraphasias: the response to the word stimulus is a French word (e.g., /tYœr/ *tueur* 'killer' > [tYmœr] *tumeur* 'tumor').

[b] For 14 of the 19 examples, word stimuli have the grapheme *h* in their orthographic representation (e.g., *ahuri* 'stunned', *dehors* 'outside').

epenthesized consonants are hardly ever coronals; it is clearly not the case with epenthesis in speech errors. In the three contexts, coronals are obviously the favored epenthetic segments.

If the higher frequency of coronals in epenthesis is a consequence of their unspecified nature, epenthetic data could provide external evidence for either the contrastive or the radical underspecification approach. In (11), the coronals are divided into three classes: (1) the anterior coronals /t/, /d/, /l/, /n/, and /r/, (2) the anterior coronals /s/ and /z/, and (3) the nonanterior coronals /ʃ/ and /ʒ/.

(11) Expected and observed frequencies of anterior and nonanterior coronals in epenthesis

	/t, d, n, l, r/	/s, z/	/ʃ, ʒ/
Expected	55.55%	22.22%	22.22%
Observed			
Word-initially	88.88% (32)	5.55% (2)	5.55% (2)
Intervocalically	97.1% (34)	(0)	2.9% (1)
Word-finally	51.4% (18)	37.1% (13)	11.4% (4)
Total	79.2% (84)	14.2% (15)	6.6% (7)

The subdivision is needed in order to see if /s/ and /z/ behave more like /t/, /d/, /n/, /l/, and /r/ or more like /ʃ/ and /ʒ/ in epenthesis. Word-initially and intervocalically, the observed distribution is significantly different from the expected one (initially: $\chi^2 = 16.201$, d.f. $= 2$, $p < .001$; intervocalically: $\chi^2 = 24.639$, d.f. $= 2$, $p < .001$), and the highest contribution to the χ^2 value comes from /t/, /d/, /l/, /n/, and /r/ in both contexts. In the final position, the observed distribution is also significantly different from the expected one ($\chi^2 = 5.446$, d.f. $= 2$, $p < .05$), but this time /s/ and /z/ are used as epenthetic consonants significantly more than /t/, /d/, /n/, /l/, and /r/ ($\chi^2 = 4.51$, d.f. $= 1$, $p < .05$). From these distributions, it is clear that /s/ and /z/ behave differently from /t/, /d/, /n/, /l/, and /r/. The frequency of the /t/, /d/, /n/, /l/, and /r/ epentheses in (11) is much higher than that of /s/ and /z/ in two of the three contexts. According to the radical underspecification approach, the latter should appear as frequently as the former. According to a contrastive underspecification approach such as the one proposed by Avery and Rice (1988), the segments /s/ and /z/ should behave more like /ʃ/ and /ʒ/ than like /t/, /d/, /n/, /l/, and /r/, which is exactly what is observed word-initially and intervocalically. In word-final position, we see the opposite tendency, with significantly more /s/ and /z/ epentheses than either /t/, /d/, /n/, /l/, and /r/ or /ʃ/ and /ʒ/ epentheses. Neither the radical nor the contrastive underspecification approach can account for the special behavior of /s/ and /z/ in this position.

The laryngeals /h/ and /ʔ/ are also inserted in the initial and the intervocalic positions. Clements (1985:234–235), reporting Lass's (1976) analysis of the reductions of full consonants to the glottal consonants /h/ and /ʔ/ (occurring commonly throughout the history of English), considers these reductions as evidence for the autonomy of the Laryngeal Node. After the deletion of everything but the Laryngeal Node, full consonants surface as phonetic /h/ and /ʔ/. In the feature geometry presented in (1), both /h/ and /ʔ/ are underspecified segments with only a Laryngeal Node in their representation. These laryngeals are the most unspecified epenthetic segments found in our epenthesis examples.

5.2. Syncopations of Coronals versus Labials and Velars

The probability of a coronal being syncopated in the initial, intervocalic, and final positions relies solely on the distribution of coronals for these contexts in our stimuli sets. Because the stimuli sets that correspond to Corpus A and Corpus B are different, the analysis of syncopation examples of the two corpora were conducted separately.

5.2.1. CORPUS A

The distribution of coronals, labials, and velars in the stimuli set of Corpus A and the number of syncopations observed for each consonant type are given in (12).

(12)   a. Distribution of coronals, labials, and velars in stimuli set: Corpus A

	Labials	Coronals	Velars
Word-initial	58 (40.5%)	70 (48.9%)	15 (10.4%)
Intervocalic	46 (33.5%)	80 (58.3%)	11 (8.02%)
Word-Final	14 (12.06%)	92 (79.3%)	10 (8.6%)

b. Distribution of observed syncopated consonants: Corpus A

	Labials	Coronals	Velars
Word-initial	5 (17.8%)	22 (78.5%)	1 (3.6%)
Intervocalic	0	5 (100%)	0
Word-Final	3 (5.6%)	42 (79.2%)	8 (15.1%)

In word-initial position, the percentage of syncopated coronals is significantly higher than the percentage of coronals in the stimuli set ($\chi^2 = 9.798$, d.f. $= 1$, $p < .01$). The percentages of the syncopated fricative coronals /s/, /ʃ/, and /ʒ/ is not significantly different from the percentages of the same segments in the stimuli set. In the intervocalic position, the only segments that have been syncopated are the liquid coronals /l/ and /r/. In the same context, the liquids /l/ and /r/ were the most frequent epenthetic coronals (/l/ = 19, /r/ = 6). Thus, there is a perfect symmetry between syncopation and epenthetic processes in this context. This fact might be taken as an indication that /l/ and /r/ are the "true" epenthetic consonants in French.

Word-finally, the distribution of syncopated coronals, labials, and velars is not significantly different from the distribution in the stimuli set ($\chi^2 = 4.409$, d.f. $= 2$, $p > .10$). Among the coronals, the anterior fricatives /s/ and /z/ as well as the nonanterior fricatives /ʃ/ and /ʒ/ are syncopated in a proportion corresponding to their distribution in the stimuli set.

5.2.2. CORPUS B

The distribution of coronals, labials, and velars in the stimuli set of Corpus B and the number of syncopations observed for each consonant type are given in (13).

(13)   a. Distribution of coronals, labials, and velars in stimuli set: Corpus B

	Labials	Coronals	Velars
Word-initial	43 (52.4%)	32 (39%)	7 (8.5%)
Intervocalic	31 (28.7%)	67 (62%)	10 (9.2%)
Word-Final	2 (5.4%)	32 (86.4%)	3 (8.1%)

b. Distribution of observed syncopated consonants: Corpus B

	Labials	Coronals	Velars
Word-initial	0	3 (100%)	0
Intervocalic	0	0	0
Word-Final	0	6 (85.7%)	1 (14.2%)

All but one of the syncopated segments are coronals. No syncopation arises intervocalically and 3 syncopations affect nonword stimuli.

5.3. Coronal Epenthesis versus Coronal Syncopation

At the beginning of Section 5.1, we suggested that the unspecified nature of epenthetic segments should render them unstable and therefore more likely to be syncopated. Our results support this hypothesis. The coronals are both the most frequent epenthetic consonants and the most frequently syncopated ones in the word-initial and intervocalic positions. The representation of epenthetic coronal segments must differ from that of labials and velars. The proposal made from the beginning is that coronals segments lack a Place Node in their representation. We now further test this hypothesis in the analysis of vowel spreading and vowel epenthesis examples.

6. CORONAL TRANSPARENCY IN VOWEL SPREADING

The special behavior of coronals in substitution, consonant epenthesis, and syncopation processes that we have exposed can be accounted for with, or without, the assumption that coronals lack a Place Node. In fact, tendencies observed in the aphasic and the normal speech errors can be accounted for by any representational system that makes visible a structural difference between coronals and labials or velars. The presence or absence of a Place Node is crucial in the cases of a number of vowel spreading examples listed in (14):

(14)   Vowel spreading across the coronals, /l/, /r/, and /t/
       /blɸi/   *bleuï*   'blued'   > [bɸlɸi]
       /plaʒ/   *plage*   'beach'   > [palaʒ]
       /gril/   *gril*   'grill'   > [gIril]
       /grwɛ̃/   *groin*   'snout'   > [gurwɛ̃]
       /bryle/   *brûlé*   'burned' > [byryle]
       /brɔs/   *brosse*   'brush'   > [bɔrɔs]
       /brɥi/   *bruit*   'noise'   > [byryɥi]
       /ɔpte/   *opté*   'opted'   > [ɔpete]

The coronals /l/, /r/, and /t/ are transparent to vowel spreading. The last example in (14) (/ɔpte/ *opté* 'opted' > [ɔpete]) gives an indication of the direction of the vowel spreading process, which is right to left. Valdois (1987:141) also reported a right-to-left direction of vowel spreading in the analysis of examples collected in aphasic speech. When the word stimulus comprises two vowels (e.g., /br̥yle/), the vowel that spreads is the one located immediately on the right of the branching onset. Examples in (15) show that vowel spreading might also be possible across the fricative coronal /s/:

(15) Vowel spreading across the fricative coronal /s/
    /apsɑ̃/   *absent*   'absent' > [apasɑ̃]
    /amsɔ̃/   *hameçon*   'hook' > [amɔsɔ̃]

If we maintain our position on the direction of the spreading (right to left), then we assume that in (15) the nasality is not spread with the vowels /a/ and /ɔ/. Such an analysis is consistent with a feature geometry approach in which the nasality is represented on a node located higher in the tree, that is, directly linked to the Root Node. We found no examples of vowel spreading across the nonanterior fricative coronals /ʃ/ and /ʒ/. Vowel spreading seems to apply across a labial in (16):

(16) /ɔbʒɛ/   *objet*   'object' > [ɔbɔʒɛ].

In fact, the epenthetic vowel /ɔ/ surfaces only when immediately preceded by a labial segment (e.g., /avny/ *avenue* 'avenue' > /avɔny/, /amne/ *amené* 'brought' > [amɔne]; /frwa/ *froid* 'cold' > /fɔrwa/) (Cf. Béland, 1990). Our hypothesis is that the vowel /ɔ/ comes from the propagation of the Labial Node on a schwa, the default epenthetic vowel in French. This analysis is consistent with a right-to-left direction of spreading and the nontransparency of the fricative /ʒ/ (/ɔbʒɛ/ *objet* 'object' > *[ɔbɛʒɛ]). In (15), the vowel /ɔ/ in [amɔsɔ̃] can derive either from a propagation of a Labial Node on a schwa or from a vowel spreading across the coronal fricative /s/. No example of vowel spreading is found across velars. With the word stimulus *squaw,* either the schwa (/skwa/ *squaw* 'squaw' > [sœkwa]) or the vowel /i/ is epenthesized between the /s/ and the velar /k/ (/skwa/ *squaw* 'squaw' > [sikwa]).[12]

Thus, only the transparency of the coronals is manifest. Examples in (15) seem to indicate that the fricative /s/ is also transparent, whereas no example of vowel spreading is found across the nonanterior fricative coronals /ʃ/ and /ʒ/. Analyses of consonant harmonies in (9) and of consonant epentheses (in word-initial and intervocalic contexts) in (11) have led us to favor the contrastive underspecification approach. The transparency of /s/ in vowel spreading, as opposed to /ʃ/ and /ʒ/, is more consistent with a radical underspecification approach, but a larger number of examples is needed to compare the transparency of the coronals /t, d, n, l, r/, as opposed to /s, z, ʃ, ʒ/, from a quantitative point of view.

7. CONCLUSION

The analyses presented here indicate that coronals have a special status in aphasic and normal speech errors. Coronals are replaced by consonants of other places of articulation more often than are labials and velars. They are, with laryngeals /ʔ/ and /h/, the most frequent epenthetic consonants. Word-initially and intervocalically, they are syncopated more often than are velars and labials. Moreover, they are the only consonants clearly transparent to vowel harmony processes.

Rather than a division between anterior (/t, d, n, l, r, s, z/) and nonanterior coronals (/ʃ, ʒ/), our analyses suggest, in some cases, a division between coronals /t, d, n, l, r/ and fricative coronals /s, z, ʃ, ʒ/. Coronals of the first subclass assimilate to labials more frequently than coronals of the second subclass. Coronals /t, d, n, l, r/ are used as epenthetic consonants significantly more than both /s, z/ and /ʃ, ʒ/ in the word-initial and the intervocalic positions.

The special behavior of coronals in speech errors is consistent with the proposal that they have no Place Node in their underlying representation. More data are needed in order to verify whether anterior fricative coronals also lack an underlying Place Node.

ACKNOWLEDGMENTS

We thank Carole Paradis and Jean-François Prunet for useful comments on earlier drafts of this article. We also gratefully acknowledge support by grant PG-28 from the Conseil de Recherches Médicales du Canada as well as fellowships to Favreau from FCAR and CRSH.

NOTES

[1] We define "aphasia" as a speech disturbance following a brain injury. Aphasic subjects described in this study are adults.

[2] "*Pure anarthria* is manifested by an isolated articulatory disturbance; that is, by a specific disorganization of the third phase of oral language [disorganization at the phonetic level]" (Lecours, Lhermitte, and Bryans, 1983:245).

[3] "Phonemic paraphasia" is the aphasiological term used to designate any phonemic error, that is, any substitution, addition, or omission of one (or more) segment(s) of a word stimulus. For instance, [pato], [brato], and [ato] are three different phonemic paraphasias produced on the word stimulus /bato/ *bateau* 'boat'.

[4] "The Broca's aphasic is laconic. The qualitative reduction of his language is obvious. He presents an articulatory disturbance. His speech is slow, laboured, often syllabic (he makes pauses between syllables) and the prosody of his propositional productions may be

greatly reduced. He may evolve towards agrammatism. His comprehension of usual, everyday language is normal or nearly so" (Lecours *et al.*, 1983:86).

"Wernicke's aphasia is identified, in its most characteristic phase, by three principal features, namely: a normal or logorrheic flow of speech which includes all types of aphasic transformations (jargonaphasia) with the exception of phonetic transformations; extremely poor repetition; and a disturbance of spoken language comprehension" (Lecours *et al.*, 1983:93).

"Three principal symptoms are associated with the most characteristic phase of conduction aphasia: when evaluated globally, the flow of speech appears normal or near normal but conversational speech includes evidence of wordfinding difficulty and numerous phonemic approximations and transformations; repetition is markedly disturbed; language comprehension is normal or nearly so" (Lecours *et al.*, 1983:93).

The case of mixed aphasias: "the aphasias may appear—and in fact often do appear at some moment in their evolution—in forms which are somewhere between the classical pictures which we have just described. In general, these intermediate forms bear a fairly clear resemblance to one or another of the classical pictures. In many cases, there is rarely any hesitation in saying whether the aphasia is clearly of a Broca's or a Wernicke's type. Nevertheless, there are certain cases in which this initial clinical judgment itself is not immediately obvious, even in the case of a relatively mild aphasia. Whatever the case, the problems of terminology are usually solved, after describing the features of all these symptom complexes, by saying that the aphasia is *mixed*" (Lecours *et al.*, 1983:100–101).

[5] The stimuli were divided into four groups according to syllabic structure. Group 1 included only CV-CV stimuli, group 2 included V-CV and CV-V, group 3 included CV-CVC, CCV-CV, CVC-CV, and CV-CCV, and group 4 included CV-CCVC, CCVC-CV, CVC-CVC, and CCV-CVC.

[6] All subjects performed significantly better on real words than on nonwords. Three of the four subjects also performed significantly better on high-frequency words than on low-frequency words. One subject was not sensitive to word frequency. The syllabic structure of the stimuli also had a significant impact on performance for three of the four subjects. One subject was not sensitive to syllabic structure.

[7] In fact, we could not eliminate the possibility of a nonword being confused with a real word. For instance, the nonword stimulus /taY/ can be confused with the word /talY/ *talus* 'embankment'.

[8] The chi-square (χ^2) is a standard statistical procedure used to test "whether a significant difference exists between an observed number of objects or responses falling in each category and an expected number based on the null hypothesis" (Siegel, 1956:43). The χ^2 value corresponds to the sum of the squared differences between each observed and expected frequency divided by the expected frequency. The number of degrees of freedom (d.f.) corresponds to the number of categories minus one. Standard statistical tables are then used to convert χ^2 to a probability (p). In this text, the observed distribution is considered as significantly different from the expected distribution when the p value is inferior or equal to .05.

[9] We put the palatal /ɲ/ together with the velar segments. This segment has a very low frequency in French and in our stimuli sets (seven occurrences in stimuli set A and five occurrences in stimuli set B). Our analysis of substitutions involving the segment /ɲ/ indicates that the substitute segment is always the coronal /n/.

[10] The number in the cell (*i*th *j*th) corresponds to the number of times a segment in the *i*th row is replaced by a segment of the *j*th column.

[11] For the cell in the *i*th row and the *j*th column, we first compute the expected value as the sum of all cells in row *i* times the sum of all cells in column *j*, divided by the sum of the entire matrix. This value times the number of segments in the class *i* in the French inventory, minus 1 and divided by 17 (number of consonant segments in the French inventory), corresponds to the expected *i*th *j*th value.

[12] The schwa surfaces as /œ/ in Montréal French.

REFERENCES

Archangeli, D. (1984) *Underspecification in Yawelmani Phonology and Morphology,* Doctoral dissertation, MIT, Cambridge, Massachusetts. Published 1988, Garland, New York.

Archangeli, D. and D. Pulleyblank (1989) "Yoruba Vowel Harmony," *Linguistic Inquiry* 20, 173–218.

Ardila, A., P. Montañes, C. Caro, R. Delgado, and H. Buckingham (1989) "Phonological Transformations in Spanish-Speaking Aphasics," *Journal of Psycholinguistic Research* 18, 163–180.

Avery, P. and K. Rice (1988) "Underspecification Theory and the Coronal Node," *Toronto Working Papers in Linguistics* 9, 101–121.

Béland, R. (1985) *Contraintes syllabiques sur les erreurs phonologiques dans l'aphasie,* Doctoral dissertation, Université de Montréal.

Béland, R. (1987) "Phonologie tridimensionnelle, représentation lexicale et productions aphasiques," *Revue québecoise de linguistique théorique et appliquée* 6, 199–226.

Béland, R. (1990) "Vowel Epenthesis in Aphasia," in J. L. Nespoulous and P. Villiard, eds., *Morphology, Phonology in Aphasia,* Springer-Verlag, New York.

Chomsky, N. and M. Halle (1968) *Sound Patterns of English,* Harper & Row, New York.

Clements, G. N. (1985) "The Geometry of Phonological Features," *Phonology Yearbook* 2, 225–252.

Clements, G. N. (1987) "Towards a Substantive Theory of Underspecification," Paper presented at the University of California, Los Angeles.

Favreau, Y. (1989) *Effet de structure et effet de fréquence dans les erreurs phonémiques des aphasiques,* MA thesis, Université de Montréal.

Favreau, Y., J. L. Nespoulous, and A. R. Lecours (forthcoming) "Syllable Structure and Lexical Frequency Effects in the Phonemic Errors of Four Aphasics," *Journal of Neurolinguistics.*

Ferreres, A. R. (forthcoming) "Phonematic Alterations in Anarthric and Broca Aphasic Patients speaking Argentinian Spanish," *Journal of Neurolinguistics.*

Grignon, A. M. (1984) *Phonologie tridimensionnelle du japonais,* Doctoral dissertation, Université de Montréal.

Hudson, P. T. W. and M. W. Bergan (1985) "Lexical Knowledge in Word Recognition: Word Length and Word Frequency in Naming and Lexical Decision Tasks," *Journal of Memory and Language* 2, 303–345.

Jakobson, R., G. Fant, and M. Halle (1963) *Preliminaries to Speech Analysis,* MIT Press, Cambridge, Massachusetts.

Kean, M. L. (1975) *The Theory of Markedness in Generative Grammar,* Doctoral dissertation, MIT, Cambridge, Massachusetts. (Distributed by Indiana University Linguistics Club, Bloomington)

Kilani-Schoch, M. (1982) "Processus phonologiques, processus morphologiques et lapsus dans un corpus aphasique," in *Publications Européennes, Série XXI Linguistique*, Vol. 17, Peter Lang, Berne.

Kiparsky, P. (1982) "Lexical Phonology and Morphology," in I. S. Yang, ed., *Linguistics in the Morning Calm*, Linguistic Society of Korea, Hanshin, Seoul.

Kiparsky, P. (1985) "Some Consequences of Lexical Phonology," *Phonology Yearbook* 2, 85–138.

Lafon, J. C. (1963) *Message et phonétique*, Presses Universitaires de France, Paris.

Lass, R. (1976) *English Phonology and Phonological Theory*, Cambridge University Press, Cambridge.

Lecours, A. R., F. Lhermitte, and B. Bryans (1983) *Aphasiology*, Baillière-Tindall, London.

McCarthy, R. and E. K. Warrington (1984) "A Two-route Model of Speech Production," *Brain* 107, 463–485.

Mester, R. and J. Itô (1989) "Feature Predictability and Underspecification: Palatal Prosody in Japanese Mimetics," *Language* 65, 258–293.

Mohanan, K. P. (1989) "On the Bases of Underspecification," ms., Stanford University, Stanford, California.

Paradis, C. and J.-F. Prunet (1989) "On Coronal Transparency," *Phonology* 6.2, 317–348.

Pérennou, G. and M. de Calmès (1987) *BDLEX: Banque de données lexicales du français parlé et écrit*, Vol. 1: *Lexique général*. Travaux du Laboratoire Serfia, Toulouse.

Piggott, G. and Singh, R. (1985) "The Phonology of Epenthetic Segments," *Canadian Journal of Linguistics* 30, 415–451.

Puel, M., J. L. Nespoulous, A. Bonafé, and A. Rascol (1980) "Etude neurolinguistique d'un cas d'anarthrie pure," *Grammatica VII* 1, 239–291.

Sagey, E. (1986) *The Representation of Features and Relations in Autosegmental Phonology*, Doctoral dissertation, MIT, Cambridge, Massachusetts.

Seidenberg, M. L. and J. L. McClelland (1987) "A Distributed, Developmental Model of Visual Word Recognition and Naming," Paper presented at the annual meeting of the Psychonomic Society, Seattle, Washington.

Siegel, S. (1956) *Nonparametric Statistics for the Behavioral Sciences*, McGraw-Hill, New York.

Steriade, D. (1987) "Redundant values," *Proceedings of CLS* 23, 339–362.

Valdois, S. (1987) *Les erreurs d'addition et d'omission dans l'aphasie: rôle du gouvernement phonologique*, Doctoral dissertation, Université de Montréal.

Zipf, G. K. (1949) *Human Behavior and the Principle of Least Effort*, Addison-Wesley, Cambridge, Massachusetts.

INDEX

A

Abkhaz, 39, 40, 43, 46
Acquisition, *see also* Child phonology, 1, 181ff.
Advanced Tongue Root, 137
Agrammatism, 219
Air Flow Node, 119, 120
Albanian, 42
Aleut, 47
Algonkian languages, 65, 76
Allen, W., 167
Amerindian languages, 42
Amharic, 21
Anarthria, 201, 202, 218
Anderson, J., 104, 162–164
Anderson, S., 52
Anomic aphasia, 202ff.
Anterior coronal, 39–41, 50, 74, 204, 215, 218
Aphasia, *see also* specific types: Anomic, Broca's, Conduction, Mixed, Wernicke's; and Anarthria, Jargonaphasia, Paraphasia, 2, 3, 20, 21, 201ff.
Apical, 32ff.
Appendix (syllable), 75
Applegate, R., 128, 140
Approximation, 219
Arabic, 13, 23, 24, 26, 53, 55, 58, 59, 118, 120, 129, 138, 140, 195
Arbitrariness, 8, 22
Archangeli, D., 3, 5, 10, 17, 23, 26, 50, 58, 59, 62, 103–105, 127, 130–132, 135, 142, 143, 147, 150, 153, 155, 161, 165, 166, 182–184, 194–196, 205, 211
Ardila, A., 202
Articulator theory, 17, 18, 89, 160ff.
Assimilation, 2, 8, 9, 11, 18, 107ff., 160ff., 181ff., 188ff., 201
Association rule, 64
Asymmetry, 210
Athapaskan, 9, 17, 122, 127ff.
Autosegmental phonology, 2
Avery, P., 2, 7–9, 14–18, 24, 49, 54, 58, 74, 75, 104–107, 114, 121, 122, 143, 165, 167, 173, 174, 176, 201, 204, 205, 210, 214

B

Baars, B., 183
Babbling, 189, 193
Bagemihl, B., 21, 128, 153, 154
Barker, M., 108
Basque, 122
Baule, 162, 164
Becker, L., 25, 176
Beeler, M., 128, 140, 142
Béland, R., 9, 10, 12, 18–21, 23, 211, 217
Berendsen, E., 99
Berg, T., 186
Bergan, M., 204

Bhat, D. N. S., 14, 39, 80, 81, 85, 91, 94
Binariness, *see also* Distinctness, 4, 18, 104, 161, 172
Bloomfield, L., 64, 65, 76
Blumstein, S., 25, 81, 91, 95, 176, 192
Bonafé, A., 2, 201
Borgstrøm, C., 93, 94
Borowsky, T., 107, 153
Boyce, S., 43
Branching constituent, 211
Broca's aphasia, 202ff.
Broselow, E., 21
Bryans, B., 218, 219
Buckingham, H., 202

C

Calmès, M. de, 203
Cambodian, 59
Campbell, L., 139
Carabane Diola, 76
Caro, C., 202
Carrier, 9
Catalan, 9, 116, 117, 122, 171, 174
Catford, J., 30–32, 34, 36, 42, 43, 115
Cerebral lesion, *see also* Aphasia, 203
Chaha, 129
Cheremis, 163
Chilcotin, 128, 139
Child phonology, 9, 19, 20, 177, 188ff.
Chinese, 35, 37, 129
Chinook, 25
Cho, S.-B., 112
Cho, Y.-M., 9, 10, 14, 17, 18, 23, 24, 111, 166, 170, 171, 177
Choctaw, 25
Chomsky, N., *see also* SPE, 2, 6, 14, 21, 25, 37, 41–43, 47, 80, 81, 161, 162, 176, 202
Christdas, P., 130, 182
Chumash, 127ff.
Class Node, 2, 4, 7
Clements, N., 2, 4, 5, 7, 13, 14, 41, 49–51, 54–56, 58, 59, 61–64, 70, 75, 76, 81–87, 92, 93, 99, 102–104, 107, 111, 115, 130, 133, 134, 153, 154, 161, 168, 175, 205, 214
Click, 99
Cluster, 61ff., 183

Cluster condition, 13, 62ff.
Coda condition, 61ff.
Coda neutralization, 173
Cole, J., 128
Collinder, B., 70, 162, 163
Compact, 202
Complement rule, 10
Conduction aphasia, 202ff.
Configurationality parameter, 18, 177
Consonant Place, 83ff., 131
Constituent structure, *see also* Feature geometry, 2
Contextual error, 184
Contrastive specification, 7, 8, 50, 58, 59, 74, 168, 194, 210, 214
Cook, E.-D., 9, 128, 140
Copying, 106, 111ff.
Cree, 65
Cruttendon, A., 189
Czaykowska-Higgins, E., 153
Czech, 38

D

D-effect, *see also* Athapaskan, 147, 148, 154
Dahl's Law, 128
Daniloff, R., 30
Dart, S., 31, 33, 42
Davis, S., 13, 22, 26, 56, 128, 129
Davy, J., 128
Debuccalization, *see also* Delinking, 110ff., 134
Deletion, *see also* Delinking, Syncopation, 2, 20
Delgado, R., 202
Delinking, 106, 110ff., 210
Dem'janeko, M., 35
Denes, P., 182, 192
Diminutives, *see also* Dutch, 96–98
Diola coda condition, 66
Diola Fogny, 62, 65–68, 74
Directionality, 185ff., 202ff.
Distinctness, 6, 7, 20, 23, 24, 183, 195, 196, 205
Distributed, 41–43, 47, 89
Distribution (relative), 202ff.
Disturbance (phonological), 203
Dorsal Node spreading, 10
Dravidian languages, 36

Dresher, E., 23, 121
Durand, J., 76
Dutch, 96–98, 117

E

Elbert, M., 1, 188
Elbert, S., 175
English, 11, 13, 18–20, 26, 33, 42, 49ff.,
    62–64, 107–109, 113, 121, 122, 129,
    162, 163, 171, 176, 182ff.
Ennemor, 25, 97
Epenthesis, 20, 21, 202
Esimbi, 88
Evers, V., 12, 14, 15, 17, 22–24, 153
Ewen, C., 104
Exchange, 19, 187, 188, 210
External evidence, *see* Speech errors, Aphasia

F

Fant, G., 25, 81, 94, 163, 176, 202
Favreau, Y., 9, 10, 12, 18–21, 23
Feʔfeʔ (Bamileke), 162, 164
Feature changing, 173
Feature filling, 172, 182
Feature geometry, 2, 3, 5, 129, 130, 204
Feature organization, *see* Feature geometry
Ferguson, C., 1, 162, 188
Ferreres, A., 11, 202
Finnish, 62, 63, 70–74, 76, 77
Forster, K., 182
Fox, 65
French, 11, 18–21, 33, 42, 76, 77, 201ff.
Frequency, 1, 10–12, 126, 181, 182, 191ff.,
    201ff.
Fricative, 11, 60, 205, 210, 215, 217
Fry, D., 11
Fudge, E., 56
Fula, 9, 21, 50, 54, 59, 74, 176
Fusion, 19, 104, 106, 188ff.

G

Gã, 92
Gaelic, 93, 94
Gamkrelidze, T., 192

Geminate, *see also* Weak gemination, 61ff.,
    104
German, 186
Germanic, 163, 164
Gewirth, L., 95
Glottal, 5
Gokana, 21
Goldsmith, J., 2
Gradation, 72
Grassman's Law, 128
Grave, 202
Greek, 62, 67, 68, 76
Greenberg, J., 13, 53, 55, 129
Grignon, A.-M., 2, 5, 211
Guere, 16, 50, 117, 176
Gussenhoven, C., 99

H

Hakulinen, L., 77
Hála, B., 38
Halefom, G., 129
Halle, M., *see also* SPE, 2, 6, 14, 21, 22, 25,
    37, 40–45, 47, 75, 80, 81, 93, 94, 130,
    161–163, 176, 202
Hamid, A.-H., 118
Hammond, M., 59
Harari, 129
Hardwick, M., 154
Hargus, S., 148
Harmony, 2, 9, 16, 17, 19, 20, 88, 125ff.,
    188ff., 201ff.
Harms, R., 70–73
Harrington, J., 128, 140
Harris, J., 76
Hausa, 163, 177
Hawaiian, 1, 175
Hayes, B., 66, 68, 109
Head-dependent constraint, 119ff.
Healy, A., 185, 192
Height feature, 79
Hewitt, M., 75
Hoijer, H., 129
Hooper, J., 51, 52, 54, 111
Howren, R., 147, 154
Hualde, J., 147
Hudson, P., 204
Hukari, T., 128
Hume, E., 176

Hungarian, 18, 162, 163
Hupa, 47
Hyman, L., 14, 21, 25, 81, 88, 139, 162, 163, 164

I

Identity, 196
Igbo, 139, 162
Indian languages, 35
Indo-European, 128
Inertia, 202
Ingram, D., 197
Inkelas, S., 175, 177
Inman, M., 175
Interdental, 60, 74
Internal evidence, 3
International Phonetic Alphabet, 11
Inventory frequency, 11
Irish, 177
Italian, 177
Itô, J., 5, 13, 23, 24, 49–51, 55, 57, 58, 62, 65, 66, 68, 70, 73–76, 97, 98, 128, 134, 135, 194, 195, 205
Iverson, G., 111, 172

J

Jacobs, H., 91
Jakobson, R., 25, 81, 94, 163, 176, 182, 197, 202
Janda, R., 52
Japanese, 2, 50, 62, 68–70, 74–76, 93, 97, 128, 134ff., 171, 177, 195
Jargonaphasia, 219
Javanese, 13, 59, 195
Jongman, A., 99

K

Kahn, D., 52
Kari, J., 129
Kawasaki, H., 89
Kaye, J., 25, 111
Kean, M. L., 1, 2, 105, 202, 205
Keating, P., 12, 25, 37, 38, 40, 45, 90, 93, 94, 161, 165, 174

Kenstowicz, M., 13, 22, 118, 154, 161, 176
Keyser, J., 56, 64, 70, 72, 76, 89
Kikuyu, 128
Kilani-Schoch, M., 202
Kim, C.-W., 170, 176
Kim, K.-H., 111, 172
Kim-Renaud, Y.-K., 170
Kimenyi, A., 129
Kinkade, M. D., 153
Kinyarwanda, 94, 129
Kiparsky, P., 2, 3, 5, 6, 9, 22, 23, 70, 72, 73, 75–77, 102, 105, 117, 162, 165, 173, 175, 182, 184, 205
Kirghiz, 47
Kisseberth, C., 154, 161, 176
Klamath, 108, 109, 113, 117, 162
Klatt, D., 185, 186, 197
Korean, 9, 10, 18, 111–113, 117, 120, 160ff.
Krauss, M., 122
Kuman, 110ff.

L

Labov, W., 162
Ladefoged, P., 30, 31, 33–35, 37, 39, 41–45, 89
Lafon, J.-C., 201
Lahiri, A., 12, 14, 15, 17, 22–25, 81, 91, 95, 153, 176
Laminal, 32ff.
Laryngeal, *see also* Glottal, Pharyngeal, 2, 65, 73, 77, 121, 134ff.
Lass, R., 162–164, 214
Lateral, 15, 16, 24, 59, 101ff., 126ff., 177
Latin, 129
Leben, W., 175, 177
Lecours, A. R., 218, 219
Lee, B.-G., 162, 164
Leer, J., 122
Length (segmental), 203
Leslau, W., 21, 129
Levin, J., 15, 59, 101, 102, 110–111, 114, 122, 149, 159, 162, 177
Levitt, A., 185, 192
Lewis, M., 189, 192
Lexical factors, 204
Lhermitte, F., 218, 219
Licensing, 73

Linear phonology, 2, 22
Linking condition, 66, 68
Linking rule, 21
Locality condition, 3, 127ff., 169
Locke, J., 189, 193
Lowenstamm, J., 25, 111
Lower Incisors Contact, 43–45
Lyman's Law, 128, 134ff.
Lynch, J., 111

M

Maddieson, I., 1, 11, 15, 25, 29, 30, 33–36,
    39, 41–45, 47, 94, 105
Mannheim, B., 129
Markedness, *see also* Radical underspecifica-
    tion, 2, 5, 6, 7, 16, 21, 22, 63, 105, 114,
    126, 147, 151, 154, 168, 172, 182, 183,
    192, 195, 204
Mascaró, J., 4, 106, 116, 173
Mattina, A., 128
Mau, 16, 50, 117
Maximal underspecification, *see* Radical
    underspecification
McCarthy, J., 4, 13, 15, 55, 59, 62, 87, 89,
    101–103, 107, 110, 114, 129, 130, 134,
    138, 139, 159, 160–162, 175, 204
McClelland, J., 182, 204
Menn, L., 177, 189
Menomini, 62, 64, 65, 74, 76
Mester, A., 5, 13, 23, 24, 49–51, 55, 57, 58,
    59, 97, 98, 118, 119, 128, 134, 135, 162,
    175, 194, 195, 205
Miletič, B., 35, 36
Minimal scansion parameter, *see also* Scansion
    parameter, 17
Mixed aphasia, 203
Modified coda condition, 13, 62ff.
Modified contrastive specification, 7ff., 104
Mohanan, K. P., 5, 19, 22, 175, 182, 195, 212
Monovalence, 7, 104, 161, 172
Montañes, P., 202
Montréal French, 220
Moravcsik, E., 2
Mordvin, 163
Morpheme structure constraint, 12–14, 23,
    50ff., 128, 138, 195
Morphemic tier hypothesis, 128

Morphological interference, 3
Morton, J., 182, 193
Motley, M., 183
Murray, R., 111

N

Nasal, *see also* Velar nasal, 11, 16, 105, 121,
    137
Nash, D., 139
Nater, H., 154
Naturalness, 22, 195
Navaho, 129, 148
Nespoulous, J.-L., 2, 201
Neutralization, 9, 10
Neyt, A., 99
Nikiema, E., 25
Nisgha, 128
Node activation condition, 173, 174, 177
Noncontextual error, 184ff.
Nonsense word, 203ff.
Nonword, *see* Nonsense word,
Nothing, *see also* Something, 183–185, 209
Nupe, 94
Nurse, D., 128

O

Obligatory contour principle, 76, 106, 161
Occurrence frequency, 11
Odden, D., 14, 25, 81, 163
Ohnesorg, K., 36
Ojibwa, 65, 75, 76
Oliverius, Z., 35, 39
Omission, 202ff.
On-line process, 182ff., 196
On-line word production, 204

P

Palatal, 10, 12, 74, 81, 174
Palatal glide, 79ff.
Palatalization, 14, 15, 39, 40, 50, 79ff., 195
Palato-alveolar, 34ff.
Panini, 81
Paolillo, J., 175
Papago, 42

Papuan languages, 111
Paradis, C., 2, 10, 16, 22, 25, 49, 50, 54, 59, ⸲
    67, 74, 75, 99, 117, 121, 148, 153, 176,
    177, 201, 204, 205
Paraphasia (phonemic), 202, 212, 218
Pérennou, G., 203
Performance error, *see* Speech errors
Peripheral Node, 18, 103
Perkell, J., 43
Pharyngeal, 5, 139ff.
Pharyngeal Node, 130, 137
Phonotactics, 49ff., 61ff.
Piggott, G., 4, 15, 25, 75, 104, 106, 121, 130,
    211
Place of articulation theory, 17, 18, 160ff.
Polish, 35–37, 39, 40, 42–44, 80, 85, 94
Pollack, K., 191
Ponapean, 74, 76, 108, 109, 113, 117, 118,
    120, 121, 176
Poser, W., 140, 141, 150, 169, 173, 175
Predictability, 5–7
Prince, A., 70, 71, 73, 75, 77
Probability, *see* Statistics
Prunet, J.-F., 2, 10, 16, 22, 25, 49, 50, 54, 59,
    67, 74, 75, 97, 99, 117, 121, 153, 176,
    177, 201, 204, 205
Psycholinguistics, 204
Puel, M., 2, 201
Pukni, M., 175
Pulleyblank, D., 5, 6, 10, 17, 23, 25, 59, 101–
    103, 105, 114, 127, 128, 130–132, 135,
    142, 143, 150, 153, 155, 161, 166, 205
Pulleyblank, E., 14, 153

Q

Quechua, 129

R

Radical underspecification, 5–7, 50, 58, 59,
    74, 165, 168, 194–196, 205, 211, 214,
    217
Rascol, A., 2, 201
Reading-aloud task, 203
Recasens, D., 37, 38
Redundancy, *see* Contrastive specification
Redundancy rule, 5, 6, 91, 105, 147, 151, 196

Rehg, K. L., 108, 118
Reichard, G., 128
Renck, G., 110
Rendaku, *see also* Japanese, 128ff.
Repetition task, 203
Retroflex, 34ff., 160ff.
Rice, K., 2, 7–9, 14–18, 22, 24, 25, 49, 54,
    58, 74, 75, 103–107, 114, 121, 122, 143,
    148, 155, 165, 167, 173, 174, 176, 201,
    204, 205, 210, 214
Ringo, C., 191
Rubach, J., 80, 81, 85, 94
Rumelhart, D., 182
Russian, 35, 39, 40, 93, 95

S

Sagey, E., 4, 49, 62, 82, 86, 87, 90–94, 103,
    104, 130, 139, 147, 149, 159, 160, 162,
    175, 204
Salish, 128
Saltarelli, M., 173
Sandhi, *see also* Sanskrit, 165ff.
Sanskrit, 18, 113, 122, 128, 160ff.
Sapir, E., 129
Sapir, J., 66, 76
Scansion parameter, *see also* Minimal scansion
    parameter, 127ff.
Schein, B., 107, 128, 169
Secondary articulation, *see also* Palatalization,
    89ff.
Seidenberg, M. L., 204
Sekani, 148
Selkirk, E., 76, 118, 119
Sequential markedness principle, 63
Serbian, 35, 36
Serbo-Croatian, 154
Sereno, J., 99
Sezer, E., 133, 154
Shattuck-Hufnagel, S., 185, 186, 197
Shaw, P., 2, 14, 15–17, 22, 24, 59, 122, 128–
    130, 146, 149, 153, 154
Siegel, S., 219
Simon, P., 33
Singh, R., 3, 211
Slave, 148
Slavic languages, 35, 36, 40, 80
SLIPS procedure, 183ff.
Smith, N., 10, 12, 17, 93, 189

Sohl, D. G., 108, 118
Something, *see also* Nothing, 183–185, 209
Sonorant, 105, 107ff.
Sonority, 76
Spanish, 11, 51, 52, 76, 202
SPE (Sound Pattern of English), *see also* Chomsky, Halle, 38, 40, 41, 43, 47, 81, 82, 86, 89, 91, 92
Speas, M., 148
Speech errors, 3, 9, 18–21, 181ff., 201ff.
Spontaneous speech, 202
Spontaneous Voice Node, 15, 16, 103ff.
Spreading, 9, 10, 90ff., 106, 202ff.
Statistics, 20, 186ff., 202ff.
Steele, S., 59
Stemberger, J., 9, 18–20, 23, 24, 75, 183–186, 188, 190, 196, 197, 209
Steriade, D., 5, 7, 17, 53, 62, 65, 67, 68, 74, 75, 107, 128, 130ff., 149, 150, 155, 162, 168, 169, 194, 205
Stevens, K., 37, 40, 43, 89, 176
Stoel-Gammon, C., 1, 18–20, 23, 24, 188–190, 196, 197, 209
Strength hierarchy, 189
Strict ajacency, 131
Structural complexity constraint, 115ff.
Structural dependency, 102ff.
Structure
  building, 189
  changing, 189
  preservation, 102
Sublingual cavity, 43–44
Substitution, 19, 20, 187ff., 201ff., 202
Švarný, O., 36
Syllable, 8, 51ff, 61ff., 203ff.
Syllable structure constraint, 51ff.
Syncopation, *see also* Deletion, Delinking, 202ff.

T

Tahltan, 17, 122, 127ff.
Tamil, 35
Tavgi, 163
Teeter, K., 128
Thompson, L., 128
Thompson, M., 128
Tier promotion, 84ff.
Toba Batak, 109, 113, 117

Tonal Node, 177
Tongue, 30–32, 44–46
Tongue Position Node, 87ff.
Transparency, 2, 10, 21, 217
Transparency hypothesis, 142
Treiman, R., 183, 184
Trigo, L., 10, 25, 73, 75, 76
Trommelen, M., 96, 117
Tulu, 139
Turkish, 132ff.
Typological inventory frequency, 11

U

Uhlenbeck, E., 13
Ulrich, C., 153
Unariness, 4, 5, 7, 18
Underlying representation (absence of), 204, 208
Underspecification, *see* Contrastive specification, Modified contrastive specification, Radical underspecification, Zero-specification
Underspecification parameter, 10, 26, 51, 175
Universality of articulators, 159ff.
Uvular, 5

V

Vago, R., 25, 81, 162–164
Valdois, S., 211, 217
Van der Hulst, H., 10, 12, 17, 25, 104
Vance, T., 76
Velar articulator, 17
Velar nasal, 69, 70, 76, 77
Velar Node, 130ff.
Vennemann, T., 111
Vergnaud, J.-R., 25, 111
Vihman, M., 1, 188, 190, 194
Vocoid Place, 83, 131

W

Walsh, L., 128, 153, 154
Warlpiri, 139
Warrington, E. K., 204
Weak gemination, *see also* Finnish, 72

Wernicke's aphasia, 202ff.
West African language, 10
Whitman, J., 18, 177
Whitney, W., 113, 167, 169
Wichita, 47
Wierzchowska, B., 36, 37, 39
Wilson, T., 121
Wintz, E., 76
Wirth, J., 2
Wiyot, 128
Wright, M., 148
Wu, Z., 35, 37

X

X-ray tracing, 35ff., 90, 93, 94

Y

Yagaria, 110, 113, 121
Yip, M., 8, 13, 14, 22, 23, 25, 50, 59, 73, 75, 121

Z

Zec, D., 175
Zero-specification, 172
Zipf, G. K., 202
Zonneveld, W., 99
Zoque, 94

PHONETICS AND PHONOLOGY

Volume 1: Rhythm and Meter
edited by Paul Kiparsky and Gilbert Youmans
Volume 2: The Special Status of Coronals: Internal and External Evidence
edited by Carole Paradis and Jean-François Prunet